RENOVATING HIGHER EDUCATION

RENOVATING HIGHER EDUCATION

Vision of Swami Vivekananda

Editors

C. Janakavalli

T. Nagavalli

K.P. Shanmugavadivu

KALPAZ

ISBN: 978-93-5128-030-9
Price : ₹ 1200

First Published, 2014

Published by

Kalpaz Publications
C-30, Satyawati Nagar,
Delhi-110052
Ph. : 9212142040
E-mail: kalpaz@hotmail.com

Laser Typesetting: Rudra Computer Graphics, Delhi
Printed at: G. Print Process, Delhi

Cataloging in Publication Data--DK
Courtesy: D.K. Agencies (P) Ltd. <docinfo@dkagencies.com>

Renovating higher education : vision of Swami Vivekananda / editors, C. Janakavalli, T. Nagavalli, K.P. Shanmugavadivu.
p. cm.
Includes bibliographical references.
ISBN 9789351280309

1. Education, Higher--India--Chennai--Case studies--Congresses. 2. Education, Higher--India--Chennai--Philosophy--Congresses. 3. Women in development--India--Chennai--Congresses. 4. Yoga--Congresses. 5. Moral education (Higher)--India--Chennai--Congresses. 6. Mind and body--India--Chennai--Congresses. 7. Vivekananda, Swami, 1863-1902--Political and social views--Congresses. I. Janakavalli, C. II. Nagavalli, T. III. Shanmugavadivu, K. P.

DDC 378.0095482 23

Contents

Editorial

The nation is paying rich tribute to Swami Vivekananda in commemorating the saint's 150th Birth Anniversary. The central and the state Governments have announced various programmes, studies on Vivekananda and have created departments, chairs in universities to take up research projects on Swamiji and his works. U.G.C. has also initiated the Higher Education institutions to focus on Swamiji's thoughts and to realise his dream of the Mother Land with the young generation. Our institution also joined in this venture by organising UGC sponsored National Seminar on Renovating Higher Education: Vision of Swami Vivekananda.

The management and the Organising Committee sincerely record their hearty thanks to the U.G.C. for approving the seminar proposal and sanctioning grant. Our deep sense of gratitude is expressed to the Vice-Chancellor and the Registrar of Tamil Nadu Teacher Education University, Chennai for giving consent to co-organise the seminar with the college. We also convey our wholehearted thanks to Kalpaz Publications, Delhi for their neat execution of the book on time and the co-operation they have extended in publishing the seminar proceedings.

The Education Board appreciates the honest effort of all the participants who took pains to prepare papers, participate in the seminar and made this occasion—a memorable one.

EDITORIAL BOARD
C. Janakavalli, Principal and Conference Director
T. Nagavalli, Associate Professor of Mathematics
Mrs. K.P. Shunmuga Vadivu, Assistant Professor of Education

List of Contributors

P. Rajalakshmi, Assistant Prof. of Computer Science Education, Krishna College of Education, Krishnagiri.

J. Vincent Thaninayagam, Assistant Professor of Education (English), Government College of Education, Komarapalayam - 638 183.

B. Kavitha, Assistant Professor of Biological Science, Kathir College of Education, Neelambur, Coimbatore.

C. Praveen, Assistant Professor, Government College of Teacher Education, Trivandrum-695 014, Kerala.

T. Padmashree, Research Scholar, Dr. B.R. Ambedkar Research and Extension Center, University of Mysore.

Chandragupta, Research Scholar, Dr. B.R. Ambedkar Research and Extension Center, University of Mysore.

G. Gayathri, M.Phil Scholar, Sri Sarada College of Education Salem.

Smt. K. Sujatha, Assistant Professor, SKMK College of Education, Kuvempu Nagar, Mysore.

C. Nandeesh, Assistant Professor, JSS Institute of Education, Suttur, Mysore.

P. Pandia Vadivu, Assistant Professor-School of Education Tamil Nadu Open University, Chennai.

M. Balasubramaniam, Ph.D. Research Scholar UGC JRF, Sri Ramakrishna Mission Vidyalaya College of Education, Coimbatore.

S. Rajaguru, Associate Professor in Education, Sri Ramakrishna Mission Vidyalaya College of Education, Coimbatore.

R. Vanniarajan, Principal (Retired), Vivekananda College, Thiruvedagam.

T. Nagavalli, Associate Professor of Mathematics, Sri Sarada College of Education, Salem.

C. Janakavalli, Principal, Sri Sarada College of Education, Salem.

L. Komathi, Ph.D. Scholar, Sri Sarada College of Education, Salem.

S. Vimala Ramani, Ph.D. Scholar, Sri Sarada College of Education, Salem.

G. Subramonian, Associate Professor, SRKV College of Education, Coimbatore.

K. Suprabha, Research Scholar, SRKV College of Education, Coimbatore.

J. Rekha, Guest Lecturer in Education, Government College of Education for Women, Coimbatore.

V. Thilagavathy, Ph.D., (UGC - JRF) Research Scholar, School of Education, Pondicherry University.

A. Kalaivani, Assistant Professor in Biological Science Education, Esther College of Education, Namakkal.

Reshmi Ramachandran, Research Scholar and Associate Professor, SRKV College of Education, Coimbatore.

G. Subramonian, Research Scholar and Associate Professor, SRKV College of Education, Coimbatore.

G. Kumutha, M.Phil Scholar, Sri Sarada College of Education, Salem.

B. Gayathri, Ph.D. Scholar, Sri Sarada College of Education Salem.

C. Janakavalli, Principal, Sri Sarada College of Education Salem.

P. Megala, Research Scholar, Sri Sarada College of Education, Salem

D.C. Vani Nayaki, Research Scholar, Kumadvathi College of Education, Shikaripur.

Y. Devaraja, Lecturer, Kumadvathi College of Education, Shikaripur.

D. Silambu Selvi, Assistant Professor, Krishna College of Education, Trichengode.

P. Sooriya, Junior Research Fellow, Sri Sarada College of Education, Salem-636 016.

C. Nandeesh, Assistant Professor, JSS PG. Center in Education (M.Ed), JSS Institute of Education, Suttur Mysore District, Karnataka.

S. Velvizhi, Physical Director, Sri Sarada College of Education Salem.

S. Santhi, Assistant Professor of History, Sri Sarada College of Education Salem.

S. Amutha, Assistant Professor, Department of Educational Technology Bharathidasan University, Tiruchirappalli-620 024.

M. Suganya, M.Phil Scholar, Department of Educational Technology, Bharathidasan University, Tiruchirappalli-620 024.

K. Subashini, Ph.D. Scholar, Sri Sarada College of Education Salem.

B. Soundiram, Ph.D., Scholar Department of Yoga, Tamil Nadu Physical Education and Sports University (TNPESU), Chennai.

R. Elangovan, Professor and Head, Department of Yoga, Tamil Nadu Physical Education and Sports University (TNPESU), Chennai.

S.D. Subadra, Ph.D. Scholar, Sri Sarada College of Education, Salem-16.

V. Usha Sri, Principal, Sengunthar College of Education, Tharamangalam.

M.N. Geetha, Assistant Professor of English, Kathir College of Education, Neelambur, Coimbatore.

D.S.N. Vimal Kumar, Assistant Professor of History, Krishna College of Education, Kattinayanapalli, Krishnagiri.

A. Balamallikadevi, Ph.D. Scholar, Sri Sarada College of Education, Salem-636 016.

Poonum Jahaly, Ph.D. Research Scholar, DOS in Education, University of Mysore.

T.S. Balakrishnan, Associate Professor, Department of Management Studies, KSR College of Arts and Science, Thiruchengode.

C. Renuga Devi, Assistant Professor in Special Education, Ramakrishna Mission, Vivekananda University Faculty of Disability Management and Special Education.

B. Kalaivani, Assistant Professor, Department of Zoology, Sri Sarada College for Women (Autonomous), Salem-636 016.

S. Priyadharsini, Ph.D. Research Scholar, Sri Sarada College of Education Salem.

Umamaheswari, Assistant Professor and Head.

M. Jayashree, Department of Botany, Sri Sarada College for Women Salem-636 016.

P. Sarvaharana, Superintendent, Teaching Learning Centre, Centre for Continuing Education, IIT Madras-600 036.

S. Manikandan, Assistant Professor, Department of Philosophy, AM Jain College, Chennai.

K.P. Shanmugavadivu, Assistant Professor of Education, Sri Sarada College of Education, Salem-636 016.

V. Priya, Assistant Professor of Physical Science, Sri Sarada College of Education (Autonomous) Salem.

R. Selvamathi Sugirtha, Assistant Professor of Bio. Science, Sri Sarada College of Education Salem-636 016.

R.R. Madankar, Associate Professor, P.G. Department of Education, Karnatak University Dharwad.

S. Logeshkumar, Ph.D. Research Scholar, Ramakrishna Mission, Faculty of Disability Management and Special Education, Vivekananda University, Coimbatore.

A. V. Karabasanagoudra, Assistant Professor, School of Education, Rani Channamma University, Belagavi-Karnataka.

P. Ranganayaki, Associate Professor, Department of Mathematics, Sri Sarada College for Women Salem.

P. Vasantha, Associate Professor of Statistics, Sri Sarada College for Women (Autonomous) Salem, Tamil Nadu.

A. Selvalakshmi, Assistant Professor of English, Sri Sarada College for Women (Autonomous) Salem.

P. Suseela, Associate Professor of History, Sri Sarada College for Women Salem-636 016.

M. Nala, Assistant Professor of History, Sri Sarada College for Women Salem -636 016.

P. Perumal, Ph.D. Research Scholar, Sri Ramakrishna Mission Vidyalaya College of Education, Coimbatore-20.

N. Muthaiah, Principal, Sri Ramakrishna Mission Vidyalaya College of Education, Coimbatore-20.

M. Senthilkumaran, Ph.D. Research Scholar, Sri Ramakrishna Mission Vidyalaya College of Education, Coimbatore-20.

B. Mohan Kumar, Research Scholar, School of Education, Pondicherry University.

G. Vinod Kumar, Associate Professor, Department of Physical Education and Sports, Pondicherry University, Puducherry.

A. Siddhartha, M.P.Ed Scholar, Department of Physical Education and Sports, Pondicherry University, Puducherry.

D. Gokulakrishnan, Assistant Professor, Selvam College of Physical Education, Namakkal.

G. Gnanagandarvan, II M.P.Ed., Selvam College of Physical Education, Namakkal.

D. Yogaraj, M.P.Ed., Selvam College of Physical Education, Namakkal-3.

K. Rajendran, (Former All-India Inter University Athlete), Assistant Professor, Department of Physical Education and Sports Sciences, Annamalai University, Chidhambaram.

Kotreshwaraswamy, A. Surapuramath, Assistant Professor, J.S.S. Institute of Education P.G. Center in Education (M.Ed), Suttur, Najangudu (Taluq), Mysore (District) Karnataka.

R. Rajeswari, Principal, Sri Sarada College for Women (Autonomous), Salem.

PART–I: SPIRITUAL VALUES IN HIGHER EDUCATION

1

Spiritual Values in Higher Education

B. Kavitha

> *"Spiritual knowledge is the only thing that can destroy our miseries forever; any other knowledge satisfies wants only for a time. It is only with the knowledge of the spirit that the faculty of want is annihilated forever; so helping man spiritually is the highest help that can be given to him."* — *Swami Vivekananda*

Introduction

The nineteenth century India produced a galaxy of great men who have enriched our national life by their talent and personality. Swami Vivekananda was one of them. Swamiji believed in essential unity of man and god. He was an eclectic educationalist. He tried to unite Indian spirituality and western materialism. No wonder that today, over a century after his death, we still try to enrich ourselves with the gems of Swamiji's spiritual thoughts on education. Let us discuss the different aspects of Swamiji's spiritual values in education.

Definition

Vivekananda was deeply spiritual and intensely human. His message is the message of humanism. But his humanism has a deeper content. He said that education which gives us intellectual energy must also give us humanistic impulse and its energy of character. Although Swamiji was an idealist and a spiritualist—emphasising realisation of divinity in man, yet he was fully aware of the need for national development to be achieved through education. Swamiji exhorted individuals to keep full confidence upon their powers. They should inculcate a spirit of self surrender, sacrifice of renunciation of material pleasures for the good of others. Education should manifest these qualities in the individual. He gave this call to his countrymen.

Aims of Spiritual Education

Swamiji has a deep and comprehensive conception of education. The ultimate goal of life and that of education is helping each soul manifest the potential divinity within it; that is Spiritual realisation.

Education for:

(i) Character building
(ii) Making people self-reliant
(iii) Serving fellow human beings and developing the spirit of renunciation.
(iv) Developing the feeling of brotherhood.

Objectives

According to Swami, "Work is worship, so to serve the man is to serve god,"

Education, he maintains should help people to build up self-confidence and self-reliance based on balanced human relationship. The ultimate goal of all educational effort is to strive towards character development characterised by the development of will-power, leading to courage, stamina and fearlessness. Though educating the individual should develop adaptability and meet the challenge of a changing society, education should lead us to acquire the spirit of renunciation.

Curriculum

According to Swami—the prime aim of education is spiritual growth and development. But this does not mean that he did not advocate material prosperity and physical well-being. His teachings advocated the inclusion, which fosters material welfare with spiritual advancement. Swami prescribed the same ancient spiritual methods of teaching, wherein the guru and his disciples lived in close association as in a family. The essential characteristics of those religions and spiritual methods were as under:

(i) To control fleeting mental faculties by the practice of yoga.
(ii) To develop the mind by concentration and deep meditation.
(iii) To gain knowledge through lectures, discussions, self-experience and creative activities.
(iv) To imitate the qualities and character of the teachings with intelligent and clear understanding.
(v) To lead the child on the right path by means of individual guidance by the teacher.

Education for Spirituality

Education is used as the higher training ground for each individual's ongoing spiritual journey.

This view includes with its scope:

1. The development of appropriate ideas and values as part of the educational process.

2. Providing individuals with the methods and practices to pursue their deeper ideals with and outside the context of day-to-day living.
3. Creating the intellectual and cultural frame that would enable individuals to harmonise and integrate with the multiplicity of ideas and ideals in a globalising society.

Role of Teacher

"Purity, Patience and Perseverance are the three essentials to success, and above all, love".

The teacher should share with the student the conviction that they are both truly one in spirit—at the same time—cultivating in the student, a feeling of dignity and self-respect. As Vivekananda said "The only true teacher is he who can immediately come down to the level of the student and transfer his soul to the student's soul and see through the student's eyes and hear through his ears and understand through his mind. Such a teacher can really teach and none else."

Contribution of Swami Vivekananda to Spiritual Education

"Arise, awake and stop not till the goal is reached"

It is in the transformation of man through moral and spiritual education that he finds the solution for all social evils. Founding education on the firm ground of our own philosophy and culture, he shows the best of remedies for today's social and global illness. Through his scheme of education, he tries to materialise the moral and spiritual welfare and upliftment of humanity, irrespective of caste, creed, and nationality.

Conclusion

"Be moral, Be brave, Be a heart—whole man—strictly moral, brave unto desperation". Try to love anybody and everybody.

Now, good dreams, good thoughts for you. You are good and noble. Instead of materialising the spirit, that is, dragging the spiritual to the material plane, convert the matter into spirit, catch a glimpse at least, everyday, of that world of infinite beauty and peace and purity-the spiritual and try to live in it-day and night.

References

- Nayak, B.K. (2006), Foundation of Education, Cuttack, Kitab Mahal.
- Pahuja, N.P. (2007), Theory and Principles of Education, New Delhi, India, Anmol Publications Pvt. Ltd.

2

Swamiji and the Guru in Renovating Education

C. Praveen

Background

When Swamiji visited Kerala in 1897, he was outraged by the overt discrimination that he saw there and he declared the place "a lunatic asylum."[1] Around that time came a saviour-Sri Narayana Guru. In a world of chaos and disorder, the Guru gave a new interpretation to life and pointed the way for universal peace, harmony and brotherhood. What Swami Vivekananda saw then, is not to be seen now. Today, Kerala is described as a tropical paradise and is being recommended by the National Geographic Magazine as one of the 50 destinations in the world that one should visit.

The Current State of Affairs in Kerala

Kerala is described as 'God's Own Country', but the fact remains that new social problems have cropped up. Corruption, glaring exploitation, cut throat competition, depressing nepotism, defiance of authority are common in Kerala. Can't we attribute this state of affairs to the failure of our educational system? A scholarly article on developmental issues in Kerala, lists the following:

- **Agriculture:** Kerala is a state blessed with wide range of natural resources. For several years, agriculture was the main occupation. But now-a-days it is hard to find the peasantry class. During 2001-2007, 887 farmer suicides were reported in Kerala.
- **Problems of aboriginals:** A recent survey conducted by the Health Department found that among 3,600 young married tribal couples 30 to 40 per cent are facing infertility problem. It has also been reported that in addition to land issues, the tribals are facing many socio-cultural, economic and health problems.
- **Changes in family pattern:** The disappearance of joint families, the preference for nuclear families, and alienation of parents during old age, growth of Old Age Homes and alienation of children are on the rise.

- **Alienation from traditional food habits:** Rise of fast food joints and the disappearance of food and rice mills are quite common today.
- **Alienation from traditional clothing:** Today, there is a marked preference irrespective of class for branded dress materials.
- **Rise of consumerism and alcoholism:** Many foreign companies are keen on opening showrooms in malls and company outlets in the townships of Kerala. And it is a pity that the State with the highest literacy level also holds the first place in consumption of liquor in the country.
- Rise of environmental issues including land mining and pollution.
- The change in employment sector lead to the rise of BPOs coupled with brain drain.

The Ezhavas of Kerala—Significance of Sri Narayana Guru

The Ezhava community, once discriminated severely by upper castes in Kerala, now forms fifty per cent of the Hindu population (3.20 Crore). The Ezhavas, today, are an empowered lot, thanks to the philosophical and spiritual teachings of the Saint-Philosopher Sri Narayana Guru who hailed from the same community. So, any talk of educational renovation in Kerala has to consider the contributions of Sri Narayana Guru. Incidentally, the recent move by the Government of Kerala to introduce the Guru's teachings into the school and college curricula is one significant milestone with regards to educational reform.

Significance of Swami Vivekananda's Teachings

Perhaps, at this moment in history-the 150th birth anniversary of Swami Vivekananda, it is appropriate indeed to consider renovation of education in Kerala. Swami Vivekananda laid great emphasis on education of the heart. He said "It is man-making education all round that we want. (III 224) We want that education by which character is formed, strength of mind is increased, the intellect is expanded, and by which one can stand on one's own feet. (V 342) Real education is that which enables one to stand on one's own legs. (VII 147-48) If the poor cannot come to education, education must go to him. (IV 363)

Sri Narayana Guru on Education

Man, according to the Guru, is the combination of three powers-intellect, body and soul. The Guru introduced a new pattern of education called the three 'H' formulas. The three 'H's Hand, Heart and Head-have to be simultaneously developed to yield fruitful results in individuals. By education, the Guru meant a process of making one able and qualified for better living in this world. The Guru reminded his followers of the extraordinary value of the reading habit. Temples were considered by the Guru as centres of social education. He believed that education in a modern industrial society should be strongly oriented towards occupational preparation. In essence, the Guru's exhortation was very simple:

vidya kondu prabuddhar avuka
sanghatana kondu shaktar avuka
prayatnam kondu sampannar avuka......[Malayalam]
Become enlightened, through education
Become strengthened, through organisation
Become prosperous, through hard work......[English Version]

Can the Swami and the Guru Help Renovate Education in Kerala?

The current state of affairs in Kerala listed earlier leaves no doubt regarding the fact that Malayalees today require an education that helps solve the problems of home, family and community. The commonality in the ideals propounded by Swami Vivekananda and Sri Narayana Guru mentioned above is in every way a beacon of hope. It is hoped that the curricula developers in Kerala, who appear to be tossing in the high sea of political and group pressures in their attempt to evolve a curricula suitable for the twenty-first century learner, succeeds in drawing inspiration from the teachings of the Swami and the Guru.

References

- New York Review of Books, 21 July 1985.
- Maclntyre, Alasdair, After Virtue Londan: Duckworth, 1981.
- Arendt, Hannah, The Human Condition, New York: Doudleday Anchor, 1959.

3

Education and Moral Values

T. Padmashree

Introduction

The two agents of moral education — families, school – are major institutions in a civil society. Today, we must add peer group to this. All these agents of education have their problems in today's society, partly as a consequence of secularisation, partly as the result of serious social changes. Even in societies in which institutional religion appears to continue to flourish there are major problems affecting the critical passing on of a moral tradition.

Students are the future of our nation. We are taught moral lessons at home and in school such as to love fellow human beings, respect elders, no wrong things should be done, never speak lies, love your country, don't be jealous etc. But, nowadays everywhere crime flourishes. We see corruption; old people are sent out of and treated badly. People are unaware of the truth. Jealousy has become the overall base of life.

The importance of life should not be taught, but should be trained. We want to have the training through which we develop the feelings of nationalism and cultivate moral values in our lives. Besides education, we should be deeply involved in such works through which we develop feelings of love and brotherhood. It is the responsibility of our parents and teachers to make the future builders of the nation.

Definitions

> *The essential purpose of education is to bring the pupil face to face with something great, so that he experiences, first awe and then curiosity.* — *Dante*

> *The problems of a civil society ... are, in essence, the problems of constituting trust in society.* — *Adam seligman*

Education: Acquisition of Useful Skills

Socrates derided the sophists for having a radically inadequate understanding of education and of philosophy. For them, education was the conveying of what would now be called 'transferable skills' : Meaning, abilities which were useful to the state or saleable commodities in the market, Education was the training in public relation, in making friends and influencing people. It gave pupils the techniques to get ahead, while accepting and operating within the present structure of things in politics and religion. The sophists were relativists. Because knowledge of the good was unobtainable, goodness could not be taught, only how to operate effectively within the system education became a market commodity, and as such, has lost its critical edge.

Moral Neutralism

Many claim that moral education today is probably impossible and certainly undesirable. We live in a morally fragmented society; there is no effective moral consensus; attempt to impose morality approved by the government or the educated elite are doomed to fail, because they will be seen as indoctrination. We are reminded that efforts over decades in the old Soviet Union and the communist states of Eastern Europe to inculcate the ideology and values of socialism met for long with the kind of rejection that has been labeled 'the vomit effect' — the best efforts of power to define truth were unsuccessful, were more or less received with a decision, and with the collapse of communist power, they disappeared almost immediately leaving hardly a trace behind. This may have left in these countries a moral and religious vacuum—which various bodies are striving to fill in, but are tending to find that the enduring legacy is either a deep-seated skepticism or an attempt to revive ancient chauvinism.

Old System of Education

In olden days, we used to have the "Gurukul" type of education system in India. The students of gurukul lived a life of tutelage and learnt everything taught by their guru with love and also by putting in lot of hard work. In the gurukul, every student was treated equally—irrespective of caste and economical status. The students are supposed to leave homes and loved ones and come and live at the Gurukul Ashram for years to learn the lessons of life from the guru. At the end of the training, the students emerged as responsible individuals, who were well learned and capable of undertaking any challenge in life. We can explain the system in the same way as mud made by God being beautifully moulded as water jug by the potter. We can further apply our own lives. Our physical body makers are our parents, like God. But our life makers are our gurus (teachers) who give us some particular turn or shape to our life, just like a potter.

Who Educates?–The School

Similar considerations apply to the schools. The formal content of education is not the only or the most important part of total educational experience. The environment, the way the school as some community operates, the human relations, the general atmosphere are important aspects of moral education. Sometime, the structure of education effectively denies the content, and forms pupils and their relationship in ways which are at odds with the proclaimed aims of the system.

Sooner or later, if our educational systems are to exemplify and support moral education which centers on reconciliation, trust and tolerance, we need to confront segregation in our education system, both religious and ethnic, and the class segregation exemplified in the prevalence of private education in Britain. School cannot be bastions of some section of the community, if they are to build trust and effective moral education.

Who Educates?–The Family

That the family is the primary loci for moral education and the formation of character is almost obvious to be worth saying. The pressures on the family today, the incidence of marriage break-up, the number of lone parents struggling in poverty to nurture children are causes of grave concern. We are all formed and influenced deeply, for better or worse, by our family and upbringing. In the family, a child receives powerful messages and examples of the kinds of behaviour, which are regarded as good or acceptable.

We learn to love.
Through being loved.
We learn how to trust.
Through being trusted.

Who Educates?–The Peer Group

In culture and morals, there is an increasingly serious gulf between generations. It is clear that many younger people take cue as to behaviour, beliefs, and belongings not so much from the home, or the school, or the tradition as from their peer. Much of this is manipulated by advertisers and by the media, and indeed by political movement. However, peer education, for all its volatile ambiguity and dangers, can sometimes nurture the trust and the vision that are essential for a healthy civil society.

Importance of Moral Education

Value-based education is needed for developing moral qualities such as humility, truthfulness, honesty, courtesy, tolerance, sacrifice among youth. It will help in developing positive social attitudes in new generation which prompt them raise their voice against social evils. Meaningful education aims at the all-round development of learner. The optimal development of moral, spiritual and aesthetic aspects of personality needs enrichment and refinement in the form of value education. The humanising role of educational process is played by the value-based education. Value education is essential for developing democratic qualities such as dignity of the individual, social justice, liberty, equality, fraternity etc. The harmonious existence of different ideologies in society requires respect for moral and ethical values. Value education inculcates these virtues in a systematic manner. Value-based education inculcates sense of cooperation and fellow-feeling among people.

Value Education

The need for value education is constantly increasing as we continue to witness increasing violent activities, behavioural disorder and lack of unity in society. Only value education would lead us attain our ultimate goal of peace on earth. Value education can strengthen students' self esteem, optimism and commitment to personal fulfillment, and help students exercise ethical judgement and social responsibility. Effective value education in schools and colleges will help students understand and apply values such as care and compassion, doing their best, fair go, freedom, honesty and trustworthiness, integrity, respect, responsibility, understanding, tolerance etc. In their daily life, value education will help the individual resolve value conflicts and fix the standard of his behaviour. Value education is needed to give direction to one's social, moral and spiritual development, thus to bring quality to life. Value-oriented education is needed to promote individual and social welfare, love, peace, goodwill and understanding. Values are the greatest unifying force in life. Inculcation of these values through education is the necessity of the hour to check the disintegration of social relation. Value education is needed to strengthen social harmony, to encourage cultural development, to instil democratic qualities and to combat social evils and injustice.

Conclusion

Today, education has become just a nine letter word as a superior term in the dictionary. Moreover Education system became a business, where it is treated like any other profession. The problem is also with us. It is we who make the society. If we improve ourselves, we can improve our society. No one is a born a criminal or a spoilt person. It is the environment—that is deviating the child away from taking the right path. Good teachers can bring the change with good education imparted to students. Education is the combination of literacy and morale values. We seldom get good quality of education if they were to be seen in isolation. Students are the future of a nation. Everyone has to prepare individually in the present for their future. They have to be mentally, physically, morally and emotionally fit for the betterment of the society. It will be a great achievement if every person can establish himself or herself as worthy person. Education includes all-round development of a person, so I think social, ethical and moral values should be included in our school's programme. Physical Education, sports and some extracurricular activities should be incorporated in our school developmental programme. We should always try to understand the rich culture and heritage of our country. We can be called as "Educated" then and not as "Literate". Well educated people can build good society and healthy nation. We can remove the present evils of our society by constantly helping one another, when our country will become a dreamland and dream destination.

References

- Jowett, B., The Four Socratic Dialogues of Plato, Oxford: Clarendon Press, 1945.
- Coulanges, Fustel de, The Anciant City, New York: Doubleday, 1956.
- Kerikegaard, S., Journals, ed. Alexander Dru, London: Fontana.

4

Moral Values in College Education

Chandragupta

Introduction

Today, the education imparted to our children is almost solely limited to what Sri Ramakrishna characterised as "education for bread and butter". Students are led to believe that by developing the ability to gather, store, and retrieve vast information, they stand educated. But, Swami Vivekananda points out, "Education is not the amount of information that is put into your brain and runs riot there, undigested all your life. We must have life-building, man-making and character-making assimilation of ideas." Mere academic knowledge without deep rooted moral and spiritual values will only fashion lopsided personalities, who may become rich in material possession, but will remain poor in aspects of self-understanding, peace, and social concern. Emphasising this fact, Swamiji said, "Excess of knowledge and power, without holiness, makes human beings; devils." As a humble step towards achieving the goal of exposing and sensitising our children to the educational vision of national heritage, Ramakrishna Mission has undertaken a project 'Be and Make - Education for Manifesting Perfection'. The concept is to reach college students with a series of books—which will be books with a difference. The main aim of these books will be to help our students imbibe certain fundamental values and internalise them in their daily life and interpersonal interaction. We intend to bring these books out at two levels: one, value education story books and two, diary-cum-personal journals. While the story books would expose the students to the philosophy and sublimity of value education ideas, the diary-cum-personal journals would form in them healthy habits calculated to develop introspection, capacity of self-evaluation, etc.

The World of College Students

The young people are being given more responsibility in their lives, facing new questions and having new experiences. They are beginning to chose their way of life, whereas much of it was chosen before for them. College students think about what kind of job they want. This is necessary so that they can select suitable colleges, subjects and job training, that give them, sense of direction and meaning in life. If they can see the necessity of universities partly in job terms, it helps them go along with more difficult aspects. For a degree, also, these students are free to chose other elements of their way of life: sports, friendship and group life, movies, TV, music, reading of different kinds, the clothes they wear. Possibly they can buy now a Walkman or a ten-speed bike with their own money. Perhaps, they can give up (or take up) a musical instrument without much adult control.

A Conception of Morality in Moral Education

Morality is based largely in human needs, of oneself and others. It is grounded in goods such as friendship, fellowship, self-respect, health, happiness, fulfillment, a sense of meaning in life. Following Aristotle, there is a strong emphasis here on human nature and basic human desires and tendencies. Many moral and social values, such as self-control, truthfulness, promise keeping, loyalty, fairness and so on is largely the means to ends rather than ends in them. They should be seen (and taught) as components within a total value system, the ultimate purpose of which is to enable humans, individually and as groups, to achieve human goods. This in no way diminishes the importance of moral and social values but shows that they like other values, must be weighed against one another rather than be seen as absolute. Members of subgroups (such as adolescents) have a right to pursue distinctive interests rather than subordinate them completely for general societal values. They also have some responsibility, of course, to integrate their values with others as much as possible and look for areas of shared values.

Religion plays an important role in morality for many people, but it is possible to be moral without being religious. This follows from the roots of morality in human nature and human life. One could develop broad definition of religion according to which it would be necessary to be religious in order to be moral. But in the everyday sense of religion, there is no necessary connection between the two. For many people, howsoever, their religion is in fact the mediator (in part at least) of their morality, and if they lost the one at the cost of other temporarily and perhaps permanently. Ethical questions are objective. Here, we part company with "values clarification" and other relativist positions. Moral issues are deeply embedded in hard realities of life, no matter how much we clarify about our values, we can still be wrong, objectively. For example, we may firmly believe that it is always wrong to tell lies, but some day, where, given all the facts, we are forced to admit that telling the truth would be wrong, since it would clearly do more harm than good. This does not mean that the same things are right or wrong for everyone: Relevant differences abound in circumstances and temperament. But for a given person or group under given circumstances, one can in principle objectively determine which action would be better and worse morally.

Issues for Study of Morals

The study of morals, as we have noted, is just one part of a school's moral education program. However, it is a very important part and working its content helps give direction to the total program. The following are some suggested topics and themes for college groups according to the subject areas wherein they might be incorporated. The word "values"" is used in the lists below rather than "morals". This is because, it is a more familiar word to students and teachers, but does not have some what negative connotation of "morals" attached. However, moral issues relevant to this age group would still be covered under the topics.

Social Studies

- What are values? What is morality?
- Differences in values
- How to solve value problems?
- Self and others
- Extended families and close communities
- From inner group to global community
- Values, regionalism, and patriotism
- Values, religion, race, culture
- Richer and poorer countries
- Values and politics
- Values and commerce

Language Arts and/or Literature

- Values and communication
- Values and the mass media
- The aesthetic side of life
- What is a good book, a good film?
- Indoctrination through literature
- Freedom as theme
- Suffering as theme

Guidance, Life Skills, Human Relation

- Friendship
- Friendship and love
- Values and Sexuality
- Sexism
- Family relationship
- Marriage
- Values and school
- Getting the most out of school
- Finding values in some job
- Choosing some way of life
- Enriching some way of life

Health, Physical Education

- Values and health
- Holistic health
- Values and stress
- Values and coping
- Valucs and sport
- Values and spectator sport

While the above topics have been listed under school subject areas, most of them could easily be studied in as separate "morals" or "values" course or in courses other than those indicated. In schools with religion program, many of the topics could be incorporated into that subject. Another possible approach is to focus on new topic throughout a grade level every three or four weeks and have different aspects dealt within a variety of college subjects. The important point is that by some means or other, most of the topics (and others) should be studied' in depth' during college years, rather than just touched on briefly and superficially or neglected entirely. Because the field of morals is so complex, students need the opportunity to build cumulatively some comprehensive system of moral ideas, principles, and skills.

Conclusion

We now have an increase in number of case studies from which we can model our attempts. But, we have been able to point some particular areas wherein we have yet to get up. In a culture on the turn, it is urgent that we maintain the momentum. Hopefully, that includes funding!

References

- Philippe Ariès, Centuries of Childhood: A Social History of Family Life, trans. Robert Baldick (New York: Knopf, 1962).
- Carl Bereiter, Must We Educate? (Englewood Cliffs: Prentice-Hall, Spectrum, 1973).
- John Farrelly, "The Human Good and Moral Choice,"
- G. McLean and F.A. Ellrod (eds.), Philosophical Foundations of Moral Education Act and Agent (The Council for Research in Values and Philosophy, 1984).

5

Educational Values of Swami Vivekananda

G. Gayathri

Introduction

Swami Vivekananda (1863-1902), a great thinker and reformer of India, embraces education, which for him signifies 'man-making', as the very mission of his life. In this paper, which purports to expound and analyse Swamiji's views on education, an endeavour has been made to focus on the basic theme of his philosophy, viz., the spiritual unity of the universe. Whether it concerns the goal or aim of education, or its method of approach or its component parts, his thoughts, we shall observe, stem from this dormant theme of his philosophy which has its moorings in Vedanta. Vivekananda realises that mankind is passing through crisis. The tremendous emphasis on the scientific and mechanical ways of life is fast reducing man to the status of machine. Moral and religious values are being undermined. The fundamental principles of civilisation are being ignored. Conflicts of ideals, manners and habits pervade the atmosphere. Disregard for everything old is the fashion of the day. Vivekananda seeks solutions of these social and global evils through education. With this end in view, he feels the dire need of awakening man to his spiritual self wherein, he thinks, lies in the very purpose of education.

The Objectives of Education

Vivekananda points the defect of the present day education as it has no definite goal to pursue. A sculptor has clear idea about what he wants to shape about the marble block; similarly, a painter knows what he is going to paint, but a teacher, he says, has no clear idea about the goal of his teaching. Swamiji attempts to establish, through his words and deeds, that the end of all education is man making. He prepares the scheme of this man-making education in the light of his overall philosophy of Vedanta. According to Vedanta, the essence of man lies in his soul, which he possess in addition to his body and mind. In true sense with this philosophy, Swamiji defines education as 'the manifestation of the perfection already in man.' The aim of education is to manifest the perfection in our lives, which is the very nature of our inner self. This perfection is the realisation of the infinite power which resides in everything and every-where–existence, consciousness and bliss (satchidananda). After understanding the essential nature of this perfection, we should identify it with our inner self. For achieving this, one will have to eliminate one's ego, ignorance and other false identification, which stand in the way. Meditation, fortified by moral purity and passion for truth, helps man to leave behind the body, the senses, the ego and other non-self elements, which are perishable. He realises thus his immortal divine self, which is of the nature of infinite existence, infinite knowledge and infinite bliss.

At this stage, man becomes aware of his self as identical with other selves of the universe, i.e., different selves as manifestations of the same self. Hence education, in Vivekananda's sense, enables one to comprehend one's self within as the self everywhere. The essential unity of the entire universe is realised through education. Accordingly, man making for Swamiji stands for rousing man to the awareness of his true self. However, education thus signified does not point towards the development of soul in isolation from body and mind. We have to remember that basis of Swamiji's philosophy is Advaita, which preaches unity in diversity. Therefore, man making for him means the harmonious development of the body, mind and soul.

In his scheme of education, Swamiji lays great stress on physical health because a sound mind resides in a sound body. He often quotes the Upanishadic dictum 'nayamatma balahinena labhyah'. However, along with physical culture, he harps on the need of paying special attention to the culture of mind. According to Swamiji, the mind of students has to be controlled and trained through meditation, concentration and practice of ethical purity. All success in any line of work, he emphasises, is the result of the power of concentration. By way of illustration, he mentions that the chemist in the laboratory concentrates the powers of his mind and brings them into one focus—the elements to be analysed—and finds out their secrets. Concentration, which necessarily implies detachment from other things, constitutes a part of Brahmacharya (celebacy), which is one of the guiding motto of his scheme of education. Brahmacharya, in nutshell, stands for the practice of self-control for harmony of impulses. By his philosophy of education, Swamiji brings it home that education is not mere accumulation of information but comprehensive training for life. To quote him: 'Education is not the amount of information that is put into your brain and runs riot there undigested, all your life.'

Method or Procedure

Having analysed the goal or objective of education, the next question that naturally arises is about the method of imparting education. Here again, we note the Vedantic foundation of Swamiji's theory. According to him, knowledge is inherent in every man's soul. What we mean when we say that a man 'knows' is only what he 'discovers' by taking the cover off his own soul. Consequently, he draws our attention to the fact that the task of the teacher is only to help the child to manifest knowledge by removing the obstacles on way. In his words: 'Thus Vedanta says that within man is all knowledge even in a boy it is so and it requires an awakening only and that much is the work of a teacher.' To drive his point home, he refers to the growth of a plant, just as in the case of a plant, one cannot do anything more than supplying it with water, air and manure, while it grows from within its own nature, so is the case with a human child. Vivekananda's method of education resembles the heuristic method of modern educationists. In this system, the teacher invokes the spirit of inquiry in the pupil, who is supposed to find things out for himself under the unbiased guidance of teacher.

Swamiji lays lot of emphasis on the environment at home and school for proper growth of the child. The parents as well as teachers should inspire the child by the way they live their lives. Swamiji recommends the old institution of Gurukula (living with the preceptor) and similar systems for the purpose. In such systems, the students can have the ideal character of teacher constantly before them, which serves as the role model to follow. Although, Swamiji is of the opinion that mother tongue is the right medium for social or mass education, he prescribes the learning of English and Sanskrit to supplement. While English is necessary for mastering western science and technology, Sanskrit leads one into the depths of our treasure of classics. The implication is that if language does not remain the privilege of a small class of people, social unity will march forward, unhampered.

Fields of Study

Swamiji in his scheme of education, meticulously includes those studies, which are necessary for the all-around development of the body, mind and soul of the individual. These studies can be brought under the broad heads of physical culture, aesthetics, classics, language, religion, science and technology. According to Swamiji, the cultural values of the country should form an integral part of the curricula of education. The culture of India has roots in her spiritual values. The time-tested values are to be imbibed in the thoughts and lives of students through the study of classics like Ramayana, Mahabharata, Gita, Vedas and Upanishads. This will keep the perennial flow of our spiritual values into the world culture. Education, according to Swamiji, remains incomplete without the teaching of aesthetics or fine art. He cites Japan as an example of how the combination of art and utility can make nation great.

Swamiji reiterates that religion is the innermost core of education. However, by religion, he does not mean any particular kind but essential character, which is the realisation of divinity already in man. He reminds us the time and that religion does not consist in dogmas or creeds or any set of rituals. To be religious for him means leading life in such a way that we manifest our higher nature, truth, goodness and beauty in our very thoughts, words and deeds. All impulses, thoughts and actions which lead someone towards this goal are naturally ennobling and harmonising, and are ethical and moral in the truest sense. It is in this context that Swamiji's idea of religion, as the basis of education should be understood. We note that in his interpretation, religion and education share similar identity of purpose.

Why religion forms the very foundation of education becomes clear in the following words: 'In building up character, in making for everything that is good and great, in bringing peace to others, and peace to one's own self, religion is the highest motive power, and, therefore, ought to be studied from that standpoint. Swamiji believes that if education with religious core can invigorate man's faith in his divine nature and the infinite potentialities of human soul, it is sure to help man become strong, yet tolerant and sympathetic.

It will also help man to extend his love and goodwill beyond communal, national and racial barrier. It is a misinterpretation of Vivekananda's philosophy of education to think that he has overemphasised the role of spiritual development to the utter neglect of material side. Vivekananda, in his plan for regeneration of India, repeatedly pressed the need for eradication of poverty, unemployment and ignorance. He says, 'We need technical education and all else which may develop industries, so that men, instead of seeking for service, may earn enough to provide for themselves, and save something against rainy day'. He feels it necessary that India should borrow from Western nations all that are good in their civilisation. However, just like a person, every nation has its individuality, which should not be destroyed. The individuality of India lies in her spiritual culture. Hence in Swamiji's view, for the development of balanced nation, we ought to combine the dynamism and scientific attitude of the West with the spirituality of our country. The entire educational program should be so planned that it equips the youth to contribute towards the material progress of the country as well as maintaining the supreme worth of spiritual heritage.

Another important aspect of Swamiji's scheme of education is women's education. He realises that had the women of our country have had the right type of education, then they will solve their problems in their own way. The main objective of his scheme of female education is to make them strong, fearless, and conscious of their chastity and dignity. He observes that though men and women are equally competent in academic matters, yet women have special aptitude and competence for studies relating to home and family. Hence, he recommends the introduction of subjects like sewing, nursing, domestic science, culinary art, etc., which was not part of education at his time.

Conclusion

The exposition and analysis of Vivekananda's scheme of education brings to light about the constructive, practical and comprehensive character. He realises that it is only through education that the uplift of the masses is possible. To refer to his own words: 'Traveling through many cities of Europe and the comforts education of even the poor people, therein was brought to my mind the state of our own poor people and I used to shed tears. When made the difference? "Education" was the answer I got.' He states emphatically that if society is to be reformed, education ought to reach everyone-high and low, because individuals are the very constituents of society. The sense of dignity rises in man when he becomes conscious of his inner spirit, and that is the very purpose of education. He strives to harmonise the traditional values of India with new values brought through the progress of science and technology.

It is in the transformation of man through moral and spiritual education that he finds the solution for social evils. Founding education on the firm ground of our own philosophy and culture, he shows the best of remedies for today's social and global illness. Through his scheme of education, he tries to materialise the moral and spiritual welfare and uplift of humanity, irrespective of caste, creed, nationality or time. However, Swami Vivekananda's scheme of education, through which he wanted to build up a strong nation that will lead the world towards peace and harmony, is still a far cry. It is high time that we give serious thought to his philosophy of education and remembers his clarion call to everybody—'Arise, awake, and stop not till the goal is reached'.

References

- Ruth Jonathan, Musory Freedoms: Liberalism, Education and Market, Oxford: Blackwell, 1997.
- New York Review of Books, 21 July !985.
- Maclntyre, Alansdair, aftcr Virtue Londan: Duckworth, 1981.
- Arendt, Hannah, The Human Condution, New York: Doudleday Anchor, 1959.
- Values in Education, Max Lerner, Phi Dalta kappa, 1976.
- Gupta. S., (2009), Education in Emerging India, New Delhi, Shipra Publications.
- Nayak, B.K., (2006), Foundation of Education, Cuttack, Kitab Mahal.
- Pahuja, N.P., (2007), Theory and principles of Education, New Delhi, India, Anmol Publications Pvt. Ltd.
- Saxena, N.R., Swaroop (2006), Philosophical and Sociological foundation of Education, Meerut, R. Laal Book Depot.

6

Moral Education in Schools

K. Sujatha and C. Nandeesh

Introduction

Education is a powerful instrument, which helps to bring about effective changes in the behaviour of children. True, education promotes harmonious development of all faculties — physical, mental, emotional, social, moral and spiritual – towards an adequate preparation for life. Many believe that the main function of education is to produce citizens with sound character and healthy personality. Good citizens are the only hope for progress and prosperity of the country. Inspiring ideals, proper conduct and life based upon good principles are very essential. It is quite common these days to find leaders in all sectors of society decrying the present climate of value crisis. Political, religious, social leaders and even educationists believe the country as going downhill because the people seem to have lost their moral integrity, sense of values, and that expediency has taken the place of pride as opposed to adherence of principles of conduct. They particularly observe that school students grow up in moral and spiritual vacuum.

The most urgent and significant reform needed is to transform not only the value system but also the basic structure and process of the educational system. It will also imply the shifting of emphasis from individual to social objectives and from mere acquisition of information to the development of skills and character formation based on knowledge. Further, the Kothari Commission (1964-66) in its report endorsed the inclusion of "moral and spiritual values" as one of the national objectives of education. Also, the Sri Prakas Committee was appointed by the Government of India in 1959 to look into the specific provision for teaching of moral and spiritual values in educational institutions. But precious little has been done to improve instruction in moral education.

Morality is not something to be taken lightly. It is a form of thought and action, parallel to other forms such as science, history and literature. One should understand that science alone cannot promote a country's progress and prosperity. Equal importance should be given to character formation education. There is no antithesis between religion and science. This has been clearly defended in the statement of Einstein that "science without religion is lame and religion without science is blind". However, it is unfortunate that the present system of education has not taken proper cognizance of this vital aspect, instead, we attach much importance to knowledge-oriented education and schools are interested just to prepare students appear public examinations. Most of the present day schools and colleges have become shops of profit and loss without giving sufficient waitage to moral education. Our graduates run after money, power, comforts, honour and titles. The mind of the youth is much contaminated by undesirable influences and our moral fibre is becoming thinner and thinner day-by-day.

True education, therefore, must teach not merely some means of earning livelihood, but must develop moral and spiritual qualities of students. The programme of moral education should help school-going children understand the significance of morality. Morality is the conformity to moral code of social group. It is the internalisation of set of virtues, ideas and values sanctioned by society which becomes an integral part of the individual self through the process of development. For many children, the school is the only source of regular moral influence they are exposed to, apart from that of their home and their peer group. We should recognise that home is on many moral values, severely limited in approach. Very many homes can offer little of direct help in promoting moral growth among children.

A mismanaged school is not only an immoral place in itself but develops in the children belief and disposition that are highly non-educative. Moral education cannot be carried out simply by imposing even the best rules and regulations through punishment and reward. Neither is it achieved simply by the children being told what to do, nor again by their having teachers as suitable role models for behaviour. The curriculum should provide enough opportunity for pupils to acquire a considerable amount of knowledge that is essential for morally responsible living in our democratic society. An understanding of the pupils is equally important. Therefore, new activities for personal understanding need to be built into school work.

Importance of Moral Education

A worthwhile education should target the total development of learner's personality. But in the present system emphasis has given to transmission of knowledge and cultivation of occupational skills. This has created a moral vacuum in the lives of the individuals. Inculcation of desirable values in the upcoming generation is felt essential for finding out answers to so many problems that humanity face today. The need for value-based education is clear from the following arguments:

- Value-based education is needed for developing moral qualities such as humility, truthfulness, honesty, courtesy, tolerance, sacrifice etc., among the youth.

- It will help in developing positive social attitudes in new generation which prompt them raise their voice against social evils.
- Meaningful education aims at all-round development of the learner. The optimal development of the moral, spiritual and aesthetic aspects of personality needs enrichment and refinement in the form of value education.
- The humanising role of educational process is played by the value-based education.
- Value education is essential for developing democratic qualities such as dignity of the individual, social justice, liberty, equality, fraternity etc.
- The harmonious co-existence of different ideologies in society requires respect for moral and ethical values. Value education inculcates these virtues in a systematic manner.
- Value-based education inculcates a sense of cooperation and fellow-feeling among the people.
- The need for value education is constantly increasing as we continue to witness increasing violent activities, behavioural disorder and lack of unity in society.
- Only value education would lead us attain our ultimate goal of peace on earth.
- Value education can strengthen the students' self esteem, optimism and commitment to personal fulfillment, and help students exercise ethical judgment and social responsibility.
- Effective value education in schools and colleges will help students understand and apply values such as care and compassion, doing their best, fair go, freedom, honesty and trustworthiness, integrity, respect, responsibility, understanding, tolerance in their daily life.
- Value education will help the individual resolve value conflicts and fix the standard of his behaviour.
- Value education is needed to give direction to one's social, moral and spiritual development, thus to bring quality to life.
- Value-oriented education is needed to promote individual and social welfare, love, peace, goodwill and understanding.
- Values are the greatest unifying force in life. Inculcation of values through education is the necessity of the hour to check the disintegration of social relations.
- Value education is needed to strengthen social harmony, to encourage cultural development, to instil democratic qualities and to combat social evils and injustice.

Conclusion

In conclusion, this paper has given the reason to take heart from what has already been done. We now have available an increasing number of case studies on which we can model our attempts. This paper points out particular areas where in which we have yet to speed up. In a culture on the turn, it is an urgent requirement that we maintain the momentum. Hopefully, that includes some funding!

References

- Sebastian A. Samay, "Affectivity: The Power Base of Moral Behaviour," in G. McLean and F.A. Ellrod (eds.), op. cit.
- Lawrence Blum, in Friendship, Altruism and Morality (London: Routledge and Kegan Paul, 1981).
- Lawrence Kohlberg, The Philosophy of Moral Development (New York: Harper and Row, 1981, pp. 14-16).

7

Role of Ethical Education

P. Pandiavadivu

Teacher Quality and Student Attainment

Efforts to improve student attainment have given rise to much international research since the 1960s. While earlier research tended to focus on socio-economic and intake factors rather than the influence of school to explain student attainment, recent studies have concentrated on the effects of teaching and teacher quality upon student attainment. Student attainment is enhanced by effective teachers who are not only competent in principle with good subject and pedagogical knowledge, but also form positive relationship and be a positive role model for students. These linked but distinct strands of teachers' behaviour, constituting what teachers do in the classroom, enhance student attainment and define teacher quality. Rowe was emphatic that teacher's quality is a key determinant of student outcome: "...the quality of teaching and learning provision is by far the most salient influence on students' cognitive, affective, and behavioural outcome..." 'what matters most is quality teachers and teaching, supported by strategic teacher professional development, maintaining that teacher quality is an important moderating factor responsible for the differences found in student performance within schools.

Attitude towards teaching as career indicates that while those who choose teaching as career are motivated mainly by factors such as wanting to make difference and working with children, the remuneration is the most significant factor that dissuades others in not choosing teaching as career or leaving it. Yet well qualified, well paid individuals are not necessarily more likely to be quality professionals, as recent global events have shown. The individuals within the finance sector, which precipitated the recent global economic crisis, were both well qualified and well paid. The education sector is often under scrutiny. Inversion and Rowe (2008) argued the concept of quality teacher is fraught with difficulties because it is almost impossible to measure directly. They suggested the measurement of teachers' quality for professional accreditation and development needs to focus upon what teachers know and should be able to do. They distinguished between successful teaching,

teaching which results in high performance outcome by students, and good teaching which provides learner with the possible opportunities to enhance their competence in a particular curriculum area, and does so in a morally defensible way. Teacher Education program is to promote growth among novices, it requires them make their pre-existing personal explicit beliefs; it must challenge the adequacy of those belief; and extended novices opportunities to examine, elaborate, and integrate new information into their belief systems.

Teacher Beliefs on Values Education

The idea that teacher's quality and quality teaching are linked with his/her values and beliefs is widely held. The significance of belief for understanding human behaviour is well documented. Cordelia Fine (2006) distilled a number of psychological research studies into a book illustrating links between belief, stereotypes and behaviour. In an earlier review of the research on teachers' belief, Pajares catalogued several sources supporting the notion that "belief are the best indicators of decisions individuals make throughout their lives" (Pajares, 1992, p. 307), noting the strong links between teachers' belief, their planning, instructional decisions, and classroom practices. She emphasised that beliefs are "far more influential than knowledge in determining how individuals organise and define tasks and problems and are stronger predictors of behaviour" (Pajares, 1992, p. 311). The social organisation of life in the classroom experienced by learners is critical to their outcome and depends upon managing the teacher's commitment. Pre-service teacher training programs must include a focus on ethics which elaborates the connection between ethics and science to help teachers deal with the challenges they meet in the classroom. In this way they can hope to enhance the quality of teaching approach and their students' engagement. Given that teachers' behaviour is substantially influenced and even determined by thought processes and that values, beliefs, and ways of thinking influence practice, an emphasis needs to be placed upon ethics education in the training of pre-service teachers.

An urgent re-focusing on morals through teacher training programmes: ...We are convinced that our attention in teacher education must shift considerably to the formation not only of knowledge and skills but also of the moral sensibility that underlies them. The moral nature of teaching cannot be conflated with the knowledge and skills important for teaching; neither can it be neatly separated from them. As we have known throughout ages yet ignore frequently, the moral is always in play in classrooms in teachers' actions, whether intentionally or not, and the complexity of the classroom environment-its immediacy and ever-changing activities-makes demands on teachers that reveal their orientation to their work in a myriad of daily acts. In sum, an ethics curriculum in pre-service teacher programmes assists teachers to tackle value education in the classroom so that they could respond to students' needs. Courses in ethics might be useful in preparing pre-service teachers for teaching, ethical decision making in the workplace and for the reflective practice required to improve the quality of their teaching.

Study Aims

The considerations outlined above were the impetus for a case study centred in a regional Tamil Nadu Open University. The study was designed in response to a workplace-integrated learning initiative to improve the quality of graduating students. Within a world wide climate of focused attention on ethics education, this study aims to:

1. Document examples of a range of ethical dilemmas faced by teachers in the workplace and pre-service teachers during, or in preparation for, practicum;
2. Examine the Bachelor of Education course curriculum for specific ethics modules/subjects across the four-year course at one School of Education in a regional university; and
3. Explore pre-service teachers' perceptions of training in ethics as a foundation for meeting the demands of teaching in school.

Methods

Ethics clearance was sought and participants' informed consent was obtained. Experiences and perceptions of ethical dilemmas were collected through focus group and individual interviews with final year pre-service teachers, recent graduates (old students) and practicing professional teachers. All participant volunteers were recruited for interview through the School of Education by the author and by invitation from school administrators in several schools. The interview protocol comprised two open-ended questions:

1. What does 'ethics' mean to you?
2. Describe any experience you have had in relation to ethical behaviour in the workplace.

All interviews were conducted by the author. They included seven Education undergraduates (in two focus groups), three recently-graduated teachers and eleven secondary and primary teachers from Chennai public schools. The number of participants in the study was dictated by the breadth of issues reported, as concept sampling was used (Creswell, 2008). Interviews were audio-taped and transcribed; all personal identifiers were removed from the written transcripts. Each transcript was read independently by two researchers in an inductive process to discover which ethical issues were being raised. Analyses focused on phrases, explanations and observations made by participants that endorsing themes under study. Ethics preparation of pre-service teachers in the School of Education was evaluated by examining subjects offered through the Bachelor of Education (BEd) degree course for ethics content. The assessment methods of subjects were also checked to ascertain if they assessed ethics or professional ethics. To determine the pre-service teachers' perception of the B.Ed course curriculum in relation to ethics training, a survey was used. It comprised 12 Likert-type questions and one free-form question; distributed during tutorial sessions at the university and completed by 86 of 120 (72 per cent) second-year pre-service teachers.

Ethical Dilemmas Reported by Experienced and Pre-service Teachers

Recent Graduate: Being aware of different cultural perspectives to behaviour management and educational expectations, indigenous cultural sensitivities.

Head of department: Providing pupils with rationale and the means with which to construct their own code of classroom behaviour; accepting the cultural and religious background of students, their practices and endorse them.

Teacher (Pre-service teacher): Behaviour management and the equity dilemma of detentions and suspensions.

Teacher (Equity issues): Avoiding racism, nepotism, giving as much access to resources (workshop) and one's time to students including those with disabilities and learning difficulties, not just to the bright students.

Teacher (Pre-service teacher): Improper grading, partiality based on who is liked, past performance, background.

Head of department (Human rights): Permitting (and teaching to the best of your abilities) a student back into your class after that student has assaulted you.

Teacher: Giving students with special needs as much time, help and resources as are necessary to help them to achieve, even if that is more than you would give to typical students and greatly increases your work load.

Conflicts between Personal and Professional Ethics

Head of department/Teacher: Teaching about the theory of evolution against the validity of students' religious doctrines. Modelling appropriate behaviours and moral values to students at all times so that there is no hidden curriculum and ambivalent messages.

Teacher(s): Teaching sex education to young students without a comparable value-moral component. To report to parents, (rather than the principal) a case of sexual misconduct between a teacher and a 16 year old same-sex student. Dealing with a suicidal, anorexic student who becomes dependent on a same sex teacher for extreme emotional support - how does a teacher support the student just enough, but does not cause her to become dependent on the teacher?

Collegial Ethical Issues

Pre-service teacher: Leering or sexual innuendos between colleagues/ principal and teachers/students. What do you do when you witness inappropriate, prolonged or unwelcome touching to comfort a distressed student?

Head of department: Plagiarising work done by other teachers and using it without acknowledgement to the author.

Teacher(s): What do you do when you see indoctrination and belittling of students' religious beliefs or practices? Malicious gossip about colleagues. Bullying behaviour; entering a colleague's class room and taking control, undermining the classroom teacher's authority.

Negotiating with Stakeholders

Head of department: Informing parents about their children's achievement and classroom behaviour when a parent does not like to hear that their child is responsible for particular behaviours.

Teacher(s): Being cautious when telling particular parents about a child's school activities when you know they will practice extreme physical punishment on a child. Take into account the personal circumstances of a child coming to school unprepared when considering the consequences for behaviour (e.g., a child who was inattentive in class due to spending the night awake and out of their home to enable the mother to conduct her prostitution "business").

Confidentiality Issues

Teacher(s): Talking about students' personal/family issues in a staff-room. Keeping school matters within school walls, particularly in cases of students at risk

Pre-service teacher: Talking about students' personal issues in a staff-room, referring to them as a 'slut'.

Head of department: Telling a parent that their under age child (16) is having a sexual relationship with another student (14) (Need the student's consent to do so).

Examples of Pre-service Teacher's Unethical Behaviour on Practicum

Teachers: Missing work ethic and being unprepared to meet the needs of the students in both the classroom and extracurricular activities. Lack of vocational attitude with respect towards profession, shows a clear bias against minority groups.

Head of department: Non-adherence to school policies in dress code and seductive behaviour with adolescents; non-adherence to school behaviour management; condoning pornographic images on students' cell phones; over-friendly behaviour with adolescent students of the opposite sex (touching, hugging), Using inappropriate language, including swearing, blaspheming in front of students and colleagues. Modelling inappropriate values in the school grounds like smoking, laughing at pornographic images on cell phones.

Hidden Curriculum

Pre-service teachers: Improper grading; partiality shown based on who is liked the most, past performance, background.

Teachers: Referring to minority groups in disparaging ways. Inclusion of students with special needs into the classroom as deemed to be "a waste of time…for one boy/girl with behaviour problems-that the time that could more usefully be spent on preparing a caring for the rest of the class".

Recent Graduate: Sexual harassment of male teacher by female students dismissed as a joke by the administration.

Head of department/Teacher(s): Indoctrinating students or promoting extreme political, controversial social or religious views.

Pre-service teacher: Right behaviour, what's right and what's wrong. Probably just following the code–I mean we've been told that when we do assignments and stuff that there's a Code of Ethics and that so getting permission to do certain things and there's right and wrong I guess ethical would be what's right and unethical would be what's wrong. I don't know but I think the definition of right and wrong would depend on the context.

Teacher: It's about how you were raised. It's a generational thing. Personal beliefs and accepted means of behaving in the community. Ethical behaviour would be to avoid gossip, not getting involved in slanging matches behind people's backs.

Systemic Power Relationships

Recent Graduate/Teachers/Pre-service Teacher

Authority in relation to students is greatly diminished—behaviour management is very difficult and you need to have parental support. Authority removed by administration and parents-no value for teaching yet expectations for discipline and moral education are firmly in place.

Ethical Dilemmas Reported by Pre-service and Practising Teachers

Audit of the Ethics Curriculum

In an examination of the subjects offered across the four-year Bachelor of Education degree course individual subject outlines were scrutinised, noting the learning objectives of each subject as well as the assessment descriptions and marking rubrics. This revealed that ethics was not taught explicitly at any particular year level. Ethics was found to be taught explicitly and assessed only in electives in the first and second years Health and Physical Education (HPE) for those specialising in HPE. Those specialising in Early Childhood Education were exposed briefly to ethics in relation to teaching in this age group, however the exposition did not involve any formal assessment. While professional standards for teachers were included in most of the subject descriptors, the ethics (philosophy) underpinning professional standards were not taught or examined in any subject of the four year degree. Professional standards and behaviours were discussed before each practicum in the second, third and fourth years and students' performance was assessed by the supervising teachers as being competent or non-competent.

Survey Results

Second year pre-service teachers reported a critical need for instruction and training in ethics, case studies, workshops, reflective journals and lectures were endorsed as useful learning experiences. The qualitative results derived from the pre-service teachers' responses to the extended-answer questions on the survey reveal a similar picture. They indicate a clearly perceived gap in their undergraduate preparation in ethics.

Discussion

A major finding of this study was the lack of explicit ethics instruction during the Bachelor of Education degree, echoing previous findings. The need for more ethics training in Education was expressed by a pre-service teacher: We can't be fuzzy on it (Code of professional ethics) because it has to be a part of our practice. Especially having a Duty of Care with the kids so I think it's very important that we know exactly what it is we should be following and not having any fuzzy areas. The ramifications of this gap are significant. Not only are newly-qualified teachers less well prepared to teach values (Lovat, 1998; Verrinder, 2007) or to demonstrate appropriate behaviours for their students, but also the status quo of existing unethical and unprofessional behaviours in schools are unlikely to be shifted. What ethics I have learnt I picked up outside university; need instruction through the B.Ed degree:

- Real life circumstances!!! Practical.
- Professional standards for HPE
- My ethical values have been developed prior to university — however it should be included in the curriculum
- More on it, like who decides what ethics and values we teach and what ethics and values we should teach
- I understand the basic idea of ethics but am not sure about how or what I would do in certain situations
- I think that it is important to discuss ethics and to be exposed to different ideas and explore what others think
- How ethics change over time - political and economic influences
- Explicit instructions on legal and preventative measures
- Dealing with subjects sensitive to adolescents, such as sex, drugs.
- How to handle family cultural matters
- Consequences of ethical breaches
- How to handle inclusion that compromise the well-being of the whole class
- More unpacking of professional standards
- All ethics should be covered instead of none being covered.
- I want to be helped to consider other viewpoints as I am becoming hyper critical of people's views; I don't want to become so narrow minded. I want to get out of my box to examine other views. Compliance

with particular behaviours may not correspond to internalisation of beliefs (Festinger, 1953), conformity effects have been found to be strong and disempowering.

Comments from interviewees about power relationships within the profession suggest the level of authority vested in teachers in India is low, in contrast to that experienced by Finnish teachers, who are applauded for exceptional quality teaching. This might be partly to do with the inability of teachers to defend their position philosophically, the weak stance of complacent relativism that is often displayed by those in the teaching profession. Alternatively it could also be something to do with forcing teachers through their training into a mould that represents teaching as simply a matter of mastering a repertoire of practical techniques. The teacher may be seen as a compliant technician with little responsibility for exercising professional discretion.

An ethics curriculum can help teachers examine their own position with greater confidence and in so doing to become better qualified to help their students do the same 'For teachers to demonstrate the values of respect, inclusion, sensitivity to difference, open-mindedness and cooperation, they need to have reflected on, and realised the value of, upholding these values'. Ethical issues arise in all academic disciplines and therefore educators need to know how to conduct discussions about ethical dilemmas with their students. Issues arising from collegial or institutional factors such as those reported in Table 1, might be better tackled in the short term if teachers were more confident in articulating their ethical concerns through robust debate. Empirical studies have shown that a persistent and eloquent minority of people can sway a majority, forcing them to consider decisions more thoughtfully and critically even when the minority is wrong. The key is the eloquence and thoughtfulness of the argument; herein lays the challenge to teachers. Long-term effects can also be anticipated as older teachers retire and are replaced by newly-qualified educators who have been given more opportunities to examine their ethical positions and how they align with their teaching.

Pre-service teachers have a simple, practical comprehension of ethics:

1. *as an ethos:* "Oh I guess the common sort of law of the school you know like what's commonly agreed upon as a good behaviour. Like at a Catholic school and the Catholic ideals would be the sort of structure there"
2. *professional standards:* "Um, I think doing the best possible job you can do, being professional about it" or
3. *relying on deontological arguments:* "ethics to me is do unto others like you would like them to do unto you, so, in fact, Christian values"

Competing arguments around ethical stances are rarely simple or static across time as, for example, the inclusion policy and corporal punishment attest. Many respondents were aware of a need for greater understanding and how to achieve this. When asked how they wanted to be taught ethics they consistently asked for context-based and practical scenarios. An HPE final-year student noted that "...in HPE we debated the issues of equity in very practical terms". These echo literature findings (Lovat & Toomey, 2007) and validate the place for an ethics curriculum in pre-service teacher education.

Limitations and Future Directions

The current study is a small scale study representing the views of pre-service teachers at one Tamil Nadu Open University. While results show that there is a need to include some ethics training in the Bachelor of Education degree course, more research needs to establish how other universities in our country are training pre-service teachers to manage ethics issues and values education. Moreover since this study has only included pre-service teachers studying a B.Ed degree, the views of those students training to teach through shorter post-graduate courses also need to be explored. To gain a better understanding of influences shaping pre-service teachers' values, beliefs and ethics, future research needs to examine the links between background variables of pre-service teachers and their perceptions of ethics education and professional ethics.

Conclusion

This study highlights a perceived need for the Bachelor of Education degree to include an ethics curriculum. As one pre-service teacher put it: "I think there should be lectures explaining them... (Ethics) Because, like the professional standards, they need to be broken down and things like practical examples given". Ethics need to be both integrated with professional standards and taught in a stand alone subject. It is clearly noted that ethics debate facilitates communication and clarification of contextual ethical issues and highlights the interplay of different personal values. Ethics understanding underpins the teaching of values, professional standards and reflective practice. This is particularly important in education with its diverse stakeholders. An ethics curriculum for pre-service teachers is a potentially sustainable intervention across political and economic times and contingencies, to 'raise the bar' by helping enhance teacher quality and, in parallel, student outcomes since positive relationships generally tend to precede learning.

References

- Alexander, R. (2009). Children, their world, their education: Final report and recommendations of the Cambridge Primary Review. Abingdon, NY: Routledge.

- Anderson, M.W., Teisl, M., Criner, G., Tisher, S., Smith, S., Hunter, M. et. al. (2007).
- Attitude changes of undergraduate university students in general education courses. Journal of General Education, 56(2), 149-168.
- Bergmark, U. and Alerby, E. (2006). Ethics of Care — a dilemma or a challenge in education? Paper presented at the Australian Association for Research in Education National Conference (AARE), Adelaide, Australia, 27-30 November, 2006.
- Bibby, M. (1999). Professional ethics and teacher practice. Ryde, NSW: NSW Department of Education and Training.
- Carr, D., (2006). Professional and personal values and virtues in education and teaching. Oxford Review of Education, 32, 171-183.

PART–II: WESTERN THOUGHTS IN HIGHER EDUCATION

8

Thoughts Behind Modern Pedagogy

M. Balasubramaniam and S. Rajaguru

Introduction

The Higher Education system in India and globe has been modernised periodically, especially in the methods advocated and practiced. Changes are only guidelines and cannot be changed on any occasion like the new innovative methods executed in the teaching and learning process. Modern methods are not new, it has strong background of philosophers.

Cooperative learning method is important method practiced in higher education system. It is a new method of teaching and owes to great Indian philosopher Swami Vivekananda. This cooperative teaching method stressed students work together (practice), share together (discuss) and learn together (experience). Cooperative method emphasise collaboration and shared understanding on any task; the evaluation is interdependent-a group must succeed for an individual to succeed. This paper is focused on the comparative approach taught by Swami Vivekananda and his thoughts about cooperative teaching.

Swamiji's View on Higher Education

Swami Vivekananda criticised the present system of higher education as materialistic. This system is not man making education, but entirely a negative education. It is based on negation worse than death. The present system of education is wrong. The mind crammed with facts before it knows how to think. We must have the education of our country—spiritual and secular, in our hands, and it must be on national lines, through national grid as far as possible. We want that education by which the character is formed, strength of mind is increased, the intellect is expanded, and by which one can stand on one's own feet.

The use of higher education is to solve the problems of life, engaged in the profound thoughts of civilised world, but it was solved thousands of years ago through the Gurukul system of education. The Gurukul system of education basically promotes holistic personality growth process by involving motor sensory activities that of-hand, mind, physical movement and reflexes with group. Vivekananda wanted the individual development done along with the group. This principle is emphasised in the cooperative teaching method.

Co-operative Learning Method

Vivekananda's thoughts of education are man making, character building and life building achieved through sharing, participating and practicing. The idea behind the method varied in the way of statement. The fundamental idea of cooperative learning is closely associated with Swami Vivekananda's thoughts such as—Empowering students take responsibility for learning, improve retention, generate more positive feelings towards the subject, provide more active learning, enhance sense of community among students, and promote inter-personal communication skills. The ideas were taken and adopted from the root and extracts of Swami Vivekananda's thoughts. Several definitions of cooperative learning were formulated. The widely used method in higher education is probably that of David and Roger Johnson of the University of Minnesota. According to Johnson and Johnson, Cooperative learning is instruction involving students in teams to accomplish common goal, under conditions that include the following elements:

1. Positive interdependence

Team members are obliged to rely on one another to achieve the goal. If any member fails to do his/her part, everyone does suffer its consequences.

2. Individual accountability

All students in a group are held accountable for their share of work and for mastery of the learning material.

3. Face-to-face promotive interaction

Although some of the group work may be parceled out and done individually, some must be done interactively with group members providing feedback, with one another challenging, reasoning and conclusions, and perhaps, teaching and encouraging one another.

4. Appropriate use of collaborative skills

Students are encouraged and helped to develop and practice trust-building, leadership, decision-making, communication, and conflict management skills.

5. Group processing

Team members set group goals, periodically assess what they are doing well as a team, and identify changes they will make to function more effectively in the future.

The elements of cooperative learning have some resemblance association with Swami Vivekananda's aims. This has been stressed and enforced by him in 1890's but it is not a primitive idea because it is still practiced in higher education.

Co-operative Learning and Swamiji's Method

The methods of teaching should be based on problem solving and life-oriented but not mechanical. As Vivekananda's methods are to reach perfection, physical and mental development, moral and spiritual development, character development, faith in ones own self and religious development. The methods and strategies adopted are, lecture method, discussion method, creative activities, self-experience, help, love, concentration and guidance methods in close association with cooperative learning, the teaching methods are think-pair-share, affinity, jigsaw, commonalities. Group investigation, three minutes, review, three step interview, STAD (Student Teams-Achievement Divisions) and round table strategies. He recommended the mode of self-experience from the group. Accordingly, practical experience is the best where one is forced to learn errors made. The strategies followed in cooperative learning methods have been; direct and indirect association with Vivekananda's methods. Life-building, man-making, character-making education can be achieved through group learnings viz.:

- Lecture Method Association with Three-minute review (CLS)
- Swami Vivekananda stressed upon the public lecture method. He emphasised the method for Arts' subjects. A three-minutes review method has some affinity with the lecture method. Lectures convey critical information, history, background, theories and equations.

Co-operative Learning Strategies

1. Three-minute Review

It is used when teachers stop during a lecture or discussion and allow the teams, review for three minutes what has been said. Students in groups can clarify question with other members or answer questions.

2. Discussion method association with Think-pair-share, Affinity, Jigsaw (CLS)

The discussion method allows the students and instructor exchange their ideas better understanding. It can be a whole period or be a part of a lesson. The discussion method for Arts and Science subjects and project methods involves think-pair-share, Affinity Jigsaw, Find the Fib method.

Co-operative Learning Strategies

Think-pair-share

The students are prompted to think about a topic or problem, record their ideas, pair with a neighbour, and share their ideas.

Affinity

Students job issues, concerns, or solutions on a card. Cards are collected and compared by the groups; "like" cards are sorted together to create categories and focus on issues, concerns, or solutions students have in common.

Jigsaw

The task and materials are divided into sections for each group member. The group members are assigned specific topics with members of other groups, notes are shared and discussed. Students re-convene with the original group to teach topic sections to one another.

Creative activities and concentration method association with Find the Fib, STAD, Group Investigations, Send-a-Problem (CLS)

Creativity can be defined "as the process of producing something original and worthwhile" through activities. Concentration is a mode to get perfect and true knowledge empowering analysis and synthesis.

Cooperative Learning Strategies

STAD (Student Teams-Achievement Divisions)

It is used among students with varying academic abilities in four or five member teams to study what has been initially taught by teacher and to help each student reach his or her highest level of achievement. Students are then tested individually.

Group Investigations

These are structured to emphasise higher-order thinking skills such as analysis and evaluation. Students work together for some group project, which may have had a hand in selecting.

Send-a-Problem (1 of 2)

Group members generate problems and write them on cards; questions are asked to other group members. If group members agree on an answer, the answer is written on the back of the card, if no consensus is arrived on, the question is revised so that an answer can be agreed upon the question cards and sent to other groups.

Self-experience, Love, Help, Guidance methods with all Cooperative Strategies

Self-experience, love, help, guidance are basic ideas in the cooperative learning, when the students involve directly in the activity. He gets some experience, when he is in a group, shares and gets the love, guidance and help.

Cooperative Learning Outcome aa Vivekananda Expected

- Critical thinking, reasoning about course content (i.e., active learning)
- Students acquire better understanding of the course content as they ought to explain topics to others in team
- Better attitudes toward courses
- Increased social skills, respect for multiple opinions and perspectives

- Higher achievement
- Higher productivity

Conclusion

The productivity of Man making, Character building, Life-education cannot be achieved through the present system of education and curriculum. When the students learn they learn from his group, learn themselves until perfection. When the students mingle with others, love spreads across. Sharing will make the human being perfect with perfect knowledge. Cooperative learning builds the Man with collaborative skill.

Love is the True Education - Swami Vivekananda

References

- Avinashilingam, T.S. (1943): Education – Swami Vivekananda, Sri Ramkrishna Math, Mylapore, Chennai (5th ed).
- Chandra, S. (1994): Swami Vivekananda's Vision of Education, In: Roy, S. and Sivaramkrishnan, M. (Eds), Reflections on Swami Vivekananda: Hundred Years after Chicago, Sterling Publishers Pvt. Ltd., New Delhi.
- Complete Works of Swami Vivekananda (8 Volumes). Advaita Ashrama, Kolkata, 1985.
- Ghosal , S., (2012): The Educational Thoughts of Swami Vivekananda: A Review, University News, 50 (09), Feb. 27 - March 04, 2012, New Delhi.
- Jitatmananda, S., (1998): Swami Vivekananda: Prophet and Pathfinder (4th ed.), Shri Ramkrishna Ashrama, Rajkot.

PART–III: WOMEN'S EMPOWERMENT

9

Education for Women Empowerment

Vanniarajan

"Where women are respected, there the gods delight... The best thermometer to the progress of a nation is its treatment of its women".
— Swami Vivekananda

Introduction

Swami Vivekananda had observed more than hundred years ago, "In India there are two great evils—trampling on the women and grinding the poor...". Women are the hub of the wheel of society. He would say "Never forget, the word is women and the people'. The two things that possessed Vivekananda's imagination was the uplift of the women and the masses. Through his deep insight he saw the success in the former owes to that of the latter. If India and the world have to rise, it has to be through women. "For this reason", said Vivekananda repeatedly, "they have to be raised first".

What did he mean by raising the women? He had a clear view on this subject. He said, "Any attempt to modernise our own women, if it tries to take them away from that ideal of Sita, it is immediately a failure, as we see it these days. The women of India must grow and develop on the footprints of Sita, and that is the only way"

"That is the only way" – his emphasis was striking and unambiguous, permitting no alternative. Trying to make women modern outside this mould of Sita has been the bane of our present education and socio-cultural striving. Every single problem that our women face today can be traced to their attempts to jump out of our age old spiritual inheritance. Swami Vivekananda could not foresee Hindu woman of the future, entirely without the old power of mediation. Modern science, women must learn, but not at the cost of the ancient spirituality.

He saw clearly enough that the ideal education exercise the smallest possible influence for direct change on the social body. It would enable every woman ahead resume into herself, the greatness of the women of the Indian past. East separate inspiration of days gone by had done its work. The Rajput story teemed with the strength and courage of the national womanhood. But the glowing metal must flow into new moulds. Ahalya Bai Rani had been perhaps the greatest woman who ever lived, whoever had come across her public works in all parts of the country, would naturally uphold so. Yet the greatness of the future, while including hers, would be no exact repetition of it. The mother's heart, in the women of the dawning age, the Vedic altar, out of which arose Savitri, with her sacred calm and freedom, was given the ideal background. But with the woman there must be a softness and sweetness, as of the south winds themselves.

Woman must rise in capacity, not fall in it. In the plans of Swamiji for a widows' home, or a girl's school and college, there were great green spaces, physical exercise, gardening, and the education on caring of animals, these always formed a part of the life lived. Religion, and an intensity of aspiration more frequently seen in the cloister was to be the heart of this new venture. And such schools, must transform themselves into pilgrimages following winter and study half of the year in the Himalayas. A race of women would be created, who could be nothing less than "Bashi-Bazouks of Religion".

And they should work on the problem. No home, but service in their work; no ties, but of religion; no love, but for Guru, and people and the motherland. Something of this sort was his dream. He saw plainly enough what was needed was a race of woman-education and this was how he contemplated in making them. Swamiji looked, naturally enough to widows as a class, the first generation of women educators. But in this respect, as in all others, he made no definite plans. In his own words, he only said, "Awake! Awake!' plans grow and work themselves." Yet, he would welcome any material, wherever it might have come from. He knew of no reason why it should be impossible for any woman—by strong and simple character and intellect, and uprightness of living—to make herself a vehicle of the highest ideals. Even burdens of conscience must be held redeemable by sincerity.

All great ends must be freely pursued says a writer on feminist movement. Our Swami had no fear of freedom, and no distrust of Indian womanhood. The growth of freedom, which he dreamt, would be no fruit of agitation, clamorous and iconoclastic. It would be indirect, silent and organic. Beginning with loyal acceptance of standards of society, more and more, as they advanced in achievement, women learn to understand the commands and the opportunities, which characterise the national life.

Swamiji regarded women as the embodiment of Shakti, the primordial energy of the feminist concept of a perpetual battle between the male and the female; he argued their roles complimentary. Education of women was essential for a nation's progress as that of men, with the difference they require to be trained differently in view of the difference in physical and mental make up and social roles.

Swamiji was aware that a number of historical and socio-economic factors had led to decline in the position of Indian women. They had not only been suppressed and exploited but also deprived of the right kind of education. Citing statistics, he regretted that even less than one percent women were educated in the country.

He believed that women could excel in fields of human activity, if treated on par with men and extended proper education and training. Although he suggested that they should be taught the rudiments of science, arts, housekeeping, cooking, sewing, embroidery, drawing, painting, photography, and other fine arts, they were equally competent to take up intellectual pursuits.

In this respect, he questioned the conservations thus: "In what scripture do you find statements that women are not competent for knowledge of celibate women, brahmacharinis, who would be instrumental in spreading education among girls. Swamiji advised that "ideal characters, must always be presented before girls to imbibe them with devotion to lofty ideals of selflessness." He felt women should be mature enough to resolve their problems instead of depending on men. He exhorted them to acquire heroic spirit and learn self-defence techniques. Swamiji was opposed to such social customs as sutte (the custom of widows entering funeral pyre of husbands), infanticide, child marriage and the confinement of women to homes. His concept of emancipation of women through education was based on spiritual and social principles.

Everywhere in the world, equality between man and woman had been sought in some legislation or external factors. But Swamiji marks the beginning of a grand shift in the equation of gender in a new way, reviving the ancient Vedantic view of human beings. Hence, the equation has to be drawn based on the divine core of both sexes, expressing as "EQUALITY". In the absence of this core shift in the way men and women look upon each other, equality based on mere legislation and external factors is bound to fail, seen everywhere even today.

The idea that men are superior to women was especially diabolical, and more so was the patronising attitude that men bore towards them. "It is wrong, a thousand times wrong". He said, "if any of you dare to say, "I will work out the salvation of this woman ... who are Lord God that you should rule over every widow and every woman? Hands off! they will solve their own problems".

Swamiji's exhortation, "Out with differences between men and women— all is Atman", may certainly be a distant goal. But that is the direction in which society ought to move. And the first step towards the attainment of this perfect state is: "To all women, every man who is not her husband, should be as her son. To all men, every woman other than his own wife, should be as his mother."

Swamiji had experienced the glory of the Divine in its feminine aspect during his tutelage under Sri Ramakrishna. Consequently, for him the women were the condensed forms of that All-Powerful Shakti. In his view, the only thing needed was to awaken this awareness in the womenfolk, and the rest would be easy. This is what constitutes true education of the women, "by which character is formed, strength of mind is increased, the intellect is expanded, and by which one can stand on one's own feet"

"With such an education", he believed, "women will solve their own problems. They will have all the time to be trained in helplessness, servible dependence on others, and so on so that they are good not only to weep their eyes out at the slightest approach of a mishap or danger. Along with other things, they should acquire the spirit of valour and heroism. In the present day, it has become necessary for them also to learn self-defence. See how grand the queen of Jhansi was".

References

- Prema Nandakumar, "He gave us back our dignity", Op-Ed, Debate @ The Hindu Social Issues (General) Discrimination, dated 10.01.2013.
- Quotations bearing the reference CW in the text are taken from: The complete works of Swami.
- Vivekananda. Volumes I-IX. Calcutta: Advaita Ashrama, 1989. (Mayavati Memorial Edition).
- "Swami Vivekananda and Women Empowerment" in Swami Vivekananda on Uplift of Women Society – Informative and researched article on Swami Vivekananda on Uplift of Women Society Published on Feb. 11, 2013.

10

Swamiji's Belief on Women Empowerment

T. Nagavalli

Introduction

Swami Vivekananda was the epitome of all that was great and good in India of the past. With Shankara's intellect he combined Buddha's heart, Christ's renunciation, and the Prophet of Arabia's spirit of equality, and the result of this holy confluence will in time flood the whole world says Swami Madhavmanda. The ideas of Swami Vivekananda have been a treasure for people across the world. In the backdrop of his 150th birth anniversary, it is imperative that one looks at his ocean of knowledge to seek more clarity. Even though he lived a century ago, some of his views are applicable even today in young India more than any other era.

There are varied opinions—Swamiji has expressed about women empowerment. He stood for it, nevertheless budged before the colonial attacks on Indian culture using the degradation of Indian women as tool to beat India. Carefully examining the two strands in his discourse, one finds that while asserting (but not advocating) the reasons for certain gender-specific Indian practices, as humanistic. Vedantist Swamiji has repeatedly emphasised his fellow countrymen remove their shackles on women and let them free. Swamiji worked effortlessly to uplift the plight of women, in particular—the Indian women. Let's browse over collection of his thoughts on women.

Swamiji on Women

- The soul has neither sex, nor caste nor imperfection.
- The best thermometer to the progress of a nation is its treatment of women.
- There is no chance for the welfare of the world unless the condition of women is improved.
- Women have suffered for aeons, and that has given her infinite patience and perseverance.
- The idea of perfect womanhood is perfect independence.

- There is no chance of the welfare of the world unless the condition of women is improved. It is not possible for a bird to fly with one wing.
- It is very difficult to understand why in this country so much difference is made between men and women, whereas the Vedanta declares that one and the same conscious self is present in all beings.
- All nations have attained greatness by paying proper respect to women. That country and that nation which do not respect women have never become great, nor will ever be in future.
- Where women are respected, there the Gods delight and where they are not, there all work and efforts come to naught. There is no hope of rise for that family or country where they live in sadness.
- Women in statesmanship, managing territories, governing countries, even making war, have proved themselves equal to men, if not superior.
- What was the way out to save and elevate Indian woman? Education was the answer.

When people are discussing as to what man and woman can do, always the same mistake is being made. They think they show man at his best because he can fight, for instance, and undergo tremendous physical exertion; and this is pitted against the physical weakness and non-combating quality of woman. This is unjust. Woman is as courageous as man. Each is equally good in his or her way. What man can bring up a child with such patience, endurance, and love as the woman can? The one has developed the power of doing; the other, the power of suffering. If woman cannot act, neither can man suffer. The whole universe is one of perfect balance. (CW V. 2, pp. 25-26)

We should not think that we are men and women, but only that we are human beings, born to cherish and to help one another. No sooner are a young man and a young woman left alone than he pays compliments to her, and perhaps before he takes a wife, he has courted two hundred women. Bah! If I belonged to a marrying set, I could find a woman to love without all that! (CW Vol. 5, pp. 412-13)

Men and women in every country, have different ways of understanding and judging things. Men have one angle of vision, women another; men argue from one standpoint, women from another. Men extenuate women and lay the blame on men; while women exonerate men and heap its entire heap on women. (CW V.7, p. 378)

Swamiji has glorified Indian women of the past for their great achievements as leaders in various walks of life. He proudly states that "Women in statesmanship, managing territories, governing countries, even making war, have proved themselves equal to men, if not superior. In India I have no doubt of that. Whenever they have had the opportunity, they have proved that they have as much ability as men, with this advantage – that they seldom degenerate. They keep to the moral standard, which is innate in their nature. And thus as governors and rulers of their state, they prove at least in India far superior to men. John Stuart Mill mentions this fact."

Swamiji views woman exactly as he views man, an individual with some destiny. In the sphere of spiritual realisation, which is the highest reach of life, woman as well as man, has to walk in a single file. Perfect freedom, independence and responsibility are involved in the individual, be it man or woman, who longs for God alone. "In India the mother is the centre of the family and our highest ideal. She is to us the representative of God, as God is the mother of the universe. It was a female sage who first found the unity of God, and laid down this doctrine in one of the first hymns of the Vedas. Our God is both personal and absolute, the absolute is male, the personal, female," he said.

Even if one amongst the women became a knower of Brahman, then by the radiance of her personality, Thousands of women would be inspired and awakened to truth, and great well-being of the country and society would ensue. Female education should be spread with religion as its centre. All other training should be secondary to religion. Religious training, the formation of character and observance of the vows of celibacy these should be attended to. Brahmacharinis of education and character should take up the task of teaching. In villages and towns, they must open centers and strive for the spread of female education. Through such devout preachers of character, there will secular education-the real spread of female education in the country.

Men and women in every country have different ways of understanding and judging things. Men have one angle of vision, women another; men argue from one standpoint, women from another. Men extenuate women and lay the blame on men; while women exonerate men and heapitsd entire heap on women. (CW V.7, p. 378). With five hundred men, the conquest of India might take fifty years; with as many women not more than a few weeks. The rise of outstanding women administrators, statesmen, scientists, writers and spiritual teachers, is gradually proving the truth of these prophetic words. Today, Swamiji words have proved true. Following the footsteps of Sarada Devi and Sister Nivedita, hundreds of women all over the world are coming forward with combination of the mother's heart and the hero's will', a combination of the purity of Holy Mother and the dynamism of Rani of Jhansi or Joan of Arc.

"Strength is life: weakness is death." It is a message for men and women of India. Yes, indeed it was Swamiji, who gave us back our dignity as women, our education, and our strength of purpose and reminded us again that no woman is a zero. Inspired by him, a host of social reformers all over India opened a new, glorious page for Indian women.

Swamiji repeatedly told that India's downfall was largely due to its negligence of women. The great images of Brahmavadinis like Maitreyi and Gargi of the Upanishad age, and women missionaries like Sanghamitra carrying

Buddha's message to Syria and Macedonia, all were laying buried deep due to millennium of foreign domination.

Women Empowerment

The progressive agenda that Vivekananda had towards women is very well known. In his own words, he says "That country and that nation which doesn't respect women will never become great now and nor will ever in future." This relentless pursuit of his to treat both genders with equality is evident through most of this discourse. At this juncture, Indian society is at a tipping point especially with the recent increase in the number of rape incidents across the country. The increase in education standards among females is triggering them to ask questions and confront the patriarchal nature of social systems which have diluted the equal space that women were offered even in our ancient scriptures. In this context, Swamiji's message of greater education and equality for female is pertinent especially with his visionary thinking of making female empowerment the benchmark for the measurement of any society's growth (Sriram Balasubramanian).

Throughout the history of Indian civilisation, it is clearly visualised that women enjoyed a very considerable position in society and their status was much better than at present. As several civilisations evolved, their status was gradually deteriorating. After the realisation of women's contribution to the development of the family in particular and the society as a whole, several attempts to empower women have been made by different social reformers, and this is an ongoing process. Swami Vivekananda, one of the great religious and social thinkers of India thought about the empowerment of women in the context of traditional Indian philosophy. His thoughts reflected throughout his work and speeches, which are more socialistic than religious in nature. He believed that in future, Indian women would cross the chapter of glorious achievements made by the ancient Indian women instead of making them only as a reflected glory. He tried to increase awareness, develop and empower women not only through education but also by enlightening them through the philosophy of Indian spiritualism, which might be considered as an effective system or approach in the process of empowering women. The word 'empowerment' is related to 'freedom', which is described in the dictionary as 'to make able'. More specifically, empowerment includes the physical, social, economic and intellectual development of human beings. Nowadays, the profession of social work also plays a very important role in this matter. But, it is also clear that in spite of best efforts, the women's empowerment movement is not up to the mark. Emphasis is given on physical and economic development rather than intellectual development. In the process of women's empowerment, the thoughts of Swamiji were very much applicable. These are related to the intellectual development of women and directed towards the total development process. After this process, women must find themselves free from superstitious beliefs, stronger and more self-confident in one hand whilst being full of love and affectionate, gentle-natured, full of mother-kind, etc., in the other (Ghosh, Raja, 2006).

Conclusion

Towards achieving women's empowerment and caste equality he faced innumerable difficulties and disappointments but he won in the end. He was able to teach even the westerners to look upon women as mothers. According to him, women are not play things, and women's problems could be solved by true education, which was, according to him, ".... a development of faculty, not an accumulation of words, or as a training of individuals to will rightly and efficiently. So shall we bring to the need of India great fearless women – women worthy to continue the traditions of Sanghamittra, Lila, Ahalya Bai, and Mira Bai – women fit to be mothers of heroes, because they are pure and selfless, strong with the strength that comes of touching the feet of God." (Prema Nandakumar, 2013).

References

- Avinashalingam, T.S. 1974. Educational philosophy of Swami Vivekananda. 3 ed. Coimbatore.
- Balasubramanian, Sriram, "Swami Vivekananda and why he is relevant a century later" retrived from his Facebook on 12.02.2013.
- Ghosh, Raja, 2006 "Swami Vivekananda's Thought on Women Empowerment: A Social Approach Rather than Religious Movement" Paper presented in McMaster University.

11

Educational Philosophies of Swamiji

C. Janakavalli and L. Komathi

Introduction

Indian society in the nineteenth century had fallen into a stage of degeneration after centuries of Afghan and Mughal, and then the British rule. At this crucial period, Swami Vivekananda strived ceaselessly to reform the Indian society, and in doing so, raised a new voice of pan-Indian nationalism. Vivekananda was unique—he was in close touch with both the core of Hindu religious thought and with the Western philosophy. He was thus able to take up the best features in his work and attempt to fuse them in his dream of the future. The message he preached in India was not the one of renunciation and mysticism that we hear. Instead he cried for work – work for the downtrodden and poor of the country, work to revitalise the society as a whole. Strength, strength was his message to Indians-physical strength, moral strength, strength to work for others. He railied against the weakness that had crept into the society, and preached self-control for the young. He strongly emphasised that the improvement and status of the society depends on the empowerment of women.

The Philosophy of Education

The real education according to Swamiji is that which prepares the individual for the struggle for existence. Education prepares man for social service, to develop his character and finally imbibes him with the spirit and courage of a Lion. For getting degree is not an education, the proper education must be viewed on the basis of character, mental powers, intelligence and inculcates self-confidence and self-reliance among people. Swamiji has emphasised that the knowledge which we get from worldly or spiritual lies embed itself in the human mind. It was covered with a veil of darkness and ignorance. Education is a tool to open from darkness and ignorance, after getting of education, the knowledge will shine out dazzlingly. The teaching and learning are the one way of process. The teacher guides, suggests, points out and helps the student. Self-learning and self getting knowledge is the real education. The teacher only motivates and encourages students to find the hidden treasure out of knowledge that lies dormant within. He condemned and refused the bookish learning and rote memory education. Condemning the theoretical and academic education, he spoke emphatically for practical and experimental education. He warned his countrymen saying "you will have to be practical in all spheres of work. The whole country has been ruined by mass theories."

The Means of Education

According to Swamiji, the means for education is love. Love and character building are the best means for education. Love is the best inspiration in character building. Love in the minds of educator is the real source of influence upon the educated. The true education, gives the growth and expansion of personality. He wanted that the education for total human development was the main vision. "Character, efficiency and humanism should be the aim of all education. Swamiji strongly pleaded that development of character through the service of his fellowmen, the utilisation of his talents for ensuring the happiness and welfare of the millions of his less fortunate fellow-citizens should be the aim of the education." The child should be taught through by love it brings in a fellow feeling and love for human beings. Education must help the individual to recognise his cultural heritage and to use it in his struggle of life. Education is a life-long process towards the fullest development of human personality, self-discovery, self-perfection, self-awareness and self-manifestation.

The Aims of Education

Swamiji wanted all-round development of education to heart and mind, to strengthen character and national consciousness, to help in the cultivation of strength and energy, nurture the brain and intellect and stir feelings of kindness and sympathy. He emphatically said: "We want that education by which character is formed, strength of mind is increased, the intellect is expanded and by which one can stand on one's own feet. What we need is to study, independent of foreign control, different branches of the knowledge that is our own and with it—the English language and Western science; we need technical education and all else that will develop industries, so that men, instead of seeking service, may earn enough to provide for them and save against for a rainy day. The end of all education, all training, should be man-making. The end and aim of all training is to make the man grow. The training, by which the current and expression of will are brought under control and become fruitful, is called education. What our country now wants are muscles of iron and a nerve of steel, gigantic will which nothing can resist, which can penetrate into the mysteries and secrets of the universe and will accomplish their purpose in any fashion, even if it means going down to the bottom of the ocean, meeting death face to face. It is a man-making religion that we want. It is man-making theories that we want. It is man-making education all round that we want."

According to Vivekananda, education is a process in which the young minds, will receive strength, energy and vigorous character. By the way of getting this process, the individual will mould themselves of their life. "All knowledge and all powers are within. What we call power; secrets of nature and force are all within. All knowledge comes from the human soul. Man manifests knowledge, discovers it with himself, which is pre-existing through eternity." Education is a man-making and nation-making process. It is the process which awakens the sleeping soul to self-conscious activity. It will become a powerful instrument to achieve the developmental qualities among the people.

The Women Empowerment

Women education is not in the hands of others, the powers are in the women. Swamiji considered that women to be the incarnation of power and asked men to respect them in every sphere. He rightly pointed out that unless Indian women secure a respectable place in this country, the nation can never march forward. The important features of his scheme of female education are to make them strong, fearless, and conscious of their chastity and dignity. He insists that men and women are equally competent not only in the academic matters, but also must have equal companion in the home and family. Vivekananda being a keen observer could distinguish the difference in perception about the status of women in the West and in India. "The ideal woman in India is the mother, the mother first, and the mother last. The word woman calls up to the mind of the Hindu, motherhood; and God is called mother."

Swamiji pleaded for the universal education so that the backward people especially women may fall in with others. To uplift women, he chose education as a powerful instrument for their life process. Thus education should spread to every household in the country, to factories, playing grounds and agricultural fields. He emphasised that "there is no chance of the welfare of the world unless the condition of women is improved. It is not possible for a bird to fly with one wing!" He strongly reasoned the cause of such degradation of Indian women. "The principal reason why our race has so degenerated is that we had no respect for these living images of Shakti. Manu says, "Where women are respected, there the Gods delight, and where they are not, there all work and efforts come to naught". There is no hope of rise for that family or country where they live in sadness. The Swami was particularly worried about the degradation of women in India.

"Swamiji strongly believes that there is a huge difference in the attitude of Indian men and their western counterpart. Indian men believe that the women are born to please them. The real Shakti-worshipper is he who knows that God is the omnipresent force in the universe, and sees in women the manifestation of that force. In America, men look upon their women in this light and treat their women as well as can be desired, and hence they are so prosperous, so learned, so free and so energetic. Swami Vivekananda said, "It is very difficult to understand why in this country so much difference is made between men and women, whereas the Vedanta declares that one and the same conscious self is present in all beings. You always criticize the women, but what have you done for their enlistment?" Swami Vivekananda glorified Indian women of the past for their great achievements as leaders in various walks of life. He proudly states that "Women in statesmanship, managing territories, governing countries, even making war, have proved themselves equal to men, if not superior. In India, I have no doubt of that. Whenever they have had the opportunity, they have proved that they have as much ability as men, with this advantage – that they seldom degenerate. They keep to the moral standard, which is innate in their nature. And thus as governors and rulers of their state, they prove-at least in India far superior to men — *John Stuart Mill*".

When people are discussing as to what man and woman can do, always the same mistake is made. They think they show man at his best because he can fight, for instance, and undergo tremendous physical exertion; and this is pitted against the physical weakness and non-combating quality of woman. This is unjust. Woman is as courageous as man. Each is equally good in his or her way. Can man bring up a child with such patience, endurance, and love as the woman can? The one has developed the power of doing; the other, the power of suffering. If woman cannot act, neither can man suffer. The whole universe is one of perfect balance. He was emphatic that women must be educated, for he believed that it is the women who mould the next generation, and hence, the destiny of the country? In Vivekananda's educational scheme for India, the uplift of women and the masses received the highest priority. The idea of perfect womanhood is perfect independence.

Swamiji views woman exactly as he views man, an individual with a destiny. In the sphere of the pursuit of spiritual realisation, which is the highest reach of life, woman as well as man, has to walk in a single file. Perfect freedom, independence and responsibility are involved in the individual, be it man or woman, who longs for God alone. "In India the mother is the centre of the family and our highest ideal. She is to us the representative of God, as God is the mother of the universe. It was a female sage who first found the unity of God, and laid down this doctrine in one of the first hymns of the Vedas. Our God is both personal and absolute, the absolute is male, the personal, female," he said.

If you do not allow one to become a lion, he will become a fox. Women are a power, only now it is more evil because man oppresses woman; she is the fox, but when she is no longer oppressed, she will be the lion. Female education should be spread with religion as its centre. All other training should be secondary to religion. Religious training, the formation of character and observance of the vows of celibacy—these should be attended to Brahmacharinis of education and character should take up the task of teaching. In villages and towns, they must open centres and strive for the spread of female education. Through such devout preachers of character, there will spread secular education. The real spread of female education in the country.

History and Puranas, house-keeping and the arts, the duties of home life and the principles that make for the development of character have to be taught. Other matters such as sewing, culinary art, rules of domestic work and upbringing of children will also be taught. Japa, worship and meditation shall form an indispensable part of the teach self-defense. . . Along with other things they should acquire the spirit of valour and heroism.

It is the strong belief of Swamiji that if the women are raised, their children will by their noble actions glorify the name of the country; then will culture, knowledge, power and devotion awake in the country. The rise of outstanding women administrators, statesmen, scientists, writers and spiritual teachers, is gradually proving the truth of these prophetic words. Today, Swami Vivekananda's words have proved true.

Conclusion

It is clearly understood from the philosophies of Swami Vivekananda that women empowerment is the basic foundation for the development of a society. His principles of sef-control, self-development and self-defense clearly indicated the importance of strength from within. We should remember his popular saying that "you must be the change you want to see"! It is the right time for educators, policy-makers and curriculum planners to incorporate more skill based education to promote self-regulatory competencies of Swamiji especially among women which certainly shall help our country reach the destination as the supreme power in world.

References

- Hossain, M., (1980). Swami Vivekananda's Philosophy of Education. Calcutta: Ratna Prakashan.
- Nivedita, Sister. (1999). The Master as I saw him. 9 ed., 12th printing. Calcutta: Udbodhan Office.
- Sengupta, S.C., (19840). Swami Vivekananda and Indian Nationalism. Calcutta: Shishu Sahitya Samsad.

12

Saintly Thoughts on Women

S. Vimala Ramani

Introduction

Women – "Be Emboldened"; "Embodiment of Goddess of Mother" There is no chance of the welfare of the world unless the condition of women is improved. It is not possible for a bird to fly on one wing."
— Swami Vivekananda

India of the Vedas entertained great respect for women amounting to worship. But during the time of Swami Vivekananda, the condition of women in Mughal-ruled and British-ruled India was deplorable. Swamiji said, "It is very difficult to understand why in this country so much difference is made between men and women, whereas the Vedanta declares that one and the same conscious self is present in all beings.

Swamiji was of the firm opinion that women should be put in positions of power to solve their own problems in their own way. The welfare of the world is dependent on the improvement of the condition of women. The mid-nineteenth century India saw women, the great mother—power shackled and degenerated to mere "child producing machines" as Vivekananda observed.

Swamiji views woman exactly as he views man, an individual with a destiny. In the pursuit of spiritual realisation, the highest reach of life, woman as well as man, has to walk in a single file. Perfect freedom, independence and responsibility are involved in the individual, be it man or woman, who longs for God alone. "In India, the mother is the centre of the family and our highest ideal. She is to us the representative of God, as God is the mother of the universe. It was a female sage who first found the unity of God, and laid down this doctrine in one of the first hymns of the Vedas. Our God is both personal and absolute, the absolute is male, the personal, female," he said. Vivekananda was against the concept of early marriage. Early marriage was the very reason for the existence of so many widows; so many women are dying early and the birth of emaciated children who would only increase the number of beggars in the country.

What was the way out to save and elevate Indian woman? Education was the answer. What kind is education? What is women's education? Sister Christine wrote that for weeks and months Vivekananda would be buried in thought, creating and recreating the splendid image of the Indian woman of the future. Would a combination of the western spirit of independence, freedom, and dynamism with Indian austerity, purity and chastity in woman's life be possible? A nation that has educated itself look upon God as Mother has learnt to invest its opinion on woman with utmost tenderness and reverence. Swami Vivekananda is the first monk to uphold and do work for the freedom and equality of women, realising her importance for the functioning of home and society.

He visited England in 1895 and met Margaret Elizabeth Noble, an Irish lady, who was in the midst of her learning about the Buddha. Influenced by Swamiji's teaching, she became the first Western woman to become a Sanyasin named Bhagini Nivedita. Nivedita played major role in promoting the rights of women in rural India. In November 1898, according to Vivekananda's instruction, she started school for girls, allowing them receive basic education. The school is today known as Ramakrishna Sarada Mission Sister Nivedita Girls' School, situated in Baghbazar of North Kolkata.

Swamiji on Women

- All nations have attained greatness by paying proper respect to women. That country and that nation which do not respect women have never become great, nor will ever be in future.
- With five hundred men, the conquest of India might take fifty years; with as many women, not more than a few weeks.
- Every nation, every man, and every woman must work out their own salvation.
- The idea of perfect womanhood is perfect independence.
- There is no chance for the welfare of the world unless the condition of women is improved.
- Women – I should very much like our woman to have your intellectuality, but not if it must be at the cost of purity."

Swamiji declared that the Western ideal of womanhood is wife, while the eastern ideal is mother. "The very peculiarity of Hindu women which they have developed and which is the ideal of their life, is that of the mother..........."

Swamiji glorified Indian women of the past for their great achievements as leaders in various walks of life. "Women in statesmanship, managing territories, governing countries, even making war, have proved themselves equal to men, if not superior. In India, I have no doubt about that. Whenever they have had the opportunity, they have proved that they have as much ability as men, with this advantage – that they seldom degenerate. They keep to the moral standard, which is innate in their nature. And thus as governors and rulers of their state, they prove-at least in India far superior to men".

— *John Stuart Mill*

The rise of outstanding women administrators, statesmen, scientists, writers and spiritual teachers, is gradually proving the truth of these prophetic words. When people are discussing as to what man and woman can do, always the same mistake is made. They think they show man at his best because he can fight, for instance, and undergo tremendous physical exertion; and this is pitted against the physical weakness and non-combating quality of woman. This is unjust. Woman is as courageous as man. Each is equally good in his or her way. What man can bring up a child with such patience, endurance, and love as the woman can? The one has developed the power of doing the other, the power of suffering. If woman cannot act, neither can man suffer. The whole universe is one of perfect balance. If you do not allow one to become a lion, he will become a fox. Women are a power, only now it is more evil because man oppresses woman; she is the fox, but when she is no longer oppressed, she will be the lion.

References

- Mac Kinnon Catherin A *"Feminism, Marxism, Method and the State: Toward a Feminist Jurisprudence",* in Pauline B. Bart and Eileen Geil Moran eds., Violence against Women: Body Footprints, New Delhi: Sage Publications, 1993.
- Maithilyananda, Swami *"The Ideal of Indian Womanhood"*, Vedanta Kesari, 1959.
- Menon, Nivedita, ed. *Gender and Politics in India,* New Delhi: Oxford University Press, 1999.
- Nair, Sukumaran. *Swami Vivekananda: The Educator,* New Delhi: Sterling Publishers, 1987.
- Nivedita, Sister. The Master As I saw Him, Calcutta: Udbodhan Office, 1977. Ranade, Eknath. *Swami Vivekananda's Rousing Call to Hindu Nation,* Calcutta: Century Publications, 1963.
- Sharma, Radha Krishna. *Nationalism, Social Reform and Indian Women,* Patna: Janaki Prakasan, 1981.

13

How Effective is Social Skills Training?

G. Subramonian and K. Suprabha

Introduction

Swami Vivekananda views that education is not information of knowledge which will be inserted into the mind of a child by force. In his own words - "Education is the manifestation of perfection already reached in man." He describes that the libraries could be the greatest saints of the world and encyclopedias have become seers and rishis. Vivekananda's concept of education was that, "it is the manifestation of the perfection already in man." He further said that the education was not of getting huge amount of information; in that case, it would be an undigested material of our brain. The good quality education must have the life building, man-making, character building, and assimilation of ideas. This would be of help to the common people to equip themselves for the struggle of life.

Saintly Philosophy of Life

The main essence of his philosophy of life is to become fearless through struggle and serve humanity with peace. He wants to make an individual without fear from enemies, face all the challenges boldly and confidently without any suppression. By synthesising the idealistic philosophy of the west and creative philosophy of the ancient Hindu Dharma, he achieved glory and greatness to the Hindu way of living.

The Means of Education

According to Vivekananda, the means for education is love. Love and character building are the best means for education. Love is the best inspiration in character building. Love in the minds of the educator is the real source of influence upon the educated. The true education, gives the growth and expansion of personality. He wanted that the education for total human development was the main vision. "Character, efficiency and humanism should be the aim of all education. Vivekananda strongly pleaded that development of character through the service of his fellowmen, the utilisation of his talents for ensuring happiness and welfare of the millions of his less fortunate fellow-citizens, which should be the aim of education." The child should be taught through by love, it makes fellow feelings and love for human beings. Education must help the individual to recognise his cultural heritage and to use it in his struggle of life. Education is a life-long process towards the fullest development of human personality, self-discovery, self-perfection, self-awareness and self-manifestation.

Saintly Views on Women Education

Women education is not in the hands of others, the powers are in the women. Vivekananda considered women to be the incarnation of power and urged men to respect them in everywhere. He rightly pointed out that unless Indian women secure respectable place in this country, the nation can never march forward. The important features of his scheme of female education are to make them strong, fearless, and conscious of their chastity and dignity. He insists that men and women are equally competent not only in the academic matters, but also must have equal role in the home and family. Vivekananda being a keen observer could distinguish the difference in perception about the status of women in the West and in India. "The ideal women in India is the mother, the mother first, and the mother last. The word woman calls up to the mind of the Hindu, motherhood; and God is called mother."

The Need

In the modern times, the history of women shows that they have come across many changing statuses. The Vedic period is said to be of complete equality for women. When the feudal period came, foreign invasions which took away women's freedom, and the national movement against foreign domination, also took women's rights and sexual equality as an important concern along with other issues. But now gone are those days and women of post independent India encounter many new problems which urge them to rise to the highest level of self-development, self-expression and self-esteem. In this millennium, equal access to education for both men and women is an important step towards greater gender equality and empowerment of women.

What are Social Skills Training?

Social skills training, is a competency-based approach to social interaction, in contrast to a deficiency-based approach. It includes an emphasis on determining people's ability to construct competencies and on offering them additional skills. The components of effective social behaviour indicate personal and situational characteristics that should be attended to. Careful assessment is necessary to identify relevant situations, to determine whether required skills are available, to find out whether there are discrimination problems in relation to, when behaviours can most profitably be displayed, and to determine whether negative thoughts or anxiety interferes with effective behaviour. It is thus important not only to identify the person's ability to construct effective behaviour, but also to identify factors that may interfere with effective social behaviours that are potentially available. Relevant information can be gathered through a variety of means, including self-report, written measures, self-monitoring, analogue or role play situations, and observations in real life situations. Ideally, multiple sources of information should be used, because one alone may not offer accurate information. These are briefly discussed below.

Means of Social Skills Training

Self-report

In self-report, descriptions of exactly what is done, said, thought, and felt in relevant situations should be obtained. The interview can be used to determine the range of situations in which interpersonal difficulties are experienced and the consequences that follow with adaptive and inappropriate social behaviours.

Written-measures

Paper and pencil inventors can be used as screening devices to identify social situations that are difficult, and they are useful to find out whether a person can identify appropriate behaviour. Self-report, paper-and-pencil inventors, such as the Assertion inventory may be used an overview of the degree of comfort in social situations as well as information on how the person usually handles a situation.

Self-monitoring

Self-monitoring, in which a person keeps track of some behaviour, thought, or feelings in certain situation, can offer helpful information for assessment as well as evaluation of progress. It is also helpful to ask people write down what they think an effective response would be, to determine whether they are aware of effective reaction.

Analogue situations

Analogue measures, where situations in the natural environment are simulated, are being used instead. A person can be asked to role-play behaviour in situations of concern, such as beginning an employment interview, with reciprocal roles assumed by the counselor after determining how significant others may act.

Observation

Role-Playing methods are artificial and may not reflect behaviour in real life situations. For this reason, role-playing may be supplemented by observation of interaction with others significant either in the office or at home. Valuable information can be gained by observing people in real-life situations.

Physiological measures

Little attention has been devoted to measuring physiological changes that may accompany social interaction. Heart-rate and pulse-measures have been used to ascertain the extent of anxiety during exchanges.

Component of Social Skills Training

Social skill training is designed to enhance observational, performance, and cognitive skills related to effective social behaviours in particular situations. It has variety of components, including model presentation or demonstrations, behaviour rehearsal or role-playing, feedback, guidance and home work assignment.

Guidance

Instructions, prompting and programming of change are used to ensure successful acquisition of skills. Each skill to be learned, including the exact verbal ands non-verbal behaviours that constitute the skills as well as situations in which the skill can be harnessed to attain certain outcome, should be described. Important components and their sequence may be noted on task cards or checklists, and participants can refer to these during rehearsal and model presentation. Thus instruction can be used to 'prompt' behaviours to encourage people engage in certain behaviours rather than in others. Use of guidance in this manner offers participants suggestions for attaining social goals such as refusing an unwanted request or initiating some conversation. It is important to clearly describe relevant verbal and non-verbal behaviours and when these should be used.

- **Demonstration**

Demonstration (model presentation) and rehearsal are usually employed when assessment indicates that a person lacks requisite behaviour to achieve certain goals. The advantage of model presentation is that an entire chain of behaviour can be demonstrated and the person asked to imitate it. Nonverbal as well as verbal behaviours can be demonstrated and attention drawn and those are especially important. The effectiveness of model presentation in establishing new behaviours, in decreasing avoidance behaviours, and in facilitating behaviours is well documented.

- **Practice**

Following model presentation, participants are requested to practice the modeled behaviour. This provides an opportunity to practice new behaviours in safe environment. It also allows others present, such as counselor or other group members, to observe behaviours, noting appropriate nonverbal or verbal components and those that still require some work. The contexts focused on should be clearly described and realistically arranged so that behaviour is practiced in some situation that is similar to the real life context.

- **Constructive Feedback**

Positive feedback should be offered following each rehearsal. Previously established criteria should be used, and checklists describing these can be referred to during feedback. These offers people a model of how to alter their own behaviour (to identify small, achievable desired changes, to practice them, and to offer praise for improvement).

- **Homework Assignments**

Much of the important work in social skills training is carried out in a real-life setting. After meeting the required skill and comfort levels, new behaviours can be tried in the natural environment through assignments. Initial assignments are high portability tasks being followed by positive consequences and entail minimal discomfort. Negative consequences can be avoided by understanding the relation and interpersonal dynamics of the situation wherein new behaviour is proposed. If negative reactions occur, a person should be prepared by variety of options available, including positive self-instruction and self-reinforcement skills.

How Effective is Social Skills Training?

There is no doubt that social skills training is a promising approach that has the advantage of clear description methods, ongoing evaluation of progress, and a systematic approach to desired outcome, making it potentially suitable for self-management programmes for many people. It is well suited for a group format, in the context of women, which will reduce costs and provide partners for new social adventures. More information is needed about the relative importance of components of skill training programmes, such as frequency of practice and kinds of demonstration. More information is required about the relative contribution of individual skills to successful performance. Continued development within social psychology among women population should enhance the effectiveness of programs that are developed.

Social Skills Training Programmes

Social skills training has been carried out with variety of population: howsoever, in some instances has behaviour analytic approach used in which situations of concern to particular population are identified by asking members and options are systematically identified and evaluated.

- with psychiatric patients,
- for children and adolescents,
- related to family interaction, and
- with other populations/situations.

Conclusion

From the analysis of Swamiji's scheme of education, the uplift of woman is possible only through education. His view on education brings some constructive, practical and comprehensive character. By giving education, he tries to materialise the moral and spiritual welfare and uplift of humanity, irrespective of caste, creed, nationality or time. By his scheme, we can get the strong nation with peace and harmony without caste or creed. He dreamt of a strong nation.

Research indicates that social skills training are effective in increasing competent behaviour. Research in this area should offer information that will help people especially women to enhance the quality of social environment as well as to offer higher-quality environment to others.

References

- Avinashilingam, T.S. (1964) *Educational philosophy of Swami Vivekananda.* Sri Ramakrishna Mission Vidhyalaya, University of Michigan.
- Larson Dale. (1984) *Teaching Psychological Skills: Models for Giving Psychology Away.* Monterey, California.
- Coughlin, L. Wingard, E. and Hollihan, K. (1999) Enlightened Power How Women are transacting the practice of Leadership. Research sponsor: Linkage, INC.
- Nithya, P. (2011) *Swami Vivekananda Views on Philosophy of Education.* Published Doctoral Thesis. Department of Philosophy, Pondichery University.
- Singh, S.K. (1983). *Religious and moral philosophy of Swami Vivekananda.* Patna: Janaki.
- Srimad Bhagavad Gita 5.25. An ancient Indian scripture.
- Basu, Sankari Prasad and Sunil Bihari Ghosh. ed., Vivekananda in Indian Newspapers and Periodicals, Calcutta: Bookland and Modern Book Agency, 1969.
- Bose, Nemai Sadhan. "Swami Vivekananda and the Challenge to Fundamentalism" in William Radice eds., Swami Vivekananda and modernisation of Hinduism, Delhi: Oxford university Press, 1998.

14

Educate Women to Elevate Our Nation

J. Rekha

Introduction

Swami Vivekananda (1863-1902), a great thinker and reformer of India, who embraces education, for signifies 'man-making', as the very mission of his life. Swamiji realises that mankind is passing through a crisis. The tremendous emphasis on the scientific and mechanical ways of life is fast reducing man to the status of a machine. Moral and religious values are being undermined. The fundamental principles of civilisation are being ignored. Swamiji seeks solutions for social and global evils through education. At any cost, educating women was the most important way of salvation for India, according to Swami. Swamiji's ideals have a strong commitment to the emancipation of women and he had great concern with the oppression of women in the contemporary Indian society. He was one of the first of his era in the field of religion to recognise the indignity and oppression to which women were subjected to in this world of men.

Child Producing Machines

During the period of the Saint, the condition of women in Mughal-ruled and British-ruled India was deplorable. Swamiji said, "It is very difficult to understand why in this country so much difference is made between men and women, whereas the Vedanta declares that one and the same conscious self is present in all beings. You always criticise the women, but what have you done for their uplift? Swami Vivekananda was of the firm opinion that women should be put in positions of power to solve their own problems in their own way. Vivekananda repeatedly told that India's downfall was largely due to her negligence of women. The mid-nineteenth century India saw women, the great mother - power shackled and degenerated to mere "child producing machines" as Vivekananda saw it.

Education for Women

Swamiji found education as the best and only device to solve problems of women and thereby their emancipation. According to him, for women problems can be many but none that cannot be solved by that magic word 'education'

He conceived of an "education by which character is formed, strength of mind is increased, and intellect is expanded. And by which one can stand on one's own feet". He said that in ancient times when... religion first began, women were distinguished for spiritual genius and great strength of mind. In spite of this, as he seemed to acknowledge, the women of the present day have degenerated. They thought of nothing but eating and drinking, gossip and scandal. According to Swamiji, one can hardly find statements that women are not competent for knowledge and devotion in the scriptures. On the deprivation of women in education he said, "In the period of degradation, when the priests made the other castes incompetent for the study of Vedas, they deprived the women also of all their rights. All nations have attained greatness paying proper respect to the women. His view reflects that of Marx's in whose theory the social progress can be precisely measured by the social status of their fair sex (woman). He quotes Mann to substantiate this, "Where women are respected, there the gods delight; and where they are not, there all works and efforts come to naught". He asserts that there is no hope for that family or country where there is no estimation of women, where they live in sadness. For this reason, they have to be raised first. He put the blame of the low status of Indian women partly on the barbarous invaders and partly on the people of India themselves. They have been trained all the time in helplessness, servile dependence on others. And so they are good only to weep their eyes out at the slightest approach of a mishap or a danger. Along with other things they should acquire the spirit of valor and heroism. In the present day, it has become necessary for them also to learn self-defense. Therefore he advised. "Educate your women first". He advised the Indian women to believe in India and Indian faith. Be strong and hopeful and unashamed. To reform Indian women he suggested such an education with which women will solve their own problems.

Education: An Eye-Opener

The aim of every system of education should be to help the mind manifest it. For this, he insisted on the old system of education, for females. He emphasised women study religion, science, art, housekeeping, cooking, sewing, hygiene, etc. Along with these, japa, worship and meditation formed an indispensable part of teaching. He said, "Their education must be an eye-opener in all matters. Ideal characters must always be presented before girls to imbue them with devotion to lofty principles of selflessness. The noble examples of Sita, Savitri, Damayanti, Lilavati, Khana and Mira should be brought home to their minds and they should be inspired to mould their own lives in the light of these. He desired that schools for girls be opened in every village. For imparting education, he finds it necessary to train Brahmacharinis who would go to the villages and other places and do hard work without any hesitation. For this, he planned to build up Math which he could not materialise during his lifetime. Later, he fulfilled his desires and Advaitha Ashram is propagating Swamiji's ideals.

In his view, educated women would inculcate virtues and values amongst children and prepare thus the new generation of people who could distinguish themselves in virtues and values. The development agenda of the twenty-first century acknowledged education as the key to women's empowerment for the same reason as Swamiji foresaw in the nineteenth century. The millennium development goals envisage that education of women "increases their productivity, raising output and reducing poverty. It promotes gender equality within households and removes constraints on women's decision making thus reducing fertility rates and improving maternal health. It increases children's chances of surviving to become healthier and better educated because educated women do a better job caring for children. It is only in the hands of educated and pious mothers that great men are born". Therefore he insisted that "daughters should be supported and educated with as much care and attention as the sons". He asserted that in ancient times, boys and girls were instructed, but now only the boys are favoured. An effort is being made to rectify the long-existing wrong. A good share of philosophy and laws of the land is the work of women during ancient times, before barbarians started to rule the land. In the eyes of the Hindu, the women now has her rights. She holds her own and has the law on her side.

Secular Education

Swamiji wished the ancient Shradha to return as remedy to solve problems of women. And we should change the parental attitude towards girl children. Somehow, they have to dispose of a girl to marriage if she be nine or ten years old, and rejoice when she deliver child at the age of thirteen. Through educating masses, this situation should change. And men and women should be married at a ripe age. But even today as Swamiji mentioned "as soon as the girl grows up a little, every one of the female sex, beginning with the mother down to the relatives and even neighbors, will begin to cry out that the father must find a groom for her, and will not leave him in peace until he does so. This is prevailing very much even today without any change. Girls are brought up so that their life is only to marry someone and not to develop as fully productive citizen by using the potentialities within her".

He prescribed the secular education for masses, that is, an education which brings the ideals slowly down among the masses and raises them to equality. He prefers to impart this secular knowledge through religion, which is Vedas. The 81st Report of the Committee on Value-Based Education-1999, did highlight the need to inculcate the principles of truth, righteous conduct, peace, love and non-violence, which are the religious values propagated by Swamiji.

Conclusion

Swami Vivekananda states it emphatically that if society is to be reformed, education ought to reach everyone-high and low, because individuals are the very constituents of society. The sense of dignity rises in man when he becomes conscious of his inner spirit, and that is the very purpose of education. He strives to harmonise the traditional values of India with the new values brought through the progress of science and technology. At present in India, violence against women, including domestic, has become a serious crime. From womb to tomb, women are under various kinds of discrimination and injustice. Subordination of women is now a universal fact and the measures for their empowerment discussing worldwide is being included in the development agenda. In such discourse, it is important to notice Swamiji's argument that men and women are equally good in her or his way. When judging them, it should be by the standard of their respective greatness. Swami Vivekananda's scheme of education through which he wanted to build up strong nation that will lead the world towards peace and harmony, is still a far cry. The best thermometer to the progress of a nation is its treatment of women.

References

- Dutta, R.S., (2001). Education in the Vision of Swami Vivekananda.
- http://vivekananda @amazon.com
- Maheshwari, V.K., (2011). Philosophical commentary on issues of today: Swami Vivekananda on Women Empowerment.
- Avinashalingam, T.S., (1974). Educational philosophy of Swami Vivekananda. 3rd ed. Coimbatore.
- Usha, K.B., (2009). Swami Vivekananda on the Women Question.

15

Women's Status in Education

V. Thilagavathy

Introduction

> *"In the Vedas and Upanishads, women taught the highest truths and received the same veneration as men."* — *Swami Vivekananda*
>
> *"Women must be put in a position to solve their problems in their own way. No one can or ought to do this for them. Our Indian women are capable of doing it as any in the world"* — *Swami Vivekananda*

Swami Vivekananda believed education is the manifestation of perfection already in men. He felt pity that the existing system of education has not enabled a person to stand on his own feet, nor did it teach him self-confidence and self-respect. To the wiseman, education was not only collection of information, but something more meaningful; he felt education should be man-making, life giving and character-building. To him, education was an assimilation of noble ideas. Education is not the amount of information that we put into your brain and runs riot there, undigested, all your life. We must have life building, man making, character making, and assimilation of ideas. If you have assimilated five ideas and made them your life and character, you have more education than any man who has got by heart a whole library.

Positive Education

Swamiji stressed on giving the public only positive education, because negative thoughts weaken men. Swami Vivekananda told, if young boys and girls are encouraged and are not criticised unnecessarily all the time, they are bound to improve in time.

In New York, Vivekananda used to observe the Irish colonists come - downtrodden, haggard-looking, destitute of all possessions at home, penniless, and wooden-headed — with their only belonging, a stick and a bundle of rags hanging at the end, fright in their steps, alarm in their eyes. Vivekananda observed a completely different spectacle in the next six months — the man walks upright, his attire is changed. In his eyes and steps, there is more fright. Swami Vivekananda tried to find out the cause, he told, if this incidence is seen by the explanations of Vedanta, that Irishman was kept surrounded by contempt in his own country — the whole of Nature was telling him with one voice — "Pat, you have no more hope, you were born a slave and will remain so". Having been thus told from his birth, Pat started believing in it and hypnotised himself that he is very low. No sooner had he landed on America than the shout went up on all sides—"Pat, you are a man as we are, it is man who has done all, a man like you and me can do everything; have courage!" Pat raised his head and saw that it was so; the self-confidence within him woke up again. Swami Vivekananda feels likewise, the education that young boys and girls receive is very negative. He thinks they do not gain confidence or self-respect from these educations, so according to Swami Vivekananda only positive education should be given to children.

Swamiji's Views

- All nations have attained greatness by paying proper respect to women. That country and that nation which do not respect women have never become great, nor will ever be in future.
- With five hundred men, the conquest of India might take fifty years; with as many women, not more than a few weeks.
- Every nation, every man, and every woman must work out their own salvation.
- The idea of perfect womanhood is perfect independence.
- There is no chance for the welfare of the world unless the condition of women is improved.
- Women – I should very much like our woman to have your intellectuality, but not if it must be at the cost of purity."
- Swami Vivekananda glorified Indian women of the past for their great achievements as leaders in various walks of life.
- India's reverence for women as the symbol of chastity brought such words from the saint.
- "I know that the race that produced Sita — even if it only dreamt of her - has a reverence for woman that is unmatched on the earth."
- The rise of outstanding women administrators, statesmen, scientists, writers and spiritual teachers, is gradually proving the truth of these prophetic words.

Swamiji concentrates and believes in the ideals that Vedanta says on women's position. He glorifies the ideals contained in the rich Indian heritage and Vedic scriptures. It is in the background of Vivekananda's understanding of the causes of degeneration of women in the modern age that he evolved his ideal of "Indian womanhood". Feminists are critical of the Indian cultural symbols, which glorify the woman's role as mother-goddess. She is projected as the symbol of productivity and welfare, spreading happiness and nullifying both wrongs and the perpetrator. This notion of motherhood has served as an institutionalised form of oppression for the subjugation of women. This view blamed the religious teaching, which advises young girls to model themselves on Sita; and this contributes to some extent to the low status of women in the society.

Vivekananda's position on women is scattered around his numerous sermons, speeches, comments, conversations, writings, etc. When he travelled through America, one of the important topics of discussion was of women's position in India. He compared the position of Indian women with those of the West. In this comparison, he found no reason for the inferior position of Indian women. In a letter written from Chicago when he was there to participate in the Parliament of World Religions, he mentioned "Nowhere in the world are women like those of this country. How pure, independent, self-relying and kind hearted! It is the women who are the life and soul of the country. All learning and culture centered in this country.... There are thousands of women here, whose minds are as pure and as white as snow of this country". Then he said about the Indian women, "Look at our girls, becoming mothers below their teens! I now see it all". He understood the paradox of Manu's dictum, "The Gods are pleased when the women are held high in esteem" and the reality of women's position and says, "We are horrible sinners, and our degradation is due to our calling women 'despicable worms', 'gateways to hell' and so forth' (CW, Vol. 6: 252- 5 53) He was aware of their subordinate position, but was not satisfied with their condition during his days.

Education for Women

Swamiji's found education as the best and only device to solve all problems of women and thereby emancipate them. According to him, for women problems can be many "but none that cannot be solved by that magic word 'education'". He conceived of an "education by which character is formed, strength of mind is increased, intellect is expanded, and by which one can stand on one's own feet". He said that in ancient times when... religion first began, women were distinguished for spiritual genius and great strength of mind. In spite of this, as he seemed to acknowledge, the women of the present day had degenerated. They thought of nothing but eating and drinking, gossip and scandal. (Ibid: 150). Therefore, he prescribed an education that would create "great fearless women - women worthy to continue the traditions of Sangamitra, Lila, Ahalya Bai, and Mira Bai—women fit to be the mothers of heroes. (CW, Vol. 5: 229). Such an education was emphasised on Swamiji's concept of true womanhood, which is vested in "the old-time intensity of trustful and devoted companionship to the husband" and hence his message to Indians was "forget not that the ideal of thy womanhood is Sita, Savitri, Damayanti". (CW, Vol. 4: 479-80). For him, the development of true ideal of womanhood was the primary goal of education.

Conclusion

Swami Vivekananda was a monk who at one time saw women as an obstacle. However, on realising the highest truth he saw no distinction between sexes and saw in women—the presence of the Divine Mother. Swami Vivekananda was of the firm opinion that women should be put in positions of power to solve their own problems in their own way. The welfare of the world is dependent on the improvement of the condition of the women. In Vivekananda's educational scheme for India, the uplift of women and the masses received the highest priority.

Reference

- Basu, Sankari Prasad and Sunil Bihari Ghosh— ed., Vivekananda in Indian Newspapers and Periodicals, Calcutta: Bookland and Modern Book Agency, 1969.
- Bose, Nemai Sadhan. "Swami Vivekananda and the Challenge to Fundamentalism" in William Radice eds., Swami Vivekananda and modernisation of Hinduism, Delhi: Oxford university Press, 1998.
- http://en.wikipedia.org/wiki/Teachings_and_philosophy_of_Swami_Vivekananda#Education
- http://www.businesseconomics.in/? p = 1061

16

Education for Women Empowerment— A Saintly Vision

A. Kalaivani

Introduction

Indian society in the nineteenth century had fallen into a stage of degeneration after centuries of Afghan and Mughal, and then British rule. The British rule, specially, had created widespread poverty and hunger, and the propaganda of missionaries created a sense of insecurity among the people about their traditional customs and beliefs. At this crucial period rose a number of important reformers like Raja Ram Mohan Roy, Swami Dayanand Saraswati and Swami Vivekananda. They strived ceaselessly to reform the Indian society, and in doing so, raised a new voice of pan- Indian nationalism. They were thus the vanguards of the Freedom Movement. This first voice of protest was not so much against the political exploitation by the British, but against their moral exploitation of Indian society, and this was to guide and provide the unique feature of the Indian Freedom struggle. Among these leaders, Vivekananda's position was unique in that he was in close touch with both the core of Hindu religious thought and with the Western philosophy. He was thus able to take up the best features of both in his work and attempt to fuse them in his dream of the future.

Swami Vivekananda is one of the most enduring icons of the rise of Indian nationalism in modern India. We know him today as being one among the first generation of leaders, who raised the voice of Indian nationality. Equally important is that he was an intensely religious man who lived a life immersed in spirituality. His position was unique in that along with a modern education which gave him a critical attitude, and his account of experience and the importance in life are as important as his work in nation building. Generally, empowerment is considered as development of skill to make a person more confident, self-reliant and to develop ability to take self-decisions. Empowerment is a process of strengthening/enhancing the authority/autonomy by giving information, delegation of responsibility, and offering share in decision-making, so that the performance life improves, in different sectors to qualify an individual an organiser and good employee in a work setting. Empowerment refers broadly to the expansion of choice and action to shape one's life. For women, freedom is being curtailed by their voiceless and powerless condition in relation particularly to the state and markets.

Women's Empowerment

Women's empowerment addresses power and relationships in society intertwined with gender, class, race, ethinicity, age, culture and history. To empower women literally speaking is to give power to women. 'Power' here does not mean some mode of domination over others, but the sense of internal strength and confidence to face life, the right to determine one's choices in life, the ability to influence the social process that affects one's life, and influence in the direction of social change, a share in decision-making and capacity-building to contribute towards national development.

Empowering women requires the removal of formal and informal institutional barriers that prevent them from taking action to improve their well-being individually or collectively — and limit their choice. The key formal institutions include the laws, rules, and regulations upheld by states, markets, civil society, and international agencies; informal institutions include norms of social solidarity, sharing, social exclusion, and corruption, among others. When women feel they can operate in society on the same terms as men, we can then call empowered women. Empowerment means very different things to different group of women, and varies according to the level of development in particular society. Every NFA should endeavour to decide for itself what empowerment means for women in the context of its own culture.

Means to Empower

In a society, there would be no gap between men and women in categories that are not based on gender opportunities and access to resources would be similar for men and women. There has been growing realisation among the world community that there would be the active participation of women side by side along with men; the goals of national development would remain a dream. The following are some of the ways to empower women:— (a) education (b) employment opportunities (c) legislations (d) development of income generating skills, (e) enhancing state of women, (f) reducing gender inequalities through change in attitudes, (g) capacity building. Education is a prime and vital mean for women Empowerment.

Education liberates women from the clutches of inequalties. Education is a force to reduce gender inequalities and access to mobility, share in decision making and contribution to national development. At home, women's education has greater effect on the family welfare than men's education. Mothers schooling also improves her own health status, and the educational attainment of her children particularly that of daughters. Violence against women at home or on streets has been associated not just with poverty but with illiteracy, which prevents women from asserting their rights. Education empowers women, it can be directly observed in enhanced productivity, wider employment opportunities and life time earning. Women's self-perception is improved by the knowledge they contribute financially and visibly to the household, and they are in a better negotiating position; should relations break down they could survive. Indirectly, education among women is widely known to have strong depressant effect on child bearing. Literate women tend to marry later than illiterate women. They tend to be more knowledgeable about family planning services. This keeps population under control and accelerate the economic development process.

Vision of Swamiji on Education for Women Empowerment

Swami Vivekananda gave Indians proper understanding of country's spiritual heritage and thus the pride in their past. Eminent leaders of India's freedom movement have acknowledged their indebtedness to Swamiji. Our first Prime Minister Jawaharlal Nehru wrote: "Rooted in the past, full of pride in India's prestige, Vivekananda was yet modern in his approach to life's problems, and was a kind of bridge between the past of India and her present... he came as a tonic to the depressed and demoralised Hindu mind and gave it self-reliance and some roots in the past." Where can you find a man like him? Study what he wrote, and learn from his teachings, for if you do, you will gain immense strength. Take advantage of the fountain of wisdom, of Spirit, and of fire that flowed through Vivekananda!

Similarly, Netaji Subhash Chandra Bose wrote: "Swami Vivekananda harmonised the East and the West, religion and science, past and present. And that is why he is great. Our countrymen have gained unprecedented self-respect, self-reliance and self-assertion from his teachings." Vivekananda strongly reasoned the cause of such degradation of Indian women "The principal reason why our race has so degenerated is that we had no respect for these living images of Shakti. Manu says, "Where women are respected, there the Gods delight, and where they are not, there all work and efforts come to naught." There is no hope of rise for that family or country where they live in sadness. The Swamiji was particularly worried about the degradation of women in India.

Swamiji was of the firm opinion that women should be put in positions of power to solve their own problems in their own way. The welfare of the world is dependent on the improvement of the condition of the women. He was emphatic that women must be educated, for he believed that it is the women who mould the next generation, and hence, the destiny of the country. In his educational scheme for India, the uplift of women and the masses received the highest priority. The idea of perfect womanhood is perfect independence. Vivekananda was against the early marriage. Early marriage was the very reason for the existence of so many widows, so many women dying early and the birth of emaciated children, who would only increase the number of beggars in the country.

Swamiji observes woman exactly as he views man, an individual with a destiny. In the sphere of the pursuit of spiritual realisation, which is the highest reach of life, woman as well as man, has to walk in a single file. Perfect freedom, independence and responsibility are involved in the individual, be it man or woman, who longs for God alone. "In India, the mother is the centre of the family and our highest ideal. She is the representative of God to us, as God is the mother of the universe. Our God is both personal and absolute, the absolute is male, the personal, female," he said. Female education should be spread with religion as its centre. Religious Training, the formation of character and observance of the vows of celibacy these should be attended to Brahmacharinis of education and character should take up the task of teaching. In villages and towns, they must open centers and strive for the spread of female education. Through such devout preachers of character, there will be secular education—the real spread of female education in the country. Along with other things, they should acquire the spirit of valour and heroism. In the present day, it has become necessary for them also to learn self-defense how grand was the Queen of Jhansi! Women - "Be Emboldened"; "Embodiment of Goddess of Mother".

Vivekananda declared that the western ideal of womanhood is wife, while the eastern ideal is mother. "The very peculiarity of Hindu women which they have developed and which is the ideal of their life, is that of the mother..........." A nation that has educated itself to look upon God as Mother has learnt to invest its observation of woman with the utmost tenderness and reverence. We must see to their growing up as ideal matrons of home in time. The children of such mothers will make further progress in the virtues that distinguishes them. It is only in the homes of educated pious mothers are being born. It is the strong belief of Swamiji that if the women are raised, their children will by their noble actions glorify the name of the country; then will culture, knowledge, power and devotion awake in the country. The rise of outstanding women administrators, statesmen, scientists, writers and spiritual teachers, is gradually proving the truth of these prophetic words. Today, Swami Vivekananda's words have proved true. Following the footsteps of Sarada Devi and Sister Nivedita, hundreds of women all over the world are coming forward with combination of the 'mother's heart and the hero's will,' a combination of the purity of Holy Mother and the dynamism of Rani of Jhansi or Joan of Arc. All nations have attained greatness by paying proper respect to women. That country and that nation which do not respect women have never become great, nor will ever be in future, men.

Conclusion

Education of women benefits individuals, families and communities. By educating women, a country can reduce poverty, improve productivity, ease population pressure, and offer children a better future. Recent studies show that the economic and social returns to the family as a result of education for women are greater than those for men. Educated mothers and father have better educated children and maternal education tends to influence a girl's education in particular. As each generation of women is educated, so are the long-term rewards for society to build quickly, so, in order to reap these benefits, empowerment of women is essential through education.

References

- His Eastern and Western Disciples. (1989). The Life of Swami Vivekananda. 2 Vols. 6th ed. Calcutta.
- Hossain, M. (1980). Swami Vivekananda Philosophy of Education. Calcutta: Ratna Prakashan.
- Nivedita, Sister. (1999). The Master as I saw him 9th ed., 12th printing. Calcutta: Udbodhan Office.
- Sengupta, S.C. (1984). Swami Vivekananda and Indian Nationalism. Calcutta: Shishu Sahitya Samsad.
- Singh, S.K. (1983). Religious and Moral Philosophy of Swami Vivekananda. Patna: Janaki.
- Srimad Bhagavad Gita 5.25. An ancient Indian scripture.

17

Education— A Catalyst in Empowering Women

Reshmi Ramachandran and G Subramonian

Introduction

From ancient times, our scriptures have given great importance to women in shaping human destiny. From the Vedic times to some thousand years back, women in India were free, educated and respected. The Upanishads contain references to women like Maitreyi, Gargi and others, who attained the highest standard of learning and challenged scholarly men. They were well-versed in religion, arts and literature. In those days, far from being treated as commodity, women enjoyed the highest respect in society.

Some blamed the downfall of women on wars and invasions, which led to restrictions on women education and mobility. Some reformers located the decline during the time of Smrities, that is, to a period when the vast body of law codes such as the Manu Smiriti was being written. Most of the reformers blamed the Muslim rule; they claimed child marriage, prohibitions on widow marriage and restrictions on female education to Muslim rule. At the time, when some social reformers were thinking of re-introducing education for women, Sri Ramakrishna demonstrated the greatness of women and sowed thus the seeds of women empowerment. He worshipped 'Shakti' as God and accepted a women as guru. He worshipped his own wife as the Mother Goddess and devotedly served his mother.

Sri Ramakrishna's greatest disciple, Swami Vivekananda followed similar path. He traced the downfall of India to the continued neglect of her women and the masses. He considered ill-treatment of women and oppression of the poor as the great evils destroying our nation. To solve these problems, he suggested uplift of women and the masses.

Swamiji's Views on Women

In West, the idea of womanhood is associated with that of the wife. In India idea of womanhood is associated with that of mother. The name 'mother' is called holy, once and forever. That is the ideal of India. Swamiji s views on ideal woman in India was the Mother, the mother first and the mother last. The word woman calls up to Indian mind—the motherhood. God is called Mother. Motherhood means tremendous responsibility. She carries a baby in her body. She is there anytime her baby wants her. It is she who creates appreciably, the physical and mental makeup of the child. "Why should mother be worshipped?" A mother made herself pure; she went harsh penances sometimes to keep herself pure. She kept her body, mind, food, clothes and her imagination pure. In the land of Sita and Savithri, women may found with character spirit of service such as affection, compassion, contentment which cannot be formed where in the world.

"Mother has been born to revive that wonderful Shakti in India and making her the nucleus, once more will Gargis and Maitreyis be born into the world". He considered women as Shakti. There is no regeneration for the world without Shakti. Our country is the weakest and the most backward of all only because Shakti is being held in dishonor. All great nations have become great because they have shown respect for women. The nation which do not respect woman have never become great nor will ever be in future. Manu says "Where women are respected there the Gods delight, where they are not, there all work and effort come to naught."

Empowerment through Education

Empowerment of women means strengthening of their capabilities in the social, political and economic sphere. Real empowerment of women lies in helping them unfold the spiritual aspect of their personality, build up their character and manifest their purity and motherhood. It is these that make up the character of the ideal Indian woman, earning capacity and public status are secondary. All women are parts of the same infinite divine power and hence divine. Empowerment of women can take place only through education.

(a) Education—The Panacea

Swamiji says "Educate your women first and leave them to themselves. Then they will tell you what reforms are necessary for them. In matters concerning them, who are you to decide?"

He emphasised the need of educating women as the first step in empowering her. He was against men deciding for women. They are matured enough to decide what is right for them. Swami Vivekananda rightly said "Our duty is to put the chemicals together; the crystallisation will come through God's law. Let us put idea into their heads and they will do the rest."

Women have to shoulder great responsibilities and she is expected to solve these problems. How can she solve these problems? Only through education. Our women are educated only to remain helpless. They are trained to be dependent on others and so they are afraid to face the world. Education will pave way to make Indian women independent. It will help her solve her own problems, her family's problems and will support the whole society.

Swamiji believed, "With 500 men, the conquest of India may take 50 years: with as many women, not more than a few weeks". The conquest he emphasised is development of a nation. The home is the world in which the child grows into adulthood. An educated women or an educated mother develops an educated society in future.

(b) Religion—the foci

Swamiji wanted women's education to be developed and spread with religion as foci. His future vision was to give full education to women in science and sports, but with an equal or more emphasis on ancient spirituality. Her infinite divine power has to be developed within her through education based on spirituality.

(c) Training in renunciation

Even if one woman attains spiritual realisation of Brahman then with her radiant personality, 1,000's of women would be inspired and awakened about the truth. He wanted such brahmacharinis of education and character to take up the task of teaching. Studying the present needs, it seems imperative to train some of them up in the ideal of renunciation.

(d) Education provided

History, Puranas, housekeeping, arts, the duties of home life and principles that make for the development of character ought to be taught. Sewing, culinary arts, rules of domestic work and upbringing of children could also be taught. Japa, worship and meditation shall form an indispensable part of such teaching.

Sports, gardening and care of animals were emphasised. He inspired young girls to develop the qualities of strength, feminine softness and sweetness, but without self-advertisement or over emotion.

Present Situation of Women

The status of women has been subject to many great changes over the past few years. From equal status with men in ancient times through low points of medieval period, it lead to the promotion of equal rights by many reformers.

The constitution of India guarantees women equality (Article 14), no discrimination by the State (Article 15(1)), equality of opportunity (Article 16) and equal pay for equal work (Article 39 (d)).

In spite of many rights and rules in favour of women, Indian women are still facing gender inequality. She has to be empowered to make herself radiant. The increased rate of crimes against women show them to have come a long way. She is being harassed at home, and at work besides before the public. She is not safe anywhere. Unless they take firm stand and push forward, it would not be possible to regain their status.

Educational attainment and economic participation are key constituents in ensuring the empowerment of women. Education is the important parameter in all spheres of activities. Without proper education, she can't fulfill her desires. Education is the only tool that can help her break the pattern of gender discrimination. It is the only way she could overcome the hurdles ahead.

Education is closely related to the development process of women and deprivation adversely affects their status. Education contributes to the development of woman but also a nation as in many ways. Educated women can provide better childcare besides earning potential and productivity. They can assert their rights and play their role effectively in national development.

Conclusion

In Swamiji's words "There is no chance for the welfare of the world unless the condition of women is improved. It is not possible for a bird to fly on only one not possible for a bird to fly on only one wing". The condition of women cannot be improved unless she is educated. Education acts like some catalyst in empowerment. Swamiji rightly pointed the importance of women that too an empowered women in the development of nation as a whole. It is just like the story that Sri Ramakrishna used to narrate about the man who went in search of light with lantern in hand. The solution to the development of nation is only through empowered women.

References

- Vivekananda, Swami. (2012) Our women. Kolkata: Advaita Asharam.
- Avinashiligam, T.S. (1964). Educational Philosophy of Swami Vivekananda. Coimbatore: Sri Ramakrishna Mission Vidyalaya.
- Burke, Marie Louise. (1986). Swami Vivekananda in the west, New Discoveries: The World Teacher. Part Two. Calcutta: Advaita Ashrama.
- Swami Vivekananda - A hundred years since Chicago: A commemorative volume. (1994). Calcutta: Swapna Printing Works (P) Ltd.
- http://www.cafindia.org/pages/CAF-19%209%202011.pdf

18

Swamiji's Thoughts for Women Education

G Kumutha

Introduction

Women education in India plays a pivotal role in the development of country. It has helped in the development of half of the population as well as the living standard of family at home and outside. Educated women support women education and give better education to their children. Educated women help in reducing the infant mortality rate in India. Educated women handle their family in a better way than illiterate women. So, we shouldn't forget the importance of women's education in India.

Swamiji said, "It is very difficult to understand why in this country so much difference is made between men and women, whereas the Vedanta declares that one and the same conscious self is present in all beings. You always criticise the women, but what have you done for their enlistment?"

As Swamiji says, the most meaningful and longest social movement still continuing in the present day is the emancipation of women. Though the main purpose for women empowerment is to enhance the quality of life for women, but have deep ramifications in social, economic and political scenario. In a country like India, we see that women have been relegated to secondary position. The vested interest of the elite class has played an important part in pushing them to oblivion. Swami Vivekananda has been very vocal about the uplift of women clan all through his life. Hence this paper much emphasises the Swami Vivekananda's thoughts on Women Education.

Saintly Observation

Vivekananda repeatedly told India's downfall as largely due to her negligence of women. The great images of Brahmavadinis like Maitreyi and Gargi of the Upanishad age, and women missionaries like Sanghamitra carrying Buddha's message to Syria and Macedonia, they were laying buried deep due to millennium of foreign donation. The mid-nineteenth century India saw women, the great mother-power shackled and degenerated to mere "child producing machines" as Vivekananda saw it.

Swamiji believes woman exactly as he views man, an individual with some destiny. In the sphere of the pursuit of spiritual realisation, which is the highest reach of life, woman as well as man has to walk in a single file. Perfect freedom, independence and responsibility are involved in the individual, be it man or woman, who longs for God alone. "In India, the mother is the centre of the family and our highest ideal. She is the representative of God, as God is the mother of the universe. It was a female sage who first found the unity of God, and laid down this doctrine in one of the first hymns of the Vedas. Our God is both personal and absolute, the absolute is male, the personal, female," he said.

The saint was against the early marriage. Early marriage was the very reason for the existence of so many widows, so many women dying early and the birth of emaciated children who would only increase the number of beggars in the country. The following are Swamiji's views on women:

- All nations have attained greatness by paying proper respect to women. That country and that nation which do not respect women have never become great, nor will ever be in future.
- With five hundred men, the conquest of India might take fifty years; with as many women, not more than a few weeks.
- Every nation, every man, and every woman must work out their own salvation.
- The idea of perfect womanhood is perfect independence.
- There is no chance for the welfare of the world unless the condition of women is improved.
- Women – I should very much like our woman to have your intellectuality, but not if it must be at the cost of purity."

Sita in the Belief of Swami Vivekananda

Swamiji considered Sita to be the ultimate sign of perfection, which stood as a testimony to the chastity of Indian Women. He said, "She will always be this glorious Sita, purer than purity itself, all patience and all sufferings. She who suffered that life of suffering without a murmur, she the ever chaste and ever pure wife, she the ideal of the people, the ideal of gods, the great Sita, our national God she must always remain.

All our mythology may vanish, even our Vedas may depart, and our Sanskrit language may vanish for ever, but so long as there will be five Hindus living here, even if only seeking the most vulgar patois, there will be the story of Sita present." Swami Vivekananda had held Indian women in high esteem and has appreciated their typical Indian features like spirit of service, compassion, affection, contentment and reverence.

Needs of Indian Women

Swamiji travelled most part of Europe, where he witnessed women driving cars, going to schools, drudging in offices and involved in professional commitments, but according to him, the chastity and feminine modesty of Indian women soothes the eye.

Swamiji wants the following to be given to the Indian women for the development of our nation:

1. He felt that modernisation of women society is possible only by following the footprints of Sita.
2. He felt that no nation can grow without taking the interest of women.
3. He said, "All nations have attained greatness by paying proper respect to women. That country and that nation which does not respect women have never become great, nor will ever be in future".
4. He felt that Indian women must be given the liberty to live an independent life.
5. They must have the right to take decisions and, when faced with problems, should learn to solve by themselves.
6. The only interference that can be made is while providing proper education and making them aware of the society.
7. He felt education of women is the only tool to move forward, and a medium which could help eradicating all grave problems and help making them the ideal women in the world.
8. There may be problems in between, but none can be serious so that cannot be solved by the magic world "education".
9. He felt that Indian women had a good understanding about chastity, because it is their heritage. So it was important to intensify that ideal within them and then all aspect would fall in place.
10. He said women, apart from knowledge about science and art, should be given training about religion, hygiene, and cooking, sewing and other simple works of life.
11. Swami Vivekananda proposed to set up a women's math, where religious literature, scriptures, grammar, Sanskrit and even some amount of English would be taught.
12. Swami Vivekananda was of the firm opinion that women should be put in positions of power to solve their own problems in their own way. The welfare of the world is dependent on the improvement of the condition of women.

Even if this step was important in order to uplift the inner virtues of women. Women, according to Vivekananda were living embodiment of the Divine Mother, and this Math would help to reach out to various people and spread female education.

The Solution

What was the way out to save and elevate Indian woman? Education was the answer. What kind is education? What is women's education? Sister Christine wrote that for weeks and months Vivekananda would be buried in thought, creating and recreating the splendid image of the Indian woman of the future. Would a combination of the western spirit of independence, freedom, and dynamism with Indian austerity, purity and chastity in woman's life be possible?

A nation that has educated itself to look upon God as Mother has learnt to invest its observation of woman with utmost tenderness and reverence. Swami Vivekananda is the first monk to uphold and do work for the freedom and equality of women and realising her importance for the functioning of home and society.

He defended the marginalisation of women and empowering women and the poor—a priority of the Ramakrishna Mission. He visited England in 1895 and met Margaret Elizabeth Noble, an Irish lady who was in the midst of her learning about the Buddha. Influenced by Vivekananda teaching, she became the first Western woman to become a Sanyasin named Bhagini Nivedita. Nivedita played a major role in promoting the rights of women in rural India. In November 1898, according to Vivekananda's instruction, she started a school for girls, allowing them to receive basic education. The school is today known as Ramakrishna Sarada Mission Sister Nivedita Girls' School, situated in Baghbazar of North Kolkata.

Conclusion

Vivekananda declared that the Western ideal of womanhood is wife, while the eastern ideal is mother. "The very peculiarity of Hindu women which they have developed and which is the ideal of their life, is that of the mother..........."

Swamiji has glorified Indian women of the past for achievements as leaders in various walks of life. "Women in statesmanship, managing territories, governing countries, even making war, have proved themselves equal to men, if not superior. In India, I have no doubt of that. Whenever they have had the opportunity, they have proved that they have as much ability as men, with this advantage—that they seldom degenerate. They keep to the moral standard, which is innate in their nature. And thus as governors and rulers of their state, they prove-at least in India far superior to men claims"— John Stuart Mill.

India's reverence for women as the symbol of chastity brought such words from Vivekananda lips: "I know that the race that produced Sita—even if it only dreamt of her—has a reverence for woman that is unmatched on the earth." The rise of outstanding women administrators, statesmen, scientists, writers and spiritual teachers, is gradually proving the truth of these prophetic words.

Today, Swamiji's words have proved true. Following the footsteps of Sarada Devi and Sister Nivedita, hundreds of women all over the world are coming forward with a combination of the 'mother's heart and the hero's will,' a combination of the purity of Holy Mother and the dynamism of Rani of Jhansi or Joan of Arc.

References

- Ghosal , S. (2012) : The Educational Thoughts of Swami Vivekananda : A Review, University News, 50 (09), Feb. 27 - March 4, 2012, New Delhi.
- Vivekananda, Swami (1993): My India : The India Eternal, Ramkrishna Mission Institute of Culture, Kolkata, (rpt. 2008).
- Vivekananda, Swami (2007): Shiksha Prasanga, Udbodhan Karjalaya, Kolkata
- Walia, Kiran Ed. (2008): My Idea of Education - Swami Vivekananda, Advaita Ashrama, Kolkata.
- His Eastern and Western Disciples. (1989). The life of Swami Vivekananda. 2 Vols. 6th ed. Calcutta.
- Hossain, M. (1980). Swami Vivekananda philosophy of education. Calcutta: Ratna Prakashan.
- Nivedita, Sister. (1999). The Master as I saw him 9th ed., 12th printing. Calcutta: Udbodhan Office.
- Sengupta, S.C. (1984). Swami Vivekananda and Indian Nationalism. Calcutta: Shishu Sahitya Samsad.

References

19

Education and Women Empowerment

B. Gayathri

Introduction

Women constitute almost 50 per cent of the world's population. As far as their social status is concerned, they are not treated equal to men in all the places, though in the Western countries, women are treated at par with men in most of the fields, their counterpart in the East suffers from many disabilities. The disabilities on one hand and the inequalities between men and women on the other, have given rise to what is known "Gender problem". Albeit the problem across the globe, the South, the East Asia and Africa, the gender problem has assumed importance during recent years the gender issue has become virtually a crucial point of argument. It is now widely believed that empowerment of women, i.e., providing equal rights, opportunities and responsibilities will go long way in removing the existing gender discrimination. The points to be considered for women empowerment in contemporary Indian Society are: in forms of their work, education, health, media images, lineage, rule of residence and domestic chores, their participation in social and political activities, their legal status in terms of marriage, divorce and inheritance of property, seeking wealth care. Empowerment in terms of knowledge and awareness of one's own life and society including legal raise their status with regarded to the lives need to enhanced. We need to build on what women think about themselves and their own abilities to rid of invisible chains of tradition and the aspects that block the moral, spiritual, social, economic and emotional development. Several persons of India has given views on education and empowerment of women. The most important and pioneer among them is Swami Vivekananda. He said, "Women must be put in a position to solve their problems in their own way. No one can or ought to do this for them. Our Indian women are capable of doing it as any in the world". We shall in this paper discuss his views on education and empowerment of women.

Reasons for Low Literacy

1. Lower Enrolment in schools. 2. Higher drop-out rate among girls from schools. 3. Girl child as second mother. 4. Bonded labour system. 5. Caste

system. 6. Dowry. 7. Child labour practice. 8. Poor school environment for girls. 9. Female age at marriage. 10. Inferiority, sub-servience and domesticity. 11. Poverty. 12. Demographic factors like rapid population growth, migration, rapid urbanisation. 13. Poor political will and conviction.

Crimes against Women

Some of the crimes against women are 1. Acid throwing. 2. Sexual harassment. 3. Dowry. 4. Child Marriage. 5. Female infanticide and sex-selective abortion. 6. Domestic violence. 7. Trafficking.

Why Education is Important ?

Education is one of the important means of empowering women with the knowledge, skills and self-confidence necessary to participate fully in the development process. Education is a potent tool in their emanicipation and empowerment. The important and significant factor which can improve the status of women in the society is education. Education gives a person particularly women-the following: 1. Develop positive self-esteem. 2. Help her get good status. 3. Courage and inner strength to face challenges in life. 4. Gain more knowledge about the world outside. 5. To procure a job and supplement the family income and achieve social status. 6. Major impact on health and nutrition to develop sustainable strategy for population control. 7. Playing an equally important role as men in nation building. The 1994 Cairo Consensus recognised education, especially for women, as a force for social and economic development. Universal completion of primary education was set as a 20-year goal, as was wider access to secondary and higher education among girls and women. Closing the gender gap in education by 2015 is one of the benchmarks for the Millenium Development Goals.

Swamiji's Observation

Swami found education as the best and only device to solve problems of women and thereby emancipate them. According to him, for women problems can be many "but none that cannot be solved by that magic word 'education". He conceived of an "education by which character is formed, strength of mind is increased, intellect is expanded, and by which one can stand on one's own feet".

He said that times when religion first began in ancient times, women were distinguished for spiritual genius and great strength of mind. In spite of this, as he seemed to acknowledge, the women of the present day had degenerated. They thought of nothing but eating and drinking, gossip and scandal. Therefore, he prescribed an education that would create "great fearless women. Women should be worthy to continue the traditions of Sangamitra, Lila, Ahalya Bai, and Mira Bai. Women should be fit the mothers of heroes. Such an education was emphasised on Swami's concept of true womanhood, which is vested in "the old-time intensity of trustful and devoted companionship to the husband" and hence his message to Indians was "forget not that the ideal of thy womanhood is Sita, Savitri, and Damayanti". For him development of true ideal of womanhood was the primary goal of education.

According to Swami Vivekananda, one can hardly find statements that women are not competent for knowledge and devotion in the scriptures. On the deprivation of women in education he said, "In the period of degradation, when the priests made the other castes incompetent for the study of Vedas, they deprived the women of their rights. All nations have attained greatness by paying proper respect to women. That country and that nation which do not respect women have never become great, nor will ever be in future. The principal reason why your race has so much degenerated is that you have no respect for these living images of Shakti." He quotes Manu to substantiate, "Where women are respected, there the gods delight; and where they are not, there all works and efforts come to naught". He asserts that there is no hope for that family or country where there is no estimation of women, where they live in sadness. For this reason, they have to be raised first. He put the blame of the low status of Indian women partly on the barbarous invaders and partly on the people of India themselves. They have all the time been trained in helplessness, servile dependence on others, and so they are good only to weep their eyes out at the slightest approach of some mishap or danger. Along with other things, they should acquire the spirit of valour and heroism. In the present day, it has become necessary for them to learn self-defense. His great heroine was the Jhansi Rani of the Indian mutiny, who led her troops in person.

To make a beginning in women's education, his argument centred on chastity, because it is the heritage of Hindu women. Firstly, "intensify that ideal within them above everything else, so that they may develop a strong character by the force of which, in every stage of their life, whether married or single, if they prefer to remain so, they will not be in the least afraid even to give up their lives rather than flinch an inch from their chastity". Therefore he advised, "Educate your women first and leave them to themselves; then they will tell you what reforms are necessary for them. In matters concerning them who are you? Liberty is the first condition of growth". He advised the Indian women to believe in India and Indian faith. Be strong and hopeful and unashamed, and remember that with something to take, Hindus have immeasurably more to give than any other people in the world".

To reform Indian women he suggested such an education with which women will solve their own problems. However, he disapproved of their modern education. According to him, "education is not the amount of information that is put into your brain and runs riot there, undigested, all your life. We must have life-building character-making, assimilation of ideas. If education were identical with information, the libraries would be the greatest sages of the world and encyclopaedias the rishis." For him, the use of higher education was to find out how to solve the problems of life. Swami Vivekananda warns that "getting by heart the thoughts of others in foreign language and stuffing the brain with them and taking some university degrees, you consider yourself educated". The education which does not bring out the strength of character, a spirit of philanthropy and the courage of a lion is not worth being called education." It is true that our modern education system in post independent India is not free from this defect. This also points out that the tendency in the feminist movement to emulate and transplanting the western theories should be taken care of for not repeating the same defect.

Swamiji supported the indigenous system of education in which the history and culture of one's own nation would be taught. He was against the alien model of education in tune with the West which compels the youth to study the alien culture, traditions and practices at the cost of what has evolved and developed in their own countries. He held that the mind of an individual is an infinite reservoir of knowledge, and all knowledge, past, present and future is within the individual, manifested or non-manifested. The aim of every system of education should be to help the mind to manifest it. For this, he insisted on the old system of education, for females also. He emphasised women studying religion, science, art, housekeeping, cooking, sewing, hygiene, etc. Along with these, japa, worship and meditation formed an indispensable part of teaching. He said, "Their education must be an eye-opener in all matters. Ideal characters must always be presented before the view of the girls to imbue them with devotion to lofty principles of selflessness. The noble examples of Sita, Savitri, Damayanti, Lilavati, Khana and Mira should be brought home to their minds and they should be inspired to mould their own lives in the light of these. He desired that schools for girls be opened in every village. For imparting education he finds it necessary to train Brahmacharinis who would go to the villages and other places and do hard work without any hesitation. For this he planned to build up Math which he could not materialise during his lifetime. Later, he fulfilled his desires and Advaitha Ashram is propagating Swamiji's ideals.

In his view, educated women would inculcate virtues and values amongst children and thus prepare the new generation of people who could distinguish themselves in virtues and values. The development agenda of the twenty-first century acknowledged education as the key to women's empowerment for the same reasons as Swamiji foresaw in the nineteenth century. The millennium development goals envisage that education of women "increases their productivity, raising output and reducing poverty. It promotes gender equality within households and removes constraints on women's decision making — thus reducing fertility rates and improving maternal health. It increases children's chances of surviving to become healthier and better educated because educated women do a better job caring for children. "It is only in the hands of educated and pious mothers that great men are born". Therefore, he insisted that "daughters should be supported and educated with as much care and attention as the sons." He asserted that in ancient times both boys and girls were instructed, but now only the boys are favoured. An effort is being made to rectify the long-existing wrong. A good share of the philosophy and laws of the land is the work of women during ancient times, before barbarians started to rule the land. In the eyes of the Hindu, the women now has her rights. She holds her own and has the law on her side. When a student returns from college, he is allowed to marry and have a household. Husband and wife must bear the work and both have their rights. The wife has her property rights also. A Hindu woman was not bound by the husband's contracts in respect of her individual property. He had no power to take her property without her consent or execute any document affecting her right to her property.

However as Gandhi says, "Hindu culture has erred on the side of excessive subordination of the wife to the husband, and has insisted on the complete merging of the wife in the husband. This has resulted in the husband sometimes usurping and exercising authority that reduces him to the level of the brute". And Swami Vivekananda's attempt was to rectify the errors by modernising Hindu culture. At present in India, violence against women, including domestic violence, became a serious crime. Its statistics is mounting day by day despite the implementation of various legislations. From womb to tomb, women is under various kinds of discrimination and injustice. Subordination of women is now a universal fact and the measures for their empowerment discussing worldwide is included in the development agenda. In such discourses, it is important to notice Swamiji's argument that men and women are equally good in her or his way. When judging them, it should be by the standard of their respective greatness.

Swamiji wished the ancient Shradha to return as remedy to solve problems of women. And to change the parental attitude towards girl children that somehow they have to dispose of a girl to marriage if she is nine or ten years old, and rejoice when she deliver a child at the age of thirteen. Through educating the masses, this situation should change. And men and women should be married at ripe age. But even today as Swamiji mentioned "as soon as the girl grows up a little, every one of the female sex, beginning with the mother down to the relatives and even neighbours will begin to cry out that the father must find a bridegroom for her, and will not leave him in peace until he does so. This is very much prevailing even today without any change. Girls are brought up so that their life is only to marry someone and not to develop as fully productive citizen by using the potentialities within her".

He prescribed the secular education for masses, that is, an education which brings all the ideals slowly down among the masses and raise them to equality. He prefers to impart this secular knowledge through religion, which is through Vedas. The 81st Report of the Committee on Value Based Education of 1999, did highlight the need to inculcate the principles of truth, righteous conduct, peace, love and non-violence, which are the religious values propagated by Swamiji. This report suggests for teaching the basics of religions and their values so that students become aware that the basic concept of religions are common, only practices differ. This shows that the modern India has to accept the virtues of religion as Swamiji reiterated in the nineteenth century.

For him without Vedanta everything was superstition, with it everything becomes religion. According to him, except Vedas every book must change. The authority of Vedas is for all time to come; the authority of every one of our other books is for the time being. For instance, one Smriti is powerful for one age, another for another age. Great prophets are always pointing to the way to work. Some prophets worked for lower classes, others like Madhva gave to women the right to study Vedas. Swamiji believed that there is infinite power of development in everything. He suggested the realisation of Vedantic ideals through constructive methods according to the need of time. Therefore, there is a need to reform to solve problems of women so as to reach its benefit to women belonging to various sections in the society. His method of solving things was "to take out by the roots the very causes of the disease and not to keep them merely suppressed". To take out the causes of female subordination, feminists seek women's identity, women's language as a means by which to secure political and social equality for women. For them, the main task is to challenge 'the foundation of social and cultural order" which made the women's situation worst. Swamiji's idea is also the same, but by using the constructive Vedic and religious methods in reforms. According to Vivekananda, every high ideal one meets with anywhere in the world had its origin in India. "From time immemorial, India has been the mine of precious ideas to human society; giving birth to high ideas herself, she has freely distributed them and broadcast over the whole world". He finds that Kantian discovery of time, space and causation are the modes of thought in the Vedantic concept of 'Maya', and Schopenhauer's reason rationalises Vedanta.

Swamiji said, "It is very difficult to understand why in India so much difference is made between men and women, whereas the Vedanta declares that one and the same conscious Self is present in all beings. Writing down Smritis, etc., and binding them by hard rules, the men have turned the women into mere manufacturing machines. If you do not raise the women, don't think that you have any other way to rise". The internal manifestation of women, such as knowledge, devotion, discrimination and passion make man omniscient, of unfailing purpose and a knower of Brahman. She, when pleased, becomes propitious and the cause of freedom of the man. Similar is the idea behind today's concept of empowerment. The process of women's empowerment will also liberate men. Empowerment freed men "from the roles of oppressor and exploiter, which distorts and limits their humanity and potential. They will be relieved of gender stereotyping and will be free to discover, develop and openly express the 'feminine' traits within them which have been suppressed or distorted". At any cost, educating women was the most important way of salvation for India according to Swamiji.

His ideals have a strong commitment to the emancipation of women and he had great concern with the oppression of women in the contemporary Indian society. He was one of the first of his era in the field of religion to recognise the indignity and oppression which women were subject to in this world of men. After having done great work for the uplift of the masses, including women. Swamiji passed away on July 4, 1902. At his death bed, he said, "I shall inspire (people) everywhere until the world shall know that it is one with God". And his work remains as he said as eternal in the modern literature.

Conclusion

With five hundred men, the conquest of India might take fifty years; with as many women not more than a few weeks. The rise of outstanding women administrators, statesmen, scientists, writers and spiritual teachers, is gradually proving the truth of these prophetic words of Swami Vivekananda. Following the footsteps of Sarada Devi and Sister Nivedita, hundreds of women all over the world are coming forward with a combination of the 'mother's heart and the hero's will,' a combination of the purity of Holy Mother and the dynamism of Rani of Jhansi or Joan of Arc. All nations have attained greatness by paying proper respect to women. That country and that nation which do not respect women have never become great, nor will ever be in future. The government of India declared 2001 as the year of women's empowerment (Swasakthi). The National Policy, for the empowerment of women was passed in 2001.

References

- Ahluwalia, B. 1983. Vivekananda and the Indian Renaissance. New Delhi: Associated Publishing Co.
- Avinashalingam, T.S. (1974). Educational philosophy of Swami Vivekananda. 3rd ed. Coimbatore.
- Burke, M.L. (1984). Swami Vivekananda in the West: New Discoveries, 6 Vols. Calcutta: Advaita Ashrama.
- Edgar Faure et al., (1972), Learning to be, Paris: UNESCO, p. 156.
- Gnatuk-Danil'chuk, A.P. (1986). Tolstoy and Vivekananda. Calcutta: The Ramakrishna Mission.

PART–IV: NATIONAL INTEGRATION AND INTERNATIONAL UNDERSTANDING

20

Swami Vivekananda and National Integration

C. Janakavalli and P. Megala

Introduction

Vivekananda was a unique towering being who did suffer joyously, vibrantly, literally for the integration of our nation. He was very positive, enthusiastic, energetic, vivacious and full of youthful energy. One can identify in him a philosopher, a singer, and commanding orator, a lover of art and architecture, a patriot, a saint besides he was a devout of humanity. He moved around the globe in the spirit of spirituality and was moved very much on visualising the pathetic state of India, where the threat of disintegration arises. Theologies endorse him as a Nararishi, whom Sri Ramakrishna brought to the earth for the welfare of mankind. The Nararishi has the main characteristics of loving man, Nara, and everything about man. Not only spirituality, but also every department in which man is functioning and moving and having its being, was very much important to him. Therefore, he was so enthusiastic about everything, be it philosophy or religion, be it literature, art, painting, engineering, technology or the development of villages—be anything. He was conversant with everything. Vivekananda was intensely interested in the overall development of man. It is obvious that Vivekananda's patriotism was rooted in something else, not merely to the fact that he was born and brought up in India, but insisted on the integration of nation. Through his lectures, starting from Colombo on one side and ending at Almora—Himalayas on the other, writings and works, he repeatedly emphasises one single point, and that is: a sense of inner unity or oneness of human beings, where India is the storehouse of spirituality and religion.

Swami Vivekananda wanted the young men to be bold and face the truth without compromise and whitewashing to actualise the endless spiritual potentialities in his 'Practical Vedanta' Vivekananda gave very powerful basis for awakening of the masses of Indian society. With the Upanishad, he declared, "Arise! Awake! And stop not until the goal is reached". He wanted a man with firm determination and good will for others and he also encouraged such types of character building. K.S. Ramasami Sastri explains the self-confidence of Vivekananda in the awakening of the nation in the following words: "The difference that I noticed between Vivekananda of 1892 and of 1897 was what struck me most. In 1892, he looked like one who had a tryst with destiny and was not quite sure when or where or how he was to keep the tryst with destiny, but in 1897, he looked like the one who clearly knew his mission and who was confident about its fulfilment."

The Ideas of National Integration

Swami Vivekananda entrusted on the dynamo of spiritual power for national integration. In one of his inspiring talks, in the Thousand Islands Park in the USA, he said, 'Do not spend your energy in talking, but meditate in silence; and do not let the rush of the outside world disturb you… Accumulate power in silence and become a dynamo of spirituality. What can a beggar give? Only a king can give, and only when he wants nothing himself." Vivekananda's idea of integrating the whole nation is not just a geographical or political integration, not even an emotional or sentimental integration, not even an integration based upon the feeling that we are Indians, but it is a spiritual integration based upon the awakening of the inner spirit, which was dormant in the ordinary human being. The touch of Swami Vivekananda will be the awakener of the potential divinity in each of us. He felt that this has to be done, and once it has been done, the entire Indian nation will be unified, integrated, not on the basis of science and technology, not on the basis of material advancement, but on the basis of spirituality, inwardness and contemplation. He also said that the nation can be integrated by uploading the national ideals. In his own words, "the national ideals of India are renunciation and service, intensify her in those channels, and the rest will take care of itself".

Swamiji visualised inequalities in society and selfishness which is the base for all evils in India tending towards exploitation. In a remarkable letter to the Maharaja of Mysore he made an appeal. "The one thing that is at the root of all evils in India is the condition of the poor. The poor in the west are devils. Compared to them, ours are angels and it is therefore so much easier to raise the poor, the only service to be done for our lower classes are to give them education, to develop their lost individuality." He trusted in the love for humanity, which is the real, living loving force of mankind that conquers all the evils in the society. He proclaimed, "India will be raised, not with the power of the flesh, but with the power of the spirits; not with flag of destruction, but with the flag of peace and love."

Even in nineteenth century Swami Vivekananda foresaw the future issues to humanity of our nation. For the solution of issues, he laid emphasis on man-making.

He served the humanity even after realising the highest spiritual truth, since his master Ramakrishna taught him serve the mankind forever. As Nehru said, "His was a kind of nationalism that automatically slipped into Indian nationalism which was a part of Internationalism." Swami Vivekananda never supported narrow nationalism. He wanted to abolish the cruel and unjust in the society by not bringing down the higher, but by raising the lower up to the level of the higher.

Conclusion

Addressing the people of India, Swami Vivekananda said, "O India! Forget not that the lower classes, the ignorant, the poor, the illiterate, the cobbler, the sweeper, are thy flesh and blood, thy brothers. Thou brave one, be bold, take courage, be proud that thou art an Indian, and proudly proclaim.

"I am an Indian, every Indian is my brother." Say, "The ignorant India, the poor and destitute Indian, and the Brahmin Indian. The Pariah Indian is my brother". Proudly proclaimed at the top of my voice, "the Indian is my brother; the Indian is my life.... Indian society is the cradle of my infancy, the pleasure garden of my youth, the sacred heaven, the Varanasi of my old age". Say brother "the soil of my India is my highest heaven: the good of my India is my good".

As per Swami Vivekananda's words, Indians have to bring in the light of national unity to remove the darkness of centuries for social progress, international understanding and world peace.

References

- Sivaramakrishna M, (2012) "Vivekananda Reader", Ramakrishna Math and Ramakrishna Mission, Belur Math, Howrah District, West Bengal.
- The Complete Works of Swami Vivekananda, Vol. I, p. 342.
- The Complete Works of Swami Vivekananda, Vol. IV, p. 362.

21

Role of Teachers in Promoting National Integration

N. Muthaiah and M. Senthilkumaran

Introduction

National integration is a positive aspect. It reduces socio-cultural and economic differences or inequalities and strengthens national unity and solidarity, which is not imposed by any authority. People share ideas, values and emotional bonds. It is feeling of unity within diversity. National identity is supreme. Cultural unity, constitution, territorial continuity, common economic problems, art, literature, national festivals, national flag, national anthem and national emblem etc promote National Integration. Dr. S. Radhakrishnan has rightly said that "National Integration cannot be built by brick and mortar; it cannot be built by chisel and hammer. It has to grow silently in the minds and hearts of men. The only process is the process of education".

The Need

The need of national integration and international understanding is felt essential across the world in modern times. India is a multi-religious (secular), multi-linguistic and multi-cultural country and its citizens, irrespective of faith/creed/caste have been granted equal status, which is already enshrined in the constitution of largest democracy in the world. Propagation of a particular religion is a fundamental right. The concept of secularism is not alien to Indian societies, but it has been misinterpreted, misused by the opposition of national development. Discrimination of a particular group/community grows hatred and it is not good for a healthy nation. For instance, it is ironical that most of the times whenever a Kashmiri visits outside Indian—Jammu and Kashmir state, he is being looked in suspicious manner and often cornered for no reasons, which is against the credentials of National Integration. Similarly, violence/crime against Dalits is still prevailing in some parts of the country even in 21st century.

The Adverse Factors

1. Casteism

Caste is an imported part of our social fabric. This was developed in the past on the basis of division of labour in the society. Casteism has segregated the society. Unity and integrity has become a dream in a caste-ridden society. The feeling of socially neglected scheduled castes under the suppression of upper caste has ruined the sense of awe, feeling and unity. It becomes a problem for national integration.

2. Communalism

Religious antagonism has posed a serious challenge to national integration in India. India is a multi-religious land. Political manipulation has projected one religion against the other which resulted in communal riot, bloodbath, mutual, distrust and disintegration of the country.

Large scale illiteracy and superstition are responsible along with other causes for raising communalism within the country. It is very difficult to promote national integration under such situation.

3. Linguistic Differences

Multi-linguism is one of the important characters of India. India has fifteen officially recognised languages. There are about 1,652 languages that are spoken in India which shows its diversities. There is conflict and riots on the languages issue. People of one language try to establish their language over others. When Hindi was declared as the national language people of South India resented against this decision supporting English language. Language issue became a barrier on the way of national integration, despite the official electronic media, cinema and cultural events.

4. Regionalism

There are several regions in India having unique traditions, food habits, dress and languages. Each region differs from the other in one or other ways, which leads to disintegration of the country. People of one region compete with the person of other regions which leads to conflict and riots. Land dispute, language problem are some of the reason, which pose hurdle on the way of to integrate.

5. Social Inequality

Social inequality among the people of different communities, castes and sometime within the community and caste sustain tension and imbalance among the people. Social disparity poses great challenge to national integration.

6. Economic Inequalities

Economic standard of people in a state depends on the fertility of land, resources available and manpower management. All the states are not equal in the above matter which leads to economic backwardness of people. Even in a particular state, distribution of wealth is not properly done. Day by day, poor becoming poorer and rich become richest—this causes tension and conflict. It is a problem for national integration.

There are many programmes and plans for removing aforesaid hindrances. Education can become a very powerful instrument or national unity provided that it is used in the right manner.

Role of the Teacher

The Teacher is one who makes the future country a blossoming nation. As teacher is treated analogous to second parents, he should make the students to love their nation and involve them for its prosperity. So, the teacher plays effective role for the promotion of national integration. Only a national minded teacher can strengthen such spirit of unity and the idea of compositeness.

1. Role Model

A teacher has been regarded as the builder of nation. He influences the students by his behavior. He should have a national outlook and reflect national consciousness, actions, conduct and behavior so that the students may receive the appropriate message on time.

2. Impartial

He should rise above petty biases and prejudices. The teacher shouldn't have partiality among the pupils and treat his students equally without distinction of caste, sex, colour and religion.

3. Love for the Nation

He should have firm faith in national unity and love for the cause. The teacher ought to make the peer and the pupil to have faith and love on one's own nation.

4. Preach and Teach

As our Father of Our Nation Mahatma Gandhiji stated—preach before you teach. The teacher should do whatever he says. There should be no difference in saying and doing. This will make the students to follow his principles.

5. Inter-disciplinary Approach

Teacher must introduce his country in his lessons. Every teacher must know the history of their own country, cities, rivers, songs; people. These things could be introduced in the classroom. The teacher should teach History, civics and geography, literature, art and music from the national point of view and the present need of the nation. This in turn influences the pupil to assimilate about the current situation.

6. Update knowledge

The teacher should update his knowledge by means of writing books and use of technology. Teacher should co-operate in framing new curricula on Indian history, civics, literature and language, lifestyle leading the students to appreciate historical, social, cultural, linguistic and religious of the people of India.

7. Organising Co-curricular Activities

These activities prepare students for National integration in direct and indirect mode. They exercise more effective and useful impact on their personality. This place is comparatively higher than other place. Following activities worth inclusion in the National Integration:

(a) Celebration of National Days
(b) Celebration of birthday's of great men
(c) Celebrating cultural festivals
(d) Celebration of festivals
(e) National Anthem
(f) Donating Blood
(g) Organising adult education programme
(h) Bulletin board
(i) Exchange of teachers
(j) Participating in social activities
(k) Respecting the National symbols

8. Newspaper and books

The teacher should stimulate students read newspapers and books of non-communal nature throwing light on the contributions from nationalists.

9. Inspiration

Teacher should inspire them for having faith and love for national language, national literature, national culture, national festivals, national symbols and national glory.

10. Behavioural change

The teacher should have keen eyes on students. If the teacher notices young minds accessible to casteism, linguism, narrow mindedness, rowdyism and damaging public property or others property, the teacher should try to mobilise the behaviour and attitude of students.

11. Supporting government projects

The directions and programmes of the government for developing national integration should be adapted more seriously. The teacher should involve students in the activity, indivually, or in groups.

Conclusion

National Integration plays a vital role for India's survival. It is the cry of the moment. The country must mobilise its resources to evolve a concrete national programme. The future of the nation is dark unless some cherished character of the people like LTTE, Taliban, but only for the cause, is encouraged. National integration is meant for developing peace in and outside of the country. Universal brotherhood tendency should be emphasised. Every citizen in a country should be treated equal in order to attain pure democracy.

As our country is divided into federal states with several languages and several community people, every individual ought to be upheld equal before the constitution.

References

- Abrams, M.H. (1999). *A Glossary of Literary Terms.* Singapore: Thomson.
- Beniwal, Anup. (2005). *"Approximating History"* Representing Partition, History, Violence and Narration. Delhi: Shakti.
- Hooks, Bell. (1993). "*A Revolution of Values: The promise of Multicultural Change.*" The Cultural Studies Reader. ed. Simon During. London: Routledge.
- Mohanty, Satya P. (1998). *"Identity, Multiculturalism, Justice"*. Literary Theory and Claims of History. New Delhi: Oxford. Quinn, Edward. 2006. A Dictionary of Literary and Thematic.
- Terms. New York: Facts on File.
- Shahane, V.A. (1972). Khushwant Singh . New York: Twayne Publisher.
- Singh, Khushwant. (1999). *Train to Pakistan: The Collected Novels.* New Delhi: Penguin.

22

Education for National Integration at Secondary Level

D.C. Vani Nayaki and Y. Devaraja

Historical Background

In the past, India was never a united country, never a nation; it never had unique language or even common religion. It was never under one ruler or political force as whole. India has possessed multifarious faiths, races, languages, religions, castes, traditions and habits. Diversity is quite natural, but there exists a fundamental unity in diversities, which has made India one country and the Indians-one nation. The unity of nation does not mean uniformity or conformity. It depends on the determination and the will of the people. It is more psychological or emotional than external or organisational. Of course, external factors like geographical contiguity, historical identity, religious similarity, linguistic, political or economic unity, greatly promote such psychological matter. The Swiss people have neither common language nor the same culture. In U.K., there are differences among the English, Welsh and the Scots, but they are united in loyalty to national ideals. The USA being mostly a land of emigrants has national unity and economic or political systems seldom stand in the way of national unity. Thus, nationhood does not depend on race or language or religion or geography, singly or collectively. The great men of modern India whether in the field of religion, philosophy, art, literature, poetry, fine arts, science or politics are all India personalities. Sri Ramakrishna, Vivekananda, Aurobindo, Swamy Dayanand, Ram Mohan Roy, Tilak, Gandhi, Tagore et al., were all India luminaries. All languages of India are sisters, Sanskrit being the common most source and link in the script structure. The Vedas, Upanishads, Manu Samhita and the great epics are still regarded as the heads of Indian culture.

The western civilisation has contributed the modern democracy, secularism, socialism, nationalism, scientific and technological knowledge, which have tied the country with common bondages. Lastly the struggle for Independence, the constitution of India and its federalism have contributed to the growth of unity in this land.

Present Position

Inspite of these favourable factors, the modern India is very often threatened by centrifugal forces. The separatist tendencies like religionalism, communalism, linguism, provincialism are raising their heads. Now, the divisive forces are working in different parts of the country—in Jammu and Kashmir, in Assam, in Mizoram, Punjab had advocated for separate land from the Indian union. Economic inequality is helping the disintegrating forces. This has led to regional rivalry and disparities. Linguism has created conflicts in many parts of the country; Southerners agitate against the so called "Hindi-Imperialism". Power seeking politicians exploit mob psychology and sustain on the ignorance and poverty of the masses. Candidates contesting in the election are sometimes elected not for their worth, but on the basis of caste or communal basis. Politicians feel that the easy road to success in election is to exploit religious or linguistic differences.

The Indian Education Commission, 1964-66 has observed in this context, 'the old values, which held society together, have been disappearing and as there is no effective programme to replace by new sense of social responsibility, innumerable signs of social disorganisation as evident everywhere are continually on the increase. These include vigils, increasing lawlessness and disregard for public property, corruption of public life and communal tensions and troubles'.

Objectives of the Mission

- To devise ways and measures for effectively control eliminating divisive tendencies based on parochialism, regionalism, linguism, casteism, communalism etc.
- To work out necessary policies and programmes for emotional integration of the people with diverse cultural, social, economic and political affiliations and aspirations.
- To curb separatist tendencies by promoting national unity and fostering national pride.
- To promote secularism so as to curb and discourage religious and sectarian forces of disintegration.
- To promote cultural integration without undermining the rich cultural diversity, in short, to bring unity in diversity.

Obstacles to the Mission

"The worth of a State is the worth of the individuals composing it". But the individuals of India are so much lost in local and regional considerations that the national causes fall short before these insignificant considerations. Even with the dawn of independence, the national solidarity of our country is in grave danger. Let us now discuss the forces that operate against the national integrations of this country.

- COMMUNALISM
- REVIVALIST TENDENCY IN SOCIAL AND CULTURAL MATTERS
- CASTEISM
- REGIONALISM
- PREJUDICE AND FANATICISM
- LANGUAGE ISSUE
- NARROW POLITICS
- ECONOMIC INEQUALITY
- NATIONAL SYSTEM OF EDUCATION
- LACK OF LEADERSHIP

National Integration Committee

So far we have discussed the major impediments in the way of integrating our nation. In order to remove these obstacles, and to achieve national integration, the Government of India appointed a Committee on National and Emotional Integration under the Chairmanship of Dr. Sampurnanand (1961) presided over by Mrs. Indira Gandhi in 1967. At Srinagar (1968), the meeting discussed to achieve communal harmony, eradicating narrow regionalism and organise education mission. For each problem, one sub-committee remained in charge and submitted constructive suggestions. Suggestions of the committee:

- Children should be acquainted with various aspects of national life.
- Children should be informed about important events of national movement for achieving freedom.
- Students should be imparted the idea about unity in diversity blending the qualities of communal harmony and fellow-feeling.

Educational Programmes:

- Scrutiny of books taught in schools.
- Items, which spoil national outlook and preach anti-national sentiments should be summarily removed.
- People of different castes and religions should willingly participate in national fairs and festivals.
- Dramas and discussions advocating national harmony should be organised across the country.
- Motion pictures. Radio, Television and Newspapers should be harnessed for national unity.
- Special films should be produced to demolish anti-national tendencies.
- All government services should be thrown open without any consideration of caste, creed, colour, sex, religion and region.
- National views and attitudes of candidates should be tested and given due credit while recruiting them for higher post and services.

- Suitable reforms may be introduced and new topics, which foster the feeling of integration, appreciation of heritage and cultural traditions may be emphasised.
- Co-curricular activities should be given importance in the government, aided and missionary schools.
- Preparing pupils for Democracy, Secularism.

Role of Teachers

Unless the teachers are infused with the spirit of democracy and secularism and inculcated with the values of Liberty, Equality and fraternity, they can't motivate and train the students in the desired direction. No programme of national integration can succeed in educational institutions unless the teachers themselves are beyond casteism, communalism and partisan activities. Teacher should set models to be formulated by pupils who think and act judiciously without any prejudice towards particular religion, language or region. Teachers should develop the patriotic spirit, broad minded approach. Such persons can strengthen the instinct of unity and idea of compositeness. Legislation alone can't develop either nationhood or national integration. Education is a powerful robot that can shape and mould the beliefs and attitudes of people. It has to take lead to produce men with undaunted intellectual courage, sense of reality, creative and critical thinking, mental eagerness, acceptance and interest in the quest of knowledge and necessary power and understanding for building a new world.

Swamiji's Thoughts

Education is the manifestation of divinity which already exists in man. Knowledge resides within the individual. He discovers that perfection is already inherent in man and education is its manifestation. He was a revolutionary in the field of education.

- Education must create faith in one's own self. This step leads to education and perfection. He must know his latent powers. This leads to completion and divine life.
- Education should create self-confidence and self-reliance. Shradda leads to self- knowledge and material prosperity. It makes him attain perfection and achieve glory of life.
- Education has to promote universal brotherhood. At man is same in all forms of life, the difference surfaces in its manifestation, education should call forth this power in every man. He should stand for national integration, internationalism and unity of mankind.
- Education should generate the spirit of renunciation. We should work for others and be able to do something for the world.
- Man is higher than all animals and none is greater than man.

- Vivekananda advocated national system of education. It must be based on our national needs, problems and aspirations. He insisted on mass education. His curricula included History, Grammar, Language, Literature, Philosophy, Theology, Vedanta, Geography, psychology, Economics, Social science, Science and Western knowledge and Technology.

Conclusion

The idea of national integration does not pre-suppose the absence of integration among people. It is a dynamic reality, not something static that ought to be achieved once and for all. In our opinion, education can and should play a very significant role through introducing common school system of public education, at all stages, developing modern Indian Languages, and taking necessary steps to enrich Hindi as quickly as possible so that it could function effectively as the official language of the Union, promoting national consciousness. It is the education which determines the level of prosperity, welfare and security of the people. Teacher as such, should develop the National Integration for students of the secondary level.

References

1. B.N. Dash, A New Approach to Teacher and Education in the Emerging Indian Society, 2005, Neelkamal Publications Pvt. Ltd., New Delhi.
2. J.C. Aggarwal, Development and Planning of Modern Education, 2004, Vikas Publishing House Pvt. Ltd., New Delhi.
3. N.R. Swaroop Sexena, Education in Emerging Society, 2000, Surya Publication, Meerut.

23

Swamiji's Formulae for National Integration

D. Silambu Selvi

Introduction

Swami Vivekananda is the world teacher, who teaches the value of life and shows ways to make one's life immortal and unite with the omnipotent. Life has no meaning until and unless lived for the service of others. Spiritual knowledge alone can destroy our miseries forever and this spirituality is meant something more than just karma, a Karma Yogi will entirely be resolved to render service as duty to the needful without motive or personal well-being and gets benefits. Because, according to Swamiji, it is noted that, he alone lives who lives for others and others are more dead than alive. Teacher Education Programme has unique ethical backgrounds which prepares the teachers in tune with values. It is the profession of all professions and the teacher is revered high in Hindu mythology, above which we worship as the God. Teacher education plays a vital role in the creation of spotless, flawless, prosperous, spiritual and high idealistic society. Education has high social concern and committed social responsibility. Much attention is required for means than the ends of the work, the more one give others the greater one gets out of it. Purity, patience and perseverance are the three essentials to success and above all, love will speaks about one's greatness. Teacher Education programme include curricular, co-curricular and extra-curricular activities meant to carve the persona of the perfect man with high ideals to serve the community. The management, the head, agencies, society and stakeholders' co-ordination, collaboration and support system will facilitate the principles of Swami Vivekananda into reality.

Saintly Wisdom

Political power or military power is never be the mission of our race, but the social well-being which includes mildness, gentleness, tolerance, forbearance, sympathy and brotherhood. The whole of Vedanta according to him is renunciation, slave to senses, pleasure, luxury and enjoyment lead to ruination. Weariness of competitions will no way support the growth of the individual and the nation but trying to excel one's good performance and co-operation will guarantee eternal peace and happiness. The future existence of the nation depends solely on respecting our traditions and cultures of the past greatness. Quarrel in any dimension will disturb the political, social and material well-being and act as the hindrance to improvement. Learning and good knowledge will work for the amelioration and elevation of human race, cares for the salvation to the downtrodden, poor, neglected, suppressed and ignorant.

If education is identical with information, the libraries are the greatest sages in the world and encyclopedias are the rishis. Education should manifest divine power that is already in man and find everything from within by introspection. Each soul is great and it should be ready at any moment to sacrifice for others. One's thoughts, word and deeds coherently need to be aligned. One should never try to imitate others as being descendants of sages and the need to maintain proper purity of food, while eating and drinking is where the true spirit of culture remains. Much attention is required in the means of work rather than the end result. He quoted the words of Lord Jesus and tries to explain the infinite power within everyone as the Kingdom of Heaven is within all and blessed are the pure in heart for they see God. Super consciousness returns with infinite power, hence concentration of mind is a prerequisite for success. Learning to control the brain will facilitate the brain centre to act consciously which gives joy of living, and accordingly, Swamiji says-laughing is better than praying, singing, surrounded with flower garden, pictures and incense and live in the natural surroundings to give happiness. The mind should be trained well to reason out and analyse critically. Faith is the essence of religions and love is the ideal, it requires no object since love is God.

Nothing is greater than work and the work should be focused to serve the poor and needy who are the children of God. Education is always advent with fullness of development of personality which cannot be attained unless the learner and teacher enjoy the synchronised and reciprocal ambivalence of love and wisdom and they are the milestone of regeneration. Introspection facilitates one to grow in love and virtue and holiness. Adjusting to the micros, will ease one to adjust to macros, because one cannot see outside what cannot be seen inside. One need to arise, awake and stop not till his goal is reached.

Teacher Education Programme

The teacher education program should extend opportunities and should arrange possible steps to grow an ideal teacher from the course. An ideal teacher should have many qualities and will be remembered by students forever. The effect of his personality on students lasts long and he should be loved and respected by every student. He must try to win the hearts of all students. He should try to establish a kind of relation and bond between the hearts and minds of himself and the students. He should make his students think and enhances their creativity. He not only passes information to them but also develops love for learning. He activates the minds of his students. He teaches them how to think and grow in logical power. He brings into play the hidden mental powers of students. He must be a man of ideas. He should explain things in a scholarly and interesting way. He need possess ideal in all respects and should be self respecting man. Thus, his students also acquire self-respect and dignity from him.

Integration of Swami Vivekananda's Principles in Teacher Education Programme

(A) Teacher Education Curriculum

Through the curricular approach, all perquisite elements can be well insisted and well developed, the aims and objectives of education can be better fulfilled through studying and awarding degree in the successful completion of course by including that in the core and elective papers. In curriculum, the rich varied cultural heritage of the Indian subcontinent, legendry heroes, prophets, saints and social activists can be included to study as compulsory papers to get through the course. This course material may also highlight the importance of students' participation in ameliorating miseries and eradication of social evils and their ways and means towards this endeavour. Assignments can be given to student-teachers to gather data locally about the prevailing problem and where help and co-operation are really wanted to set right the situation can be discussed such as ill-treatment of women, child labour, female infanticide, students' drop out, absenteeism in school, pollution control, health, sanitation, preservation of natural resources and growing trees etc.

(B) Co-curricular Approach

Giving training for Yoga, meditation, *Griya* and breathing will be useful for the student-teacher to grow in conscience, mental alertness, sensitive to adoption of values, develop leadership skills, gain inner awareness, creativity and above all, grow in love. Knowing the self and to go in the practice of introspection promotes peace of mind and concentration and will-power. The B.Ed course may be made compulsory to pursue in residential-based programme, so that right habit can be formed when involved continuously in such values for at least a minimum period of time. It will impact one's character and sustain forever in the life, because anything can be turned permanent at least that good thing practiced for more than three months. Time management, service attitude, humbleness, obedience, adjustment, accommodation and value of each and everything can be better inculcated and grown with good ideals in their life. Personality development and soft skills development can be imparted and necessary work can be done in this aspect. Physical exercise, sports and games need to be encouraged more to keep the students strong and fit and they can be encouraged to participate in inter-collegiate, state and national level. Educational and cultural tour program remain green in their memory to glorify the richness of the nation's tradition. They should be encouraged to live simple and take responsibility to care the brethren.

(C) Extra Curricular Activities

Community orientation in higher education system has been emphasised continuously. Todays' students are tomorrow's citizen and the society and education is inseparable. The future is being shaped in the present student mass. They are very well identified with the society. They should be made aware about social welfare programs such as, pulse polio, education for all, voters' awareness, hygiene, anti-aids, education for all, child care, anti-alcohol, corruption, adulteration, save environment, grow trees, save water, save electricity and so on. The local non-governmental organisations can be made known, the support expected can be made clear will facilitate students to render participation to their level best during study or in future. Teacher education institutions can adopt any village or the needy to grow in a happy and peaceful life. If possible, they can arrange free medical camp to render service to the society.

(D) Other Aspects

National youth day can be celebrated and cultural activities can be conducted to renovate the ideals of Swami Vivekananda and facilitate them understanding the role and responsibility to work. M.Ed and M.Phil research can contain the topics related to social concern, case studies and action research can be undertake. Best practices implemented by some institutions can be collected and the same can be followed to possible extent in the local setting. Alumni association has to be revived and their participation should be welcome in future endeavours of the institution.

Conclusion

Education is the manifestation of perfection, already in man and no knowledge comes from outside and infinite power and wisdom is present from within. Complete self-sacrifice will lead one to godlines, because reciting God's names, doing rituals and observing ceremony will have no meaning when the children of God are dying of poverty, diseases and ignorance. Hence the education in general and teacher education in particular need take active role in the integration of Swami Vivekanada's principles to get this dream into reality.

References

1. Allahabad, Feb. 14, 2013, (PTI).
2. http:/teaching.org. top 10 qualities of a great teacher.
3. Mohit Chakrabarti (2005), "Swami Vivekananda Education of Love" Kanishka Publishers, Distributors, New Delhi.
4. Sharma, S.R., (2004), "Life and Works of Swami Vivekananda", Book Encllave, Jaipur.

5. Swami Vivekananda (2008), My India the India Eternal, Published by Ramakrishna Mission Institute of Culture Kolkata -700 029, India.
6. Dr. Dancoder Mohapatra (2009) Swami Vivekananda on Education relevance to contemporary India, Neel Kamal Publications Pvt. Ltd. Educational Publisher's Sultan Bazar, Hyderabad-500 095.
7. T. Pradeep Kumar (2011) Encyclopaedia of Education in the New Millennium, (Vol. IV) great (philosophers of education), APH Publishing Corporation, New Delhi-110 002.
8. Journal of International Women's Studies Vol. 10 #2 November 2008 225.

24

Cultural Intelligence: A Key Perspective

P. Sooriya

Introduction

"Culture is a combination of thoughts, feelings, attitudes, beliefs, values, customs, behaviours, artifacts, understandings, assumptions, and goals that shared by racial, ethnic, religious, or social groups of people". Today, the advancement of science and improvements in the technology of transport and communication, the different races, cultures and nations were beginning to come closer and interact with one more effectively than before at different levels. Even though globalisation increases intercultural interaction leading the world as flat, which increases the probability of cultural misunderstanding, tensions and conflicts. In fact, National integration and international understanding is the crying need in modern times. However, culture is encountered as main factor in building national integration and international understanding. Culture brings unity and not uniformity. Lack of understanding of this strength leads to conflicts; clear understanding leads to meaningful, sustainable and harmonious development. Therefore, Cultural intelligence quotient (CQ) was conceived at the turn of twenty-first century to culminate ideological clashes and cultural conflict. In fact, great philosophers like Swami Vivekananda who have struggled strongly for national integration and international understanding have high level of cultural intelligence. So in this article, I would like to discuss about cultural intelligence of Swamiji and how it will become key perspective in building national integration and international understanding by providing some evidence from Swamiji's life history.

Cultural Intelligence of the Saint

Swami Vivekananda, an authoritative spokesman of Indian culture, suddenly leapt into fame at the parliament of religions held in 1893, at which he represented Hinduism. His vast knowledge of eastern and western culture as well as his deep spiritual insight, fervid eloquence, brilliant conversation, broad human sympathy, colourful personality and handsome figure made an irresistible appeal to many Americans who came in contact with him. So, he became India's ambassador in America and pleaded eloquently for better understanding between India and the new world in order to create a healthy synthesis of east and west, of religion and science. All these happened due to his cultural intelligence. The term cultural intelligence was introduced only in 2003 by Earley and Ang. Cultural intelligence is defined as the recognising and understanding of beliefs, values, attitudes and behaviours of a group of people and the capability to apply such knowledge towards achieving of specific goals. It is a multidimensional construct, with four dimensions i.e. Meta-cognitive CQ, Cognitive CQ, Motivational CQ, and Behavioural CQ.

Recent research has shown Vivekananda's warm appreciation of Christ. According to the erudite, Christ was a Bhakta and essentially a Sanyasin. Vivekananda believed Christ believed to have been the reincarnation. Hence, the Ramakrishna Mission finds no difficulty in quoting liberally the sayings of Jesus such as 'I and my Father are one'. It is significant that Swami Vivekananda inaugurated the Ramakrishna Mission after his master's death, on Xmas Eve. This shows the Meta cognitive CQ of Swami Vivekananda which upholds the mental capability of individuals to acquire and evaluate cultural knowledge. It occurs when people make judgments about their own thought processes and those of others.

The saint first travels across the length and breadth of the country finding out the pain of our nation and acquired an intimate knowledge not only of the socioeconomic conditions of his countrymen but the spiritual and cultural values they had cherished for thousands of years. After the parliament of religions, Vivekananda toured extensively in the west for nearly two years preaching the essence of universal brotherhood and he assiduously studied the spiritual and cultural values that guided the lives of the people of those countries. This shows the cognitive CQ of Swami Vivekananda which refers to an individual's general knowledge and knowledge structures about cultural institutions norms, practices and conventions in different cultural settings.

Swamiji warned Indians against trying to adopt Western culture. 'He struggled to introduce India's spiritual power into bloodstream of the West, and to infuse the West's generous democratic spirit into the Indian consciousness. On the other hand, Swamiji has taught Indians how to master Western science and technology and at the same time develop spiritually. Swamiji has also taught Indians how to adapt Western humanism to Indian ethos. He tried and achieved considerable success in the difficult task of reconciling with the cultural values of the East and the West, which have together come to shape the destiny of mankind. This shows the Motivational CQ of Swami Vivekananda which refers to the mental capacity directing attention and sustaining energy toward learning about, functioning and performing in intercultural situations.

At the end of the nineteenth century, India in general, and Hinduism in particular, faced grave challenges from the western materialistic life, the ideas of the western free society, and the proselytising activities of Christians.

Vivekananda met these challenges by integrating the best elements of western culture in Hindu culture. Furthermore, he pointed out to Indians about the drawbacks of Western culture and the need for India's contribution to overcome them. Swami Vivekananda's communicative style was spontaneous and sprang from inner vision of unity. This shows the Behavioural CQ of Swami Vivekananda which reflects the capability to flex behaviours fit into different cultural contexts. It also refers to an individual's capability to enact a wide repertoire of verbal and non-verbal actions when interacting with people from different cultures. The individuals know when to adapt and when not to adapt, while engaging cross-culturally.

Why does it Matter?

When individuals relocate to unfamiliar cultures, they often experience stress because norms and behaviours are unfamiliar and confusing. Misunderstanding concepts about the role of culture in behaviour, communication, and learning often lead to conflicts. So, Cultural intelligence is necessary because it focus on the capability of knowing about oneself, others and the situation in different cultural contexts. It provides people with an organising framework for thinking about possible ways that cultures might be similar and different. It is also valuing culturally diverse experience in and of itself, because it is inherently satisfying. It allows people to manage and regulate social behaviours in inter-cultural encounters so there is minimal misperception and misattribution. It focuses on the capability to flex verbal behaviour which includes speaking faster or slower, louder or softer, and varying the amount of inflection and communication conveyed via gestures, facial expressions and body languages, rather than through words, because some cultures are neutral and others are expressive. It also gave some flexibility in manner of communicating specific types of messages such that requests, invitations, apologies, gratitude, disagreement and saying 'no' are expressed appropriately based on local standards.

In the Context of Nation Building

A nation is an imagined community-based on one or more of the following: race, ethinicity, religion, customs, political memory, culture and ancestry. Nation building should focus on the accommodation of cultural diversity in different states. The terms-international understanding, co-operation and peace are to be considered as indivisible, whole-based on the principle of friendly relations between people and States of different social and political systems.

The Swami's mission was both national and international. A lover of mankind, he strove to promote peace and human brotherhood on spiritual foundations of Vedantic oneness of existence. Swami Vivekananda felt the greatest misfortune of the world is we do not tolerate and accept other religions. He told not only to tolerate other religion, but positively embrace them, and that the truth is the basis for all religions. In building up national integration and international understanding, in bringing peace to others, and peace to oneself, religion is the highest motive power. He believed that it is sure to help man becoming strong, yet tolerant and sympathetic. It will also help man to extend his love and good will beyond the communal, national and racial barriers. Actually, the problem pointed out by Vivekananda is not merely related to the nature of diversity itself. Instead, everything depends upon the manner in which we look at diversity: as a creative power or a destructive force. Therefore, the question of what ought to be our behaviour towards others in order to achieve religious harmony becomes more important than the existence of diversity of religions itself.

India is the only country, where the sublime truth of unity in diversity has been understood, appreciated and also practiced from time immemorial. We have done this with regard to various castes, communities and religions within India; we have also accepted and assimilated people from across the borders, whether they came to India as invaders, traders or refugees. As Swami Vivekananda stated "We have never been a conquering race, and this blessing is with us". This is because, we never believed that we have to bulldoze humanity into one, uniform, monotonous moulds.

Cultural Intelligence for the Cause

- Education for intercultural citizenship related to rights and social justice, building inclusive public spaces and the capacity of all cultural or faith based groups to make their voices heard and their practices more visible.
- Knowledge about other cultural systems, as a means of understanding the diversity of human realities. Owing to the messages of peace, justice and solidarity enshrined in their own culture, spiritual leaders are uniquely positioned to help youth understand and respect diversity.
- Youth involvement in the promotion and safeguarding of cultural heritage as an effective means to familiarise with their own and other culture.
- Culturally responsible media coupled with media literacy education. Youth recognise that, while the media often generate new ideas and social change, they can also streamline prejudices into public debates and deepen social cleavages.
- Investing in sport as a means to "foster peace and development" exposing youth to diversity as well as engaging them in promoting intercultural understanding through innovative ways and approaches.
- Education through the school is a social institution that can be exploited to promote cultural intelligence which leads to the appreciation and tolerance of others who are culturally different leading to sustainable living. This contributes to national stability which is an essential ingredient in nation building.

- Nurture and amplify Swami Vivekananda message of pride in culture and country to a whole new generation in a way that is personal, that reaches out and captures the youth.
- Compilation of available published material on the cultural life of world.
- Organise periodic lectures, seminars, workshops, discussion and exhibitions, which directly deal with the concerned communities.
- Undertake research start a data bank on the basis of field data collected through various documentation projects to record the multifarious elements of culture life, along with the current trends.
- An effort has been made at "Vivekanandar Illam" through exquisite paintings by eminent artists to chronologically depict the so grand traditions from the past to the present times, illustrating turning points of our cultural heritages.
- The cultural tourism has developed with the efforts to gain new information and experiences as well as knowing about different cultures.

Conclusion

Cultural intelligence sets an enabling environment for sustainable development. It highlights the importance of an approach through education that promotes the appreciation and tolerance of cultural diversity in an attempt to uphold the presence of a multicultural society. Living for a short span of four decades, Vivekananda left his footprints on the sands of time. His teachings will inspire the lives and times for generations to come. Now, if we, as followers or admirers of Swami Vivekananda, want to develop unity and harmony in our societies, let us put his ideas into practice, firstly in our personal lives, then by helping and supporting people who trod in this direction.

References

- Ang, S., and Van Dyne, L. (2008). Conceptualisation of cultural intelligence: Definition, Distinctiveness, and Nomological network. In Ang, S., and Van Dyne, L. Handbook on Cultural Intelligence: Theory, Measurement, and Applications (3-15). Armonk, NY: M. E. Sharpe.
- Ang, S., and Van Dyne, L. (Eds.) (2008). Handbook on Cultural Intelligence: Theory, Measurement, and Applications. Armonk, NY: M. E. Sharpe.
- Ang, S., Van Dyne, L., Koh, C., Yee Ng, K., Templer, K. J., Tay, C., and Chandrasekhar, N. (2007). Cultural intelligence: Its measurement and effects on cultural judgment and decision making, cultural adaptation, and task performance. Management and Organisation Review, 3, 335-371.

- Van Dyne, L., Ang, S., and Livermore, D. (2010). Cultural intelligence: A pathway for leading in a rapidly globalising world. In K. Hannum B.B. McFeeters, and L. Booysen (Eds.), Leading across differences, 131-138. San Francisco: Pfeiffer.
- Van Dyne, L., Ang, S., Yee Ng, K., Rockstul, T., Ling Tan, M., and Koh, C. (2012). Sub-dimensions of the four factor model of cultural intelligence: Expanding the conceptualisation and measurement of cultural intelligence. Social and personality compass, 6/4, 295-313.

25

Education for National Service: A Comparative Study on Patriotic Attitude and National Integration among the NCC Cadets and Non-NCC Students

B. Mohan Kumar

Stipulated Definition-Patriotism

Accordingly, patriotism is supposed to be a fundamental element of individual and group life, and it is believed to fulfil such basic needs as the needs for security, for a positive identity, for effectiveness and control, for a positive connection to other people connection to other people, and for comprehension of reality (Staub, 1997).

Operational Definition-Patriotic Attitude

Patriotic Attitude can be defined as the level of attitude of an individual's love towards nation, welfare of one's country, the virtues and actions of a patriot, the passion which inspires one to serve one's country.

NCC Cadets

NCC Cadets refers to the "first, second and third year National Cadet Corps (NCC) students pursuing their under graduate course".

NON-NCC Students

NON-NCC students refers to the "first, second and third year students pursuing their undergraduate course out of NCC training".

Objectives of the Study

1. To find out the Level of Patriotic Attitude and National Integration among the National Cadet Corps (NCC) cadets and Non-NCC Students.
2. To Compare NCC and Non-NCC Students with respect to their Level of Patriotic Attitude and National Integration

Hypothesis

1. There will be no significant difference in the overall level of Patriotic Attitude and National Integration among NCC and NON-NCC College Students with respect to various dimensions.

Need for Patriotic Attitude

Patriotism is love of country. For most people, it is not a passionate exclusive and life-altering love. It's more like love for a blood-relative, perhaps an aunt. It doesn't involve choice. It doesn't require a tremendously high estimate of the object's intrinsic qualities. We may put our family first, but to love only them is too exclusive. Loving all of humankind is good, but it doesn't mean the same thing as love for a concrete object. For instance, you cannot have an obligation to know many details about humankind.

A nation works as an object of love. One can identify and feel with it consequent obligations and entitlements, including the obligation to know its history, culture, constitution, and geography. Love for a country inspires, enlarges one's sympathies, and gives one a sense of support and solidarity.

1. Patriotism promotes participation in national politics, including such acts as voting, joining national social movements, litigating in federal court, and enlisting in the military or serving in the civil service. In turn, broad participation makes national politics work better and more justly.
2. Patriotism is a flexible concept, it involves allusions and reinterpretations of shared traditions; and patriotism provides a rich and diverse store.
3. It seems that a democratic government can legitimately decide to instil love of country, Local democratic governments can also promote love of their own local communities, and that is common enough--but it doesn't negate the right of a national democracy to promote patriotism.
4. Patriotism has a role in a theory of human development.

Research Design

Sl. No.	*Type*	*Sources*
1.	Nature of Research	Normative Survey
2.	Variables	Patriotic Attitude and National Integration
3.	Tools used	National Integration and Patriotic Attitude Scale (PAS) was developed and standardised by the investigator.
4.	Sampling Technique	Convenient Sampling
5.	Sampling Population	NCC and NON-NCC Students of Chennai Colleges
6.	Size of the Sample	468
7.	Statistical Techniques used	Descriptive Analysis Differential Analysis

Research Analysis

Table values indicating mean, standard deviation and t-test values of overall level of Patriotic Attitude and National Integration with respect to various dimensions.

Dimensions	*Group*	*N*	*Mean*	*S.D*	*t-value*	*Level of Significance*
National Affinity	NCC	234	12.23	1.61		
	NON NCC	234	11.28	2.11	5.4301	Significant 0.01
National Development	NCC	234	20.82	3.00		
	NON NCC	234	18.52	3.91	7.1183	Significant 0.01
National Integration	NCC	234	12.01	1.98		
	NON NCC	234	10.23	2.51	8.4786	Significant 0.01
Patriotic Attitude	NCC	234	45.06	4.75		
	NON NCC	234	40.04	7.17	8.9210	Significant 0.01

From the above table, the calculated 't' value of National Affinity (5.4301), National Development (7.1183), National Integration (8.4786), Overall Patriotic Attitude (8.9210) of NCC and NON-NCC College Students is found greater than the table value 2.58 at 0.01 level. There exists significant difference between NCC and NON-NCC College Students, with respect to various dimensions of "Patriotic Attitude". Hence, null hypothesis finds rejected.

Research Outcome

- There is a significant difference among NCC and NON-NCC College Students in the overall Level of Patriotic Attitude for the dimensions National Affinity, National Development and National Integration.
- There is a significant difference among NCC and NON-NCC College Students in the overall Level of Patriotic Attitude.

Suggestion

- The students should be sensitised to develop moral values.
- The students should be taught to identify moral issues in the society.
- The students should be motivated to read biographies of great people, national leaders and moral stories.
- Students should be motivated to join uniformed services training like NCC, RSP, Scouts and Guides etc.
- Importance and benefits of uniform services (NCC) should be explained by conducting motivational classes.
- National Integration camps should be organised on national level for the NON-NCC College students also; it will help the students to know about the other State language, culture, etc.
- Policy makers may consider importance of Patriotic attitude, Social Maturity and value education, while framing curriculum and educational policies.

Limitation

1. The study was conducted with the sample of only 234 NCC Cadets and 234 NON-NCC College Students of Government and Govt. aided colleges only.
2. The study has conducted with Colleges present in Chennai Metropolitan city.

References

- Bar-Tal, D., and Staub, E. (1997). Introduction: Patriotism: Its Scope and Meaning. In D. Bar-Tal and E. Staub (Eds.), Patriotism: In the Lives of Individuals and Nations. Chicago: Nelson-Hall. pp. 1-21.
- Gail P. Kelly (1982). Schooling and National Integration: The Case of Interwar Vietnam. Journal of Comparative Education. V18 (2), pp. 175-195.
- Mohanty, J. (1986). Indian education in the Emerging society, 3rd edn. New Delhi, Sterling Publisher's Private Limited. Chapter 4 and 24, pp. 19-25, 152-161.

PART–V: EDUCATION FOR NATIONAL SERVICE

26

Value-Based Education for Rural Development

C. Nandeesh

Introduction

The role of education in national development and in individual and social well being has been well recognised. Its importance in capacity building and in improving the quality of life has generated a demand by planners throughout the world for a high priority to education, lager public sector allocations, and the strengthening of elementary education. Outlay(s) on education are considered as 'investments in human capital' as they help to build the human resource so vital for economic growth, reduction of poverty, equalisation of opportunities, and social empowerment. The level of education has shown a high degree of correspondence with earning(s), upward social and economic mobility, a wider range of choices in economic and social spheres, greater adaptability in adjusting to changing labour markets, enhanced ability to acquire new skills and competencies, greater social awareness and a better quality of life.

To most of us, the twenty-first century will hopefully bring much peace, solace, comfort, progress, productivity, information technology, etc. This century is looked at as a knowledge-based, technologically advanced and informative period. In order to fulfill and realise these dreams and expectations, we have to go through a series of actions and processes, which would take us to some logical end. One of the very important vehicles of attaining these goals is vocational education, which through its inherent problem solving approach of middle level skilled human resource in unorganised sector-particularly the service sector.

Basic human values: Words used to express and describe values are notoriously hard to define. What is love to one person may be self-sacrifice to the other, truth and duty often overlap, and may be interwoven with goodness or perfection. The variety of definitions and expression however, should not hide the fact that certain values have endured through centuries of human experience. For purpose of conceptualisation and instruction, one may identify as basic values—the five: Truth, righteous action, peace, love and non-violence.

It is felt that five basic values include in a balanced way, profound moral insight of all the world's great enduring civilisations. Other values too:

The Concept

'Vidya' is of two types. The first type is worldly education which teaches skills and various disciplines and imparts knowledge and information useful for earning one's livelihood, attaining and maintaining some standard of living. The second type is moral and spiritual education, which imparts equanimity, tolerance, control, gratitude, devotion to god, and dedication to the realisation of reality. The first is the 'Apara' or secular, mundane, and the second is 'para' or transcendental and spiritual (Sadri, Dastoor and Jayashree 2001). While both types are important, the present scenario in the country and the world reveals all the emphasis being laid on the first type.

Approaches to Value Education

The continuous erosion of moral values in public life has shocked educationists and they are now thinking of reintroducing value education in school curricula so as to rebuild social life on sound ethical ground. A student should develop a sort of personality that would be able to resist all evil influences and will stand unshaken. If the students of today are succumbing to immoral ways, the reason is that their moral base in school was not well laid out. The education in human values programmed aims at the development of an integrated personality of the student. So, all the activities and experiences to which children will be exposed either in the class room or outside the class-room, on the play field, in the laboratory and the library should be value-oriented. The every atmosphere in the school is such that the students imbibe the values of silence, discipline, and a sense of order, cleanliness, beauty and such other values.

Catalyst for Rural Development

Mahatma Gandhi had sought to build India from bottom, that is, from the poorest and the weakest, and hence his concept of development followed the centrality of the village. He stood for the integrity and foundations of the villages. In his own word, "Under my scheme of things, nothing will be allowed to be produced by the cities which can be equally well produced by the villagers. The proper function of cities it is to serve as clearing houses of village products." He was pained to see the contrast between the two: the poor villagers and exploited by their own countrymen — the city dwellers. They produce the food and go hungry. They produce milk and their children have to go without it. He advocated value education exposed to various knowledge, disseminating media, fostering leadership building, developing rural entrepreneurship, undertaking participation in social and culture activities, and engendering keen interest in undertaking a high level of interest in community activities in its totality all of which together would contribute to accelerated rural development.

Self-reliance, oriented rural development can take place only if the citizen of village develop into an empowered and enlightened development force and medium and what better ways to ensure this for the future at least than by educating the village children and youth to take care of their future, themselves. An educated child is an empowered child and tomorrow's empowered citizen.

Village Reconstruction

Following may be the developing programs needed for a village reconstruction (Singh 2006):

- The construction of all-weather roads in rural area and their proper maintenance without fail.
- The establishment of the educational institutions of all types and for different stages of education with special emphasis on the quality and Value Education in life. The staff must have proper residential facilities near the Institution.
- The establishment of adequately equipped hospital and nursing home within affordable price of villagers. The complete staff has to live within the establishment or nearby.
- A carefully planned development of Dairy Farming with special emphasis on cow, as its products serve as medicines for large number of diseases.
- Developing rural entrepreneurship capabilities by organising training programs and hobby clubs to serve as Interest Groups in suitable vocational areas.

Role of Teachers and Students

It is essential for the school teacher to be not only an effective instructor but a skilful motivator, communicator, social educator and appreciably, a good instructor who makes even the difficult subjects easy. There is no better way to reach the community than through schools, wherein students are the real change agents. Students, in fact are the pivotal actors of such societal change as could very well facilitate the initiation of chain-reaction in spreading the message of safe-guarding the community's health and knowledge wealth. Students can act as catalysts change agents and facilitators for including change at least in their immediately related families thereby reflecting the village school as model unit of holistic community life in the villages. The children when they attend school should learn something about cleanliness, public health and sanitation, environmental conservation besides acquiring outside-the-class vocational skills under this model.

Value-Oriented Vocational Education

The teaching-learning of a vocational education involves acquisition of knowledge and understanding about a particular vocation, development of skills and competencies to perform the related tasks as well as development of such personality traits required for the success of learner both as an individual and a worker. In vocational education, more emphasis is given on practice or skill learning through practical education in school through on-the-job training and apprenticeship training in an industry/collaborating institution.

In this process, the learners are expected to imbibe certain values and qualities such as:

- Dignity of labour (respect for manual work and regard for manual workers) and work ethics.
- Punctuality, regularity, sincerity, diligence, dedication, discipline, honesty, integrity.
- Self-reliance, cooperation, team work, perseverance, tolerance.
- Deeper concern for the environment, safety, health, hygiene and sustainable development.
- Quality consciousness, excellence and sense of perfection for production of globally competitive quality goods and services.
- Self-esteem through achievements in productive work and service.
- Judicious use of the raw material and care of tools.
- Sense of belonging, responsibility and commitment to the society and the nation.

Conclusion

It is the dream of India to attain the status of one of the most developed nations of the world by the year 2020. In order to attain this goal, what the country needed most is to prepare a solid base for building "Village India" into a self reliant entity so as to turn each "Tiny Republic" into a potential catalyst of nation building for achieving the noble goal.

The paper suggests that the quality education should blend the need of the present with the anticipated needs of the future. We have inherited a golden era of our heritage enriched by highest ideals of human values. At the same time, we have to give rights to the newly emerging techno-economic pattern, which are so essential for the developing villages into vibrant units of society.

References

1. Batra, G.S. and Dangwal, R.C. (Ed. 2001), Entrpreneurship and Small Scale Industries: New Potentials, New Delhi: Deep and Deep Publications P. Ltd., pp. 101-110.
2. Guru, G. and Singh, D.P. (Ed. 1998), Environment and Development; PSSCIVE (NCERT), New Delhi.
3. Sadri Sorab, Dastoor Dhun S., and Jayashree S. (2001). The Theory and Practice of Managerial Ethics. Mumbai: Jaico Publishing House, 111-234.

4. Sharma, G.D. (2001). Management and the Indian Ethos New Delhi: Rupa and Co., 28-91.
5. Singh, D.P. (2001), Value Inculcation through Work Experience and Vocational Education, Journal of Value Education, Vol. I, No. I, pp. 114-119.

PART–VI: YOGA EDUCATION

27

Vision of Swamiji on Raja Yoga

S. Velvizhi

Introduction

"Take up one idea. Make that one idea your life; dream of it; think of it; live on that idea. Let the brain, the body, muscles, nerves, every part of your body be full of that idea; and just leave every other idea alone. This is the way to success, and this is the way great spiritual giants are produced."

— Swami Vivekananda

The word "Raja" comes from the Sanskrit word for royal or king, and the word "yoga" means union. The main preoccupation of Raja Yoga is cultivation of the mind. It concentrates heavily on training the mind, connecting with the life force and withdrawing into the highest states of spiritual life. All forms of yoga have a goal of release from the mundane physical world, which is achieving "moksha". Raja yoga is the science of physical and mental control. It is a system for attaining perfection of mind and body through systematic physical exercises.

Swami Vivekananda suggested that Raja Yoga is one of the four yogas of Hinduism, along with Jnana, Bhakti and Karma. Raja-Yoga proposes to start from the internal world, to study internal nature, and through that, control the whole, both internal and external. With yoga comes knowledge; knowledge again helps the Yogi. He who combines in himself both yoga and knowledge, the Lord is pleased with him. The goal of Raja Yoga is how to concentrate the mind, how to discover the innermost recesses of our own mind and how to generalise their contents and form our own conclusions. In order to obtain the goal, practice is absolutely necessary. This human body is the greatest body in the universe, and a human being—the greatest being. Man is higher than all animals, than all angels; none is greater than man.

Need for Raja Yoga

Raja Yoga is predicated on the notion that thoughts, feelings, perceptions and memories, along with external things, distort the true Self. Practicing Raja Yoga helps to dissolve these barriers to becoming your true Self, connecting with and controlling the life force and elevating toward the infinite and eternal Self.

A report by Lander University's Oriental Philosophy includes caution advocated by practitioners that when you abuse the Raja Yoga practice, "it can create a hell past human imagining." Premature awakening of latent forces can cause mental instability, the report says. These include psychic powers, reading other people's thoughts, control of forces of nature, becoming "almost all-knowing," living without breathing, power to levitate and control of others bodies.

As a certain commentator on yoga philosophy says, "When one proof is obtained, however little that may be, it will give us faith in the whole teaching of yoga." For instance, after the first few months of practice, you will begin to find you can read another's thoughts; they will come to you in picture form. You will hear something happening at a long distance, when you concentrate your mind with a wish to hear. These glimpses will come, by little bits at first, but enough to give you faith, and strength, and hope. For instance, if you concentrate your thoughts on the tip of your nose, in a few days you will begin to smell most beautiful fragrance, which will be enough to show that there are certain mental perceptions that can be made obvious without the contact of physical objects.

The aim, the end, the goal, of this training is liberation of the soul. Absolute control of nature, and nothing short of it, must be the goal. We must be the masters, and not the slaves of nature; neither body nor mind must be our master, nor must we forget that the body is mine, and not I the body.

The Components of Raja Yoga

Raja Yoga's precepts are concerned with moral, physical and mental discipline, taught in a set of eight stages. There are eight components to practicing Raja Yoga.

- **Yama:** Non-killing, truthfulness, non-stealing, continence, and non-receiving of any gifts.
- **Niyama:** Mental and Physical cleanliness — self-surrender to God.
- **Asana:** Physical Posture to maintain during meditation
- **Pranayama:** Breath control and heartbeats to calm your mind and direct energy.
- **Pratyahara:** Practice of withdrawing from physical senses, making the mind more introspective.
- **Dharana:** Concentration and involves fixing attention on one thing to the exclusion of everything else.
- **Dhyana:** Total concentration and deep meditation.
- **Samadhi:** The sacred power that is the source and sustainer of the universe.

Word and Wisdom—Primordial Vibration

The Seven Lotus "Chakras"

Following Patanjali, Vivekananda describes seven spiritual energy- centers, or "chakras," located at various points at the back of the body cavity and arranged along the spinal column. The following list should be read upward, starting at the bottom:

- **Sahasrara:** At the crown of the head, with a thousand petals;
- **Ajna:** Between or just above the eyebrows, with two petals;
- **Vishuddha:** In the region of the throat, with sixteen petals;
- **Anahata:** Near the heart, with twelve petals;
- **Manipura:** Near the solar plexus, with ten petals;
- **Svadhisthana:** Usually visualised as just above the genitals, with six petals;
- **Muladhara:** Located in the sacrococcygeal plexus at the base of spinal cord, close to the genitals and anus, visualised as a lotus flower with four petals.

The two most important chakras for meditation purposes are the starting and ending points, the Muladhara and the Sahasrara, In the Muladhara, coiled up in a triangular area, is the serpent-like Kundalini, which contains the individual's reservoir of psychic energy. The goal of Raja Yoga is to awaken the Kundalini and send it upward along the chakras until it reaches the Sahasrara and opens the thousand-petaled lotus blossom there. Inside of that lotus think of the Golden One, the Almighty, the Intangible, He whose name is Om, the Inexpressible, surrounded with effulgent light. Meditate on that.

He who has given up all attachment, all fear, and all anger, he whose whole soul has gone unto the Lord, he who has taken refuge in the Lord, whose heart has become purified, with whatsoever desire he comes to the Lord, He will grant that to him. Therefore worship Him through knowledge, love, or renunciation.

Raja Yoga—The Detergent

According to the Raja-Yogi, who has said that there are two sorts of purification:

- External Purification
- Internal Purification

External Purification: The body by water, earth, or other materials is the external purification, as bathing.

Internal Purification: The mind by truth, and by all the other virtues, is what is called internal purification.

It is not sufficient that a man should be internally pure and externally dirty. When both are not attainable, the internal purity is the better, but no one will be a Yogi until he has both. Worship of God is by praise, by thought, by devotion.

Swami Vivekananda said that "the goal is to manifest this divine within, by controlling nature, external and internal. Do this either by work, or worship, or psychic control, or philosophy, by one, or more, or all of these-and be free. This is the whole of religion. Doctrines, or dogmas, or rituals, or books, or temples, or forms, are but secondary details."

A Yogi must avoid the two extremes of luxury and austerity. He must not fast, nor torture his flesh. He who does so, says the Gita, cannot be a Yogi: He who fasts, he who keeps awake, he who sleeps much, he who works too much, he who does not work, none of these can be a Yogi (Gita, VI, 16).

Good for Health

If the body is not in a fit state, the practice will be obstructed. Therefore, we have to keep the body in good health; we have to take care of what we eat and drink, and what we do. Always use a mental effort, what is usually called "Christian Science," to keep the body strong. That is all-nothing further of the body. We must not forget that health is only a means to an end. If health were the end, we would be like animals; animals rarely become unhealthy.

- Yoga is to make men live long
- Some of you will find it a good thing for headaches to drink cold water through the nose as soon as you get up in the morning; the whole day your brain will be nice and cool, and you will never catch cold. It is very easy to do; put your nose into the water, draw it up through the nostrils and make a pump action in the throat.
- He is determined not to fall sick, and he never does. He lives long; a hundred years is nothing to him; he is quite young and fresh when he is 150, without one hair turned grey
- *Pranayama:* First the nerves are to be purified, then comes the power to practice Pranayama.
- Stopping the right nostril with the thumb, through the left nostril fill in air, according to capacity; then, without any interval, throw the air out through the right nostril, closing the left one.
- Again inhaling through the right nostril eject through the left, according to capacity;
- Practicing this exercise, three or five times at four hours of the day, before dawn, during midday, in the evening, and at midnight, in fifteen days or a month purity of the nerves is attained; then begins Pranayama."

Practice Peacefully

- When you practice, first salute ancient Yogis, and your own Guru, and God, and then begin.

- You have to practice when the body feels very Energetic,
- To practice when the mind is very Joyful.
- Go to well hidden place, where people seldom come to disturb you.
- To choose clean places. Rather choose beautiful scenery, or a room in your own house which is beautiful.

Conclusion

"When I Asked God for Peace, He Showed Me How to Help Others
God Gave Me Nothing I Wanted, He Gave Me Everything I Needed."
— Swami Vivekananda

Raja yoga teaches that—The man who thinks that he is receiving a response to his prayers does not know that the fulfillment comes from his own nature, that he has succeeded, by the mental attitude of prayer, in waking up a bit of this infinite power which is coiled up within himself. Raja Yoga is the science of religion, the rationale of all worship, all prayers, forms, ceremonies, and miracles. In human society, in the same way, too much wealth or too much poverty is a great impediment to the higher development of the soul. It is from the middle classes that the great ones of the world come. Here, the forces are very equally adjusted and balanced.

References

- Banhatti, G.S. (1995). Life and philosophy of Swami Vivekananda. New Delhi: Atlantic. p. 145.
- Sen, Amiya P. (2006). "Raja Yoga: The Science of Self-Realisation". The Indispensable Vivekananda. Orient Blackswan. pp. 219-227.
- Feuerstein, Georg; Ken Wilber (2002). "The Wheel of Yoga". The Yoga Tradition. Motilal Banarsidass Publishers.
- Akhilananda, Swami; Gordon W. Allport (1999). Hindu Psychology. Routledge.
- Vivekananda, Swami (1980). Raja Yoga. Ramakrishna-Vivekananda Center.
- Wood, Ernest (1951). Practical Yoga, Ancient and Modern, Being a New, Independent Translation of Patanjali's Yoga Aphorisms. Rider and Company.
- Prabhavananda, Swami; Christopher Isherwood. How to Know God. Vedanta Press and Bookshop.

28

Concentration—The Method of Education

S. Santhi

Introduction

Thus, the secret of a strong mind — exercise and meditate.

"The more this power of concentration, the more knowledge is acquired, because this is the one and only method of acquiring knowledge. Even the lowest shoeblack, if he gives more concentration, will black shoes better; the cook with concentration will cook a meal all the better. In making money or in worshipping God, or in doing anything, the stronger the power of concentration, the better will that thing be done. This is the one call, the one knock, which opens the gates of nature, and lets out floods of light."

Thinking is the hardest thing to do in this world." — *Gandhi*

Newton didn't discover gravity by lasing under apple trees in a garden nor thinking about the, perhaps, delicious red apples. He was successful because he concentrated all his energy for some time on just one subject. That's the power of concentration — effective thinking — is all about, here's what Vivekananda, one of India's great spiritual gurus said more than a 100 years ago on the subject:

"To me, the very essence of education is concentration of mind, not the collecting of facts. If I had to do my education over again, and had any voice in the matter, I would not study facts at all. I would develop the power of concentration and detachment, and then with a perfect instrument I could collect facts at will."

Power of Concentration

"The more this power of concentration, the more knowledge is acquired, because this is the one and only method of acquiring knowledge. Even the lowest shoeblack, if he gives more concentration, will black shoes better; the cook with concentration will cook a meal all the better. In making money or in worshipping God, or in doing anything, the stronger the power of concentration, the better will that thing be done. This is the one call, the one knock, which opens the gates of nature, and lets out floods of light."

"How has all the knowledge in the world been gained but by the concentration of powers of the mind? The world is ready to give up secrets, if we only know how to knock, how to give necessary blow. The strength and force of the blow come through concentration. There is no limit to the power of the human mind. The more concentrated it is, the more power is brought to bear on one point; that is the secret."

"Free! We, who cannot, for a moment, govern our own minds, nay, cannot hold our minds on a subject, and focus it on a point to the exclusion of everything else, for a moment! Yet we call ourselves free. Think of it! ... The mind uncontrolled and unguided will drag us down, and down, forever—rend us, kill us; and the mind controlled and guided will save us, free us."

Meditation strengthens the mind and makes it less susceptible to distraction thus improving one's concentration. But before we start meditating, it is necessary to strengthen our body. If our body is weak, our brain will keep distracting us, because its priority is a fit body — it depends on healthy body for its own survival and functioning.

Concentration and Learning

Concentration is learning to train our mind to disregard any distraction. Thus the first step towards strengthening our mind is to first strengthen our body — that is by exercising. Once our body is fit the mind will have less to worry about its own health, and thus can be better utilised and directed by our own will. That is why; even just exercising daily will improve your concentration. But to really strengthen it, to learn to constructively use our emotions by ensuring that they aren't uncontrollable, physical exercises aren't enough and one also needs to meditate. Thus, the secret of a strong mind – is exercise and meditation.

The main focus in learning is to make the hidden ability of a learner manifest. As Vivekananda said, 'what a man "learns" is really what he "discovers", by taking the cover off his own soul, which is a mine of infinite knowledge. According to the Vedanta philosophy, knowledge is inherent in a human being 'Manifestation' indicates spontaneous growth, provided that the impediments, if any, are removed. Next in importance in the Swami's definition of education is the expression 'already in man'. This refers to a human being's potential, which is the range of his abilities and talents, known or unknown that he was born with. 'Potential' speaks of the possibility of awakening something that is lying dormant.

Rabindranath Tagore's propensity, expressed in his Gitanjali, indicates his strong aspiration to discover the wonder behind this creation; and the capability—i.e., a person's motivation and efficiency in working towards an position, and says, 'You are pure and perfect, and what you call sin does not belong to you.' Sins are very low degrees of Self-manifestation; manifest your Self in a high degree." We should look upon God as the whole of reality, and ourselves as parts of that reality; God as the divine Fire, and ourselves as sparks of that Fire.

There have been many changes in the field of education since Swamiji left the mortal core one hundred years ago, but not as many changes as in other areas of society. One such noticeable change in education is that it is now engaged in preparing human beings for a new type of society, and it is trying to create a new type of human being for it. Interestingly, Swamiji had envisioned a society with a new type of human being in whom knowledge, action, work and concentration were harmoniously blended, and he proposed a new type of education for achieving this. The right to education for everyone, guaranteed by the Constitution of India, was Vivekananda's dream, but it is still a far cry from its goal. His idea of continual, or lifelong, education, however, has been adopted in many countries already. Moreover, because of the adoption of continuous education in these countries, our idea of what constitutes success and failure has altered, raising new hope for the weak, underprivileged section of these societies — the very people who for various reasons cannot complete their education when they are young. Vivekananda's cry for the uplift of the downtrodden masses, particularly of the long-neglected women has evoked a favourable response from different quarters, but societies tailor make education to meet their own needs, thereby often robbing the weak of their freedom to determine their own destiny. Unless radical changes are made in all the societies, the poor will never be able to raise upon themselves. This was a major concern of the Swami. It is remarkable by the extent to which there were similarities between Vivekanada's thoughts and actions taking place one century ago and the present concerns of UNESCO.

Conclusion

His vision of education, science and culture are the essential instruments of human development. That education should be a lifelong process. And we need to move away from routine learning. He was a visionary and an original thinker, Vivekananda pointed out in his first public lecture in Asia, on 15 January 1897: "but education has yet to be in the world and civilisation—civilisation has begun nowhere yet" (CW, Vol. III, p. 114). This is true. If we consider civilisation to be the manifestation of the divine in human beings, as Vivekananda conceived it to be, no society has made much progress so far. This is why we find that mildness, gentleness, forbearance, tolerance, sympathy and so forth—the signs of a healthy civilisation—have not taken root in any society on an appreciable scale, although we prematurely boast of a global village. The lack of basic necessities among the underprivileged all over the world is no less striking than the lack of morality among the educated privileged ones. To squarely meet this great challenge, Vivekananda prescribed 'man-making and character-building education'

References

- "Awakening India". http://awakeningindia.org. Retrieved 30 March 2012.
- Vivekananda, Swami (1996). In Swami Lokeswarananda. My India: the India eternal (1st ed.). Calcutta: Ramakrishna Mission Institute of Culture. pp. 1-2. ISBN: 81-85843-51-1.
- "Swami Vivekananda: Life and Teaching". Belur Math. Retrieved 30 March 2012.
- "The Future of India". Wikisource. Retrieved 3 April 2012.
- "Swami Vivekananda quotes". http://jnanagni.com. Retrieved 3 April 2012.
- "The Complete Works of Swami Vivekananda/Volume 7/Conversations And Dialogues/X". Wikisource. Retrieved 30 March 2012.
- "The Education that India needs". Wikisource. Retrieved 30 March 2012.
- "Universal teachings of Swami Vivekananda". http://www.ramakrishna.org. Retrieved 30 March 2012.

29

Yoga: An Urgent Need

S. Amutha and M. Suganya

Introduction

Swami Vivekananda (1863-1902) a great thinker and reformer of India, embraces education as "Man Making". The saint treats yoga as science. Today, the teachers and the students lead their life in a mechanical way like that of some machine. Moral and religious values are being undermined. The fundamental principles of civilisation are being ignored. Swamiji seeks the solution of these entire social and global evils through education by awakening humans' spiritual self in turn to attain a purpose of education. The four pillars of education are learning to know, learning to do, learning to live together and learning to be. Learning to live together is one of the major issues in today's education. Education must prepare every individual for managing life with peace and harmony in a rapidly changing world.

Learning to live together in peace and harmony requires a coherent and integrated approach to ensure learner involvement towards achieving this which involves an integrated curriculum framework, appropriate teaching strategies, a variety of approaches, techniques and resources, access to key international documents and the direct involvement of students in internalising and practicing these values in realistic situations (Amutha, 2012).

Objectives

Vivekananda points out that the defect of the present-day education is that it has no definite goal to pursue. A sculptor has a clear idea about what he wants to shape out of the marble block; similarly, a painter knows what he is going to paint. But a teacher, he says, has no clear idea about the goal of his teaching. Swamiji attempts to establish, through his words and deeds, that the end of all education is man making. He prepares the scheme of this man-making education in the light of his overall philosophy of Vedanta. According to Vedanta, the essence of man lies in his soul, which he possesses in addition to his body and mind. In true essence with this philosophy, Swamiji defines education as 'the manifestation of the perfection already in man.' The aim of education is to manifest in our lives the perfection, which is the very nature of our inner self. This perfection is the realisation of the infinite power which resides in everything and every-where-existence, consciousness and bliss (satchidananda). After understanding the essential nature of this perfection, we should identify it with our inner self. For achieving this, one will have to eliminate one's ego, ignorance and all other false identification, which stand in the way. (Sudipa Dutta Roy, 2001). Therefore, yoga education aims to impart physical, mental, emotional, intellectual, social and spiritual well being of any individual.

Need for Yoga Education

The utility of yogic science is to bring out the perfect man, and not let him wait and wait for ages, just a plaything in the hands of the physical world, like a log of drifty-wood carried from wave to wave, and tossing about in the ocean. This science wants you to be strong to take the work in your hand, instead of leaving it in the hands of nature and get beyond this little life. This is the great idea.

> *"We want that education by which character is formed strength of mind is increased, the intellect is expanded and by which one can stand on one's own feet."* — *Swami Vivekananda.*

Swamiji's method of education resembles the heuristic method of the modern educationists. In this system, the teacher invokes the spirit of inquiry in the pupil. Vivekananda lays a lot of emphasis on the environment at home and school for the proper growth of the child. The parents as well as the teachers should inspire the child by the way they live their lives. Vivekananda recommends the old institution of Gurukula (living with preceptor) and similar systems for the purpose. In such systems, the student can have the ideal character of the teacher constantly before them, which serves as the role model to follow. Philosophy of education is especially interested in the relationship between theory and practice. Value education comprises all those experiences that affect the growth and development of some person throughout his life. In building up character in making for everything that is good and great in bringing peace to others and peace to one's own self. It also helps man to extend his love and good beyond the communal and national.

Implications of Yoga

Yoga in Education provides the following advantages to the users:

- respecting self and others
- positive outlook
- good health and mind
- relaxation of body and mind
- manage stress
- regulate energy levels

- enhance learning
- enhanced concentration
- physical well-being
- reduced problem behaviour
- less test anxiety and anger
- increased self-regulation and focus

Conclusion

Though we live in the technological era, everyone wants to live in peace and harmony. Teachers should play a vital role in maintaining peace and harmony in educational institutions and in the global level. This transformation can be achieved through imparting Yoga in education. It is high time for the teachers and teacher education institutions to take cognizance of the Swami Vivekananda's quote "Arise, awake, and stop not till the goal is reached" and work towards the world with peace and harmony.

References

- Amutha, S., (2013) Yoga: A Gateway to Global peace and Harmony, International Conference proceedings, Servite College of Education, Thoogaimalai.
- Yoga in the Classroom a New Kind of Education, National Center on Health, Physical Activity and Disability (NCHPAD), retrieved from www.ncpad.org/881/5004.
- Sudipa Dutta Roy (2001). Education in the Vision of Swami Vivekananda, retrieved from www.esamskriti.com/essay-chapters/Education-in-the-Vision-of-Swami-Vivekananda-1.aspx.

30

Human Values in Karma Yoga

K. Subashini

Introduction

Swami Vivekananda is the famous philosopher and great educationist in the history of India. His thoughts and ideas have influenced the philosophy of life. Swami Vivekananda believed in the Vedanta philosophy which considers that the ultimate goal of human life is to attain 'Unity with the Creator'. According to him 'God resides in every human heart', so that, the best worship of God is service to mankind. Swami Vivekananda who, will proclaiming the sovereignty of the advaita philosophy, as including that experience in which all is one, without a second .

Swami Vivekananda was the great preacher of karma yoga, not divorced from but as expressing as Jnana and Bhakthi yoga. According to Swami Vivekananda, worship the study, the farm yard and the field as true and fit scenes for the meeting of God with man as the cell of the monk or the door of the temple. To Him, there was no difference between service of man and worship of God, between manliness and faith, between true righteousness and spirituality.

Swami Vivekananda always believed that the development of a nation is not possible without real education. According to him, development of good personality in every human being is very essential in case of nation building. That's why, Swami Vivekananda emphasised on Man making education by which we can make a good citizen for national development. According to Swami Vivekananda 'Man making means a harmonious development of the body, mind and soul'

Objectives of Study

- To identify the human values advocated by Swami Vivekananda on karma yoga.
- To adopt the strategies advocated by Swami Vivekananda to practice these human values.
- To analyse the relevancy of values in present day school education.

Methodology

Content analysis was adopted to investigate the study.

Swami Vivekananda and Karma Yoga

Karma-Yoga, therefore, is a system of ethics and religion intended to attain freedom through unselfishness, and by good works. The Karma-Yogi need not believe in any doctrine what soever. He may not believe even in God, may not ask what his soul is, nor think of any metaphysical speculation. He has got his own special aim of realising selflessness; and he has to work it out himself. Every moment of his life must be realisation, because he has to solve by mere work, without the help of any doctrine or theory.

Swami Vivekananda himself was a karma yogi; he stressed the importance of duty and its various sectors. No man can be so without doing work. The word karma is derived from the Sanskrit word kri, to do, all action is karma. Technically, the word also means the effect of actions. In karma yoga we simply mean work. Swami Vivekananda spoke karma yoga in eight chapters. These eight chapters were carefully analysed.

Table I: Human Values Identified

Sl. No.	*Chapter I*	*Chapter II*	*Chapter III*	*Chapter IV*
1.	Character	Equilibrium	Spirituality	Duty is universal
2.	Self-lessness	Morality	Non-attachment	Respect others
3.	Love	Resist not evil	Liberation	Adjustment
4.	Truth	Renunciation	Work through love	Work is worship
5.	Work for work's sake	Unity in variety	Kindness	Chastity
6.	Happiness	Universal humanity	Charity	Respecting parents
7.	Self-restraint	Affection	Self sacrifice	Do your duty sincerely
8.	Cause and effect	Friendship	Renunciation	
9.	Equanimity	Speak truth		
S. No.	*Chapter V*	*Chapter VI*	*Chapter VII*	*Chapter VIII*
1.	Unity in thought, word and deed	Cause and effect	Perfect equilibrium	Liberation
2.	Helping others	Doing duty with care	Dynamism	Follow ethics
3.	Non-Attachment	Struggle to become perfect	Self-lessness	Be good and do good
4.	Believe in Infinity	Sacrifice	Work incessantly	Work, do not expect fruit
5.	Sympathy	Equanimity	Spirituality	Serve for the humanity
6.	Courageous	Head in the forest and hand in society	Cause and effect	Equality
7.	Self confidence	Yoga	Self-confidence	Self-less
8.		Perfection		

Chapter I: Karma yoga and its effect.

Chapter II: Each is great in its own place.

Chapter III: Secret of work.
Chapter IV: What is duty.
Chapter V: We help ourselves, not the world.
Chapter VI: Non-attachment is self-abnegation.
Chapter VII: Freedom Chapter VIII: Ideal of karma yoga.

Table II: Strategies Advocated to Practice

Sl. No.	*Human values listed*	*Strategies advocated by swami Vivekananda*
1.	Character	It can be developed by practicing Yama and Niyama
2.	Truth	This can be adhered by having role models like parents, teachers and elders
3.	Humanity	Citation of moral stories, incidents and biographies of great personality
4.	Renunciation	Pictures and sayings of noble saints from all religions to be depicted
5.	Kindness	Learning through parables
6.	Self sacrifice	By giving inspiring talks
7.	Respecting others	By observation and through dramatic shows
8.	Duty	By group activities and austerity
9.	Unity in thought, word and deed	By telling stories
10.	Spirituality	By observing severe austerity
11.	Self-confidence	By motivational talks and developing positive attitude
12.	Adjustment	By group work
13.	Work is worship	By direct and indirect method
14.	Cause and effect	Atmosphere of the school and society
15.	Liberation	By practicing yogic disciplines
16.	Helping others	By daily activity
17.	Equanimity	Training in acquirement of balanced mind
18.	Unity in diversity	By day to day activity

Table III: Relevance of Human Values

Sl. No.	*Relevant human values identified to the present day context*
1.	Character
2.	Duty
3.	Work is worship
4.	Helping others
5.	Kindness
6.	Morality
7.	Love
8.	Truth
9.	Self-confidence
10.	Respecting parents

The above values have great relevance for the present day context. These exhibit the order of life. Quality of life can be enhanced by adhering to these values. An individual can be identified as good or bad based on the values they practice. In the present scenario, it is very necessary to balance the society. The modern technology equipped world should keep abreast of controlling the body, mind and spirit of an individual.

Role of school in fostering human values

The school plays vital role in developing students with human values. The major part of students time is being spent in school, therefore school develop the attitude in children. The following programmes can be adopted to foster human values in students:

- Establishing different subjects club, so that students work together to perform various activities.
- Establishing students union to represent their activity.
- Conducting various co-curricular activities to develop their value system.
- Extracurricular activities will be conducted to develop their potential and various values in students.
- Giving exposure to various kinds of activities like debate and discussion. on value to understand the significance to practice in daily life.
- Present suitable examples of ideal persons before students.
- Giving inspiring talks about the importance of human values.

Outcome of the study

- The eight chapters on karma yoga have been analysed.
- The human values have been identified in each chapter. Five to ten values have been identified in these chapters and listed in the Table I.
- The values like character, love, truth, non-attachment, kindness, duty, self-confidence etc., have been listed.
- Table II depicts the strategies adopted to practice the values in daily life. The strategies like practicing yama and niyama, by depicting pictures and sayings of noble personality, by observing severe austerity and yogic disciplines, learning through stories, parables, biographies, by giving inspiring talks and by daily practice have been listed.
- In Table III, the human values which are relevant to practice in the present day context have been listed. The significance of these values in day to day life has been highlighted.

Conclusion

Swami Vivekananda emphasised the reality of karma yoga in a simpler sense to make our life meaningful and purposeful. It is said that even God cannot give anything, but we attain anything through hard work. Try, try and try until you succeed. How much ever you work, you deserve the fruit accordingly. Hard work gives you pleasure and sense of satisfaction. It is said that duty with love is desirable. That is we have, "Duty is God and work is worship".

References

- Avinashlingam, T.S (2010), "Education-Swami Vivekananda" Sri Ramakrishna Printing Press Limited, Mylapore, Chennai.
- Swami Swananda (1989), "Complete works of swami Vivekananda Vol. 1" Swapna Printing Works Private Limited, Calcutta.
- Swami Budhananda (2008), "How to Build Character", Advaita Ashrama, Kolkata.
- Didyendu Bhattacharyya, Pranab Barman (2012), "Vivekananda's Thoughts on Man-making Through Moral Values and Character Development and its Present Relevancy in School Education" International journal of multidisciplinary educational research.

Conclusion

Swami Vivekananda emphasised the [illegible] work [illegible] our life [illegible] and [illegible] [illegible] work gives you pleasure and [illegible] [illegible] [illegible]

References

[illegible] (2010) [illegible] Vivekananda [illegible]

[illegible]

[illegible]

31

Effect of Pranayama on Selected Physiological Variables

G. Vinod Kumar and A. Siddhartha

Introduction

With increased awareness and interest in health and natural remedies, yogic techniques including pranayama are gaining importance and becoming increasingly acceptable to the scientific community. Pranayama literally means control of prana. Prana, in Indian philosophy, refers to all forms of energy in the universe. Life force is one part of this (Urban J.A, 2005). Life force in an individual is symbolised by breathing. That is why pranayama is generally considered to mean regulated breathing. A yogi, through pranayama, can, at some stages, control other functions of his body and finally control manifestations of prana even outside his body (Bijlani, 2004). As a technique, pranayama can assume rather complex forms of breathing, but the essence of practice is slow and deep breathing. Such breathing is economical because it reduces dead space ventilation. It also refreshes air throughout lungs, in contrast with shallow breathing that refreshes air only at the base of the lungs (Bijlani, 2004). Slow and deep breathing itself has a calming effect on the mind and helps an individual to de-stress (Sandeep et al., 2002). This study investigated the immediate effect of a type of slow pranayama called as surianabhedana, chandrabhedana and anulom vilom on heart rate, blood pressure and mathematical problem solving ability in young healthy subjects.

Materials and Methods

This study was carried out in Dr. Sivanthi, Aditanar College of Education, Tiruchendur, and Tamilnadu. Thirty healthy volunteers were recruited and separated into experimental and control groups. They were aged between 21-23 years. All were doing B.Ed first year. They were highly motivated to participate and allowed to quit any time during the study. In the experimental group, 15 subjects (10 males and 5 females) were found to be highly motivated in the treatment as well could perform the exercise as instructed. The control group, 15 subjects (10 males and 5 females) were found to be untreated group. Their average body mass index was 21.59 ± 2.83. The control group subject's that matched for age, sex, and body mass index to the experimental group. The physiological variables selected for this study included heart rate, systolic and diastolic blood pressure, simple problem solving ability to explain the cardiopulmonary function and mental efficiency. The physiological variables tested and assisted by lab technicians from P.G. Hospital, Tiruchendur.

Experimental Protocol

The trainer involved in this study explained 30 students on the purpose the procedure to be followed, and willingness of the subjects to participate. And the trainer demonstrated the mode of surianabhedana, chandrabhedana and anulom vilom pranayama. Among 30 students, only 15 subjects met the treatment criterion. Another 15 subjects matched for sex, age, and body mass index of subjects in the experimental group were selected as control group. Each subject was treated separately and twice at the same time (4.00-5.00 pm) for seven working days. In the control group, recording was done before starting to relax breathing with closed eyes and immediately after (within 5 minutes) 20 minutes of exhaling. In the experimental group, pre-test recording was done before performing in any sugasana posture (within 5 minutes) after 10 minutes quiet breathing, and the post-test was recorded followed by 'surianabhedana, chandrabhedana and anulom vilom pranayama' training for 20 minutes (within 5 minutes).

Test Administration

Heart rate was measured by counting radial pulse for a minute. Three readings were taken and their average was recorded. Systolic and diastolic blood pressures were measured with the auscultatory method by using sphygmomanometer and stethoscope. Three readings were taken and their average was recorded. The mathematical simple problem solving ability was estimated as follows: A simple arithmetical problem of three-digit numbers involving addition, subtraction, multiplication, and division was given. Two sets of questions comprise 10 problems each. Each was prepared and students were asked to pick up any set by 'draw'. The time taken to solve the questions was noted down.

Statistical Analyses

All the values obtained before and after performing 'surianabhedana, chandrabhedana and anulom vilom Pranayama', rest and quiet breathing were expressed as mean ± SD. The student paired t' test was used to compare variables within groups. P value of less than 0.05 indicates a significant difference.

Results

There were 10 males and 5 females in either groups. The average body mass index of the control group was 21.43 ± 2.49 and that of the experimental group was 21.75 ± 2.77. The baseline heart rate, blood pressure and times taken to solve the arithmetic problems were comparable between experimental and control groups. Among the physiological variables the experimental group, a significant decline in heart rate (P< 0.0001) and systolic blood pressure (P<0.001) was observed (Table 1). In control group displayed no significant change in heart rate, systolic blood pressure and diastolic blood pressure following 20 minutes rest and quiet breathing (Table 2). Although, experimental and control subjects could solve problems correctly, the time taken to solve decreased significantly only after practice of surianabhedana, chandrabhedana and anulom vilom pranayama (P<0.0001, Table 1). Twenty minutes rest and quiet breathing had no significant effect on the time taken to solve the problems (Table 2).

Table 1. Immediate Effect of Surianabhedana, Chandrabhedana and Anulom Vilom Pranayama on Physiological Variables and Arithmetic Problems Solving in Experimental Group

	Experimental Group				
Physical Variables	*Pre test Mean SD*	*Post Test Mean SD*	*Mean Difference*	*t-Value*	*P Value*
Basal heart rate (beats/minute)	85.9 ± 4.6	74.6 ± 4.1	11.3 ± 4.0	8.92*	<0.0001
Systolic blood pressure (mmHg)	120.9 ± 5.8	116.6 ± 4.6	4.3 ± 2.2	6.14*	<0.001
Diastolic blood pressure (mmHg)	79.0 ± 2.3	78.2 ± 2.1	0.8 ± 1.4	1.81	NS
Arithmetic Problems Solving (second)	90.8 ± 24.9	69.5 ± 21.8	21.3 ± 10.0	6.72*	<0.0001

*Significant at 0.05 level of confidence with df 2, 28 table value is 2.048.

NS - No Significant difference.

Table 2. Pre-Test and Post-Test Mean and Standard Deviation on Physiological Variables and Arithmetic Problems Solving in Control Group

	Control Group				
Physical Variables	*Pre test Mean SD*	*Post Test* Mean SD*	*Mean Difference*	*t-Value*	*P-Value*
Basal heart rate (beats/minute)	84.8 ± 4.4	83.9 ± 4.3	0.9 ± 1.8	1.58	NS
Systolic blood pressure (mmHg)	121.7 ± 4.3	120.6 ± 3.4	1.1 ± 1.9	1.82	NS

Diastolic blood pressure (mmHg)	79.2 ± 2.7	79.1 ± 2.6	0.4 ± 2.1	0.61	NS
Arithmetic Problems Solving (second)	90 ± 21.9	89.0 ± 21.9	1.0 ± 1.6	1. 94	NS

*Post Test means After 20 Minutes Quit Breathing.

Significant at 0.05 level of confidence with df 2, 28 table value is 2.048.

NS - No Significant difference.

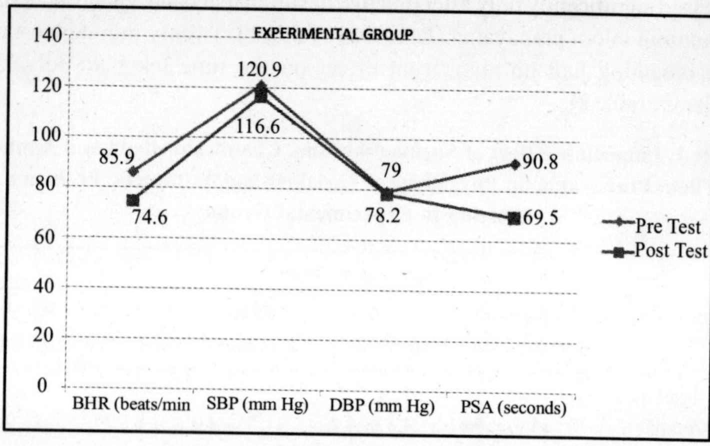

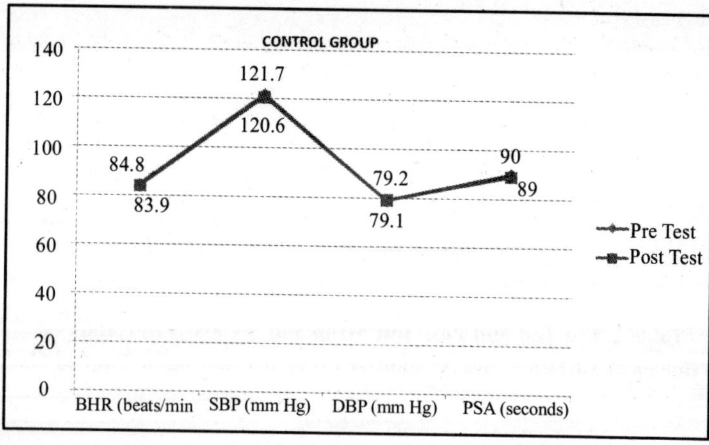

Conclusions

1. This study investigated the immediate effect of surianabhedana, chandrabhedana and anulom vilom pranayama on some selected physiological variables indicative of cardio-respiratory function and mental efficiency.

2. A practitioner of pranayama not only tries to breathe, but at the same time, also tries to keep his/her attention on the act of breathing, leading to concentration. This stress free state of mind evokes relaxed responses (Bijlani, 2004). In this relaxed state, parasympathetic nerve activity overrides sympathetic nerve activity (Udupa et al., 2003). Therefore, the significant decline in basal heart rate and systolic blood pressure in the pranayama practice could be largely due to better parasympathetic control over the heart.
3. Diastolic blood pressure mainly varies with the degree of peripheral resistance (Guyton, 1996) and heart rate. The non-significant change in diastolic blood pressure observed in the present study suggests that 'surianabhedana, chandrabhedana and anulom vilom Pranayama' might have no any immediate effect on peripheral vascular resistance or it has some roles, but is obscured by a slow heart rate.
4. In the present study, the students following pranayama took significantly less time in solving problems compared to that for solving problems prior to training ($P<0.0001$). In the present study, while performing breathing practice, subjects were also emphasised to concentrate on the act of breathing. This act of breathing removes his attention from worldly worries and de-stress. This stres-free individual adapts better to the daily emotional, physical, and mental stresses. Therefore, the significantly less time taken to solve mathematical problems could be due to better adaptability for mental stress induced by breathing act for 20 minutes.
5. The positive results found in the present study might apply to work places to improve work efficiency and to educational institutes to improve learning ability. A few minutes practice daily may help in setting the mind better on works and studies.

References

1. Bijlani R.L. The Yogic Practices: Asanas, Pranayamas and Kriyas. In: Bijlani R.L. (ed). Understanding Medical Physiology, 3rd edition. New Delhi-India: Jaypee Brothers Medical Publishers (P), pp. 883-889, 2004.
2. Udupa K., Madanmohan, Ananda B.B., Vijayalakshmi P., and Krishnamoorthy N. *Effect of pranayama training on cardiac function in normal young volunteers.* Indian J. Physiol Pharmacol 47:27-33, 2003.
3. Guyton A.C. *Textbook of Medical Physiology*, 9th edition. Philadelphia: W.B. Saunders, pp. 161-169, 1996.
4. Sandeep B., Pandey U.S., and Verma N.S. *Improvement in oxidative status with yogic breathing in young healthy males.* Indian J. Physiol Pharmacol 46:349-354, 2002.

32

Effect of Aerobic Training and Aeroyoga

D. Gokulakrishnan and G. Gnanagandarvan

Introduction

Today's life mostly depends more on science and technology. Sportsmen are being exposed to the exercises and training methods, beneficial for achieving high standards. The modern trends in sports and games reflect advanced technological developments and scientific methods of training.

The term yoga stands for unity or joining of two aspects, which are self and God, or in other words construed to mean about mind and body. It is a misnomer to label yoga as merely a science of physical exercise yoga not only trains and controls the body, it also trains healthy mind which resides in healthy body as an old adage. Asana: Asana means a steady comfortable posture. Various yogic asanas are the most popular aspect of yoga.

Aerobic exercise (also known as cardio) is physical exercise of relatively low intensity that depends primarily on the aerobic energy-generating process. Aerobic literally means "living in air", and refers to the use of oxygen to adequately meet energy demands during exercise via aerobic metabolism. Generally, light-to-moderate intensity activities that are sufficiently supported by aerobic metabolism can be performed for extended periods of time.

The word aerobic literally means with oxygen. This is a reference to the fact that aerobic activities require the use of oxygen to perform. Aerobic training is exercise that requires the heart and lungs to work harder to meet the increased demand of the body's oxygen needs. Examples include running, cycling and swimming. The aero yoga—a complete new fitness regime was developed and implemented on controlled and experimental group in comparison with yogasana and aerobic battery for relevance. The aero yoga aims primarily on the self-realisation, fighting negative effects of stress and modern lifestyle such as the sedentary lifestyle that is very degenerative for body and mind (premature aging). Moreover the aero yoga swing is adaptable for possible use by health professionals in rehabilitation and physical therapy through special foam embeddable, and for artists and Air Dancers by special ropes who need longer ropes, for more precise movements. Aero Yoga is the only aerial system that includes in design and protocol—training professionals from medicine and physiotherapy to contemporary dance and fine art.

Methodology

To achieve the purpose of the study, One hundred and five female subjects were selected at random and their ages ranged from 17 to 25 years. The subjects were divided into three equal groups. The study was formulated as a true random group design, consisting of a pre-test and post-test. The subjects (n=105) were randomly assigned three equal groups of thirty five subjects each. Group I was treated with yogasanas; the Group II was with the regime of aerobics and the Group III with aero yoga for fitness for a period of six weeks. Cardio vascular efficiency was selected as a criterion variable. The Harvard Step test was selected as a criterion measure. All the subjects were tested immediately prior and after the experimental programme. Analysis of co variance (ANCOVA) was applied to analyse the significant difference. The .05 level of confidence was fixed as the level of significance to test the F ratio obtained by the analysis of covariance, which was considered as an appropriate.

Data Analysis and the Result

Analysis of Variance on Pre-Test, Post-Test and Analysis of Covariance on Adjusted Post-Test Means of Yogasana Training Group (YT), Aerobic Training and Aeroyoga Groups (AYG) on Cardiovascular Efficiency

Table 1. Cardiovascular Efficiency

Tests	*YT*	*AT*	*AYG*	*Source of Variance*	*Sum of Squares*	*Df*	*Mean Squares*	*F-ratio*
Pre-Test				B	88.77	2	44.50	2.01
Means in	47.30	46.03	45.60					
inches				W	2259.38	102	22.14	
Post-Test				B	115.48	2	57.50	2.52
Means	48.24	49.91	47.38					
in inches				W	2322.94	102	22.77	
Adjusted				B	115.01	2	57.51	3.79*
Post-Test	47.54	49.97	48.02					
Means in				W	1532.16	101	15.17	
inches								

An examination of the above Tables 1 indicated that the results of ANOVA for pre-test scores of the Yogasana training group, aerobic training group and aeroyoga group. The obtained F-ratio for the pre-test was 2.01. It was found to be lesser than the required 'F' ratio of 3.09.

In the post-test data analysis, the F-test was applied to test the significance of mean difference if any among the yogasana training group, aerobic training group and aeroyoga on cardiovascular efficiency. The obtained F-ratio for the post-test was 2.52. The F-ratio needed for significant differences on the mean, for degrees of freedom 2, 102 was 3.09 at 0.05 level of confidence. Since the observed F-ratio on this variable was found to be higher than the F-ratio needed for significance, it was inferred that the mean differences among the three groups on the cardiovascular efficiency used in the study at the end of the treatment period was statistically significant.

The F-ratio obtained from the testing the adjusted post-test means among the three groups namely yogasana training group, aerobic training group and aeroyoga on cardiovascular efficiency was 3.79.

The obtained F-ratio on cardiovascular efficiency among the three groups was statistically significant since they exceeded the needed F-ratio (3.09) for degree of freedom 2 and 101, at 0.05 level of confidence. From this it was concluded that the measurements of cardiovascular efficiency was significantly influenced by the treatments used in this study.

Table. 2

Scheffe's Test for the Differences between the Adjusted Means of Yogasana Training Group (YT), Aerobic Training and Aeroyoga Groups (AYG) on Cardiovascular Efficiency

	YTG	*ATG*	*AYG*	*MD*	*Obtained F value*	*Table F value*
Cardio	47.55	49.97	—	2.42	6.76	3.09
Vascular	47.55	—	48.02	0.47	0.26	3.09
Efficiency	—	49.97	48.02	1.95	4.38	3.09

Table 2 shows the mean differences between yogasana training group and aerobic training group, aerobic training and aeroyoga training group and yogasana training and aeroyoga training group were 2.42, 0.47 and 1.95 respectively on cardiovascular efficiency

The sheffe's post hoc test obtained F-ratio for the above comparisons were 6.76, 0.26, and 4.38 respectively the Table F-ratio was 3.09. Hence, the first and third comparisons were significant and third comparison was insignificant. The result of the study was supported by the findings of Sunitha Arora which stated as youth undergoing through aeroyoga, aerobics and yogasana. No significant difference was found in Ht and MHR, except that in subjective assessment.

Conclusion

1. Aerobic training was found to be more suitable for the development of cardiovascular efficiency.
2. Yogasana was found to be more suitable fitness for people irrespective of physical and mental condition.

3. Aeroyoga was found to produce maximum workout in minimum time frame when compared with other two fitness regime.

References

- Donald K. Mathews, *Measurement in Physical Education,* Philadelphia: W.B saunders Company, 1958.
- Harrison H. Clarke, *"Application of Measurement to Health and Physical Education"* (5th Edition) Englewood cliffs: N.J. Prentice Inc., 1976.
- Aladar Kogler, *Yoga for Every Athlete,* Mumbai: Jaico Publishing House, p. 2, 2003.
- Iyenger, B.K.S. *Lights on Yoga,* Unwin Paperbacks, 1974, pp. 21-24.
- Swami Satyananda Saraswathi, *Asana Pranayama,* Bihar: Mudra and Bandha Publications, 1961, p. 223.

33

Influence of Bhastrika Pranayama on Stress

D. Yogaraj

Introduction

Pranayama is the control of life-forces by realising naught but brahman in all things as the mind. The negation of the Universe is the outgoing breath. The thought 'I am Brahman' itself is called the incoming breath. The permanence of that thought thereafter is the restrained breath. This happened to be the Pranayama of the wise, while the pressing of nose is only for the unknowing. Bhastrika relieves inflammation of the throat, increases gastric fire, destroys phlegm, removes diseases of the nose and chest and eradicates asthma, consumption.

It gives good appetite, it breaks the three granthis or knots viz., Brahma Granthi, Vishnu Granthi and Rudra Granthi. It destroys phlegm which is the bolt or obstacle to the door at the mouth of Brahma Nadi (Sushumna). It enables one to know the Kundalini, removes diseases which arise from excess of wind, bile and phlegm. It gives warmth to the body.

Stress is a complex Psychological construct that encompasses the physiological and motor element of performance. Stress is a substantial imbalance between demand [Physical and/or Psychological] and response capability under conditions, where failure to meet that demand has important consequences (Mc Grath 1970). Stress may be produced by particular situation and anxiety-producing stimuli that do not have similar effect on everybody.

Methodology

The purpose of the study was to find out the influence of bhastrika pranayama on stress. To facilitate the study, thirty intercollegiate players were selected as subjects at random and their ages hung between 18 to 25 years. The subjects were divided into two equal groups. The study was formulated as a true random group design, consisting of a pre-test and post-test. The subjects (n=30) were randomly assigned to two equal groups of fifteen subjects each. The groups were assigned as experimental group and control group in an equivalent manner.

Experimental group participated for a period of six weeks and the post-tests were conducted. The training programme was scheduled from 6.30 to 7.30 am for three days in a week for experimental group. In this study, Everly and Girdano's stress questionnaire was used to find out the stress of the intercollegiate players.

In this study, pranayama was given to experimental group for the period of 6 weeks. The pre-tests were taken from the subjects before administrating training. The subjects were involved with respective training for a period of 6 weeks.

At the end of sixth weeks, post-tests were undertaken. The significant difference between the means of experimental group and control group for the pre-test and post-test scores were determined by paired *'t'* ratio. The level of significance was fixed at 0.05 level of confidence for the degree of freedom 14.

Results and Discussion

Table 1. Descriptive Analysis on Pre and Post Test Means of Experimental and Control Group on Stress

S.No	*Variables*	*Pre-Test Mean*	*Post-Test Mean*
1.	Stress	Exp: 41.53	Exp: 35.87
		Con: 40.53	Con: 40.20

Table 2. Computation of 't' Ratio Between the Pre Test and Post Test Means of Stress of Experimental and Control Groups

S. No	*Variables*	*Mean diff*	*SD*	*σDM*	*'t' ratio*
1.	Stress	Exp: 5.67	1.50	0.39	14.67*
		Con: 0.33	0.72	0.17	1.78

*Significant at 0.05 level.

An examination of Table 2 indicates that the obtained a 't' ratio was 14.67 for stress of experimental group. It was found to be greater than the required Table value of 2.14 at 0.05 level. And there is significance for the degrees of freedom14. So, it was found to be significant. It was observed that the obtained *'t'* ratio was 1.78 for stress of control group. It was found to be lesser than the required Table value of 2.14 at 0.05 levels. And there is significance for the degrees of freedom 14. So, it was found to be not significant.

The mean scores of stress of experimental and control groups were shown graphically in Fig. 1.

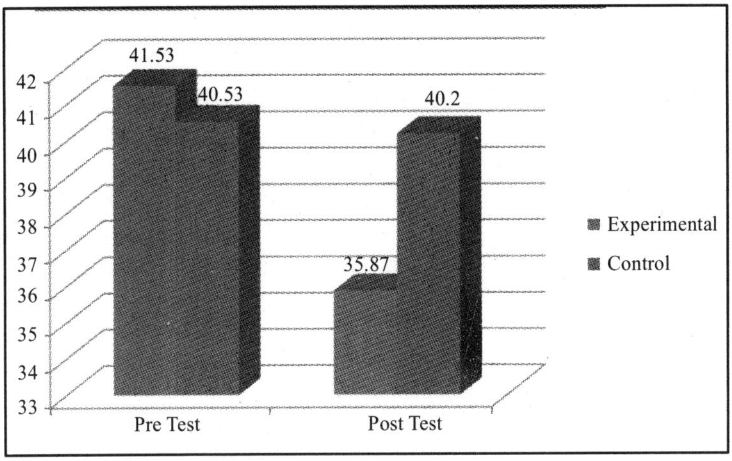

Fig. 1. Bar Diagram Showing the Pre Mean and Post Mean of Stress of Experimental and Control Group.

Conclusion

Within the limitation of the present study, the conclusions were drawn.

1. The stress of experimental group showed significant difference when compared to control group.
2. There was no significant difference in stress of control group.

References

- Ananda, (1982), *The Complete Book of Yoga Harmony of body mind*, Delhi, India: Orient Books Pvt. Ltd.
- Selvarajan Yesudian Elizabeth haich (1987), *Yoga and Health,* London 7th Edition Unwin Publishers. 93
- Sharma, P.D., 1984, *"Yogasana and pranayama for health,"* Bombay, India: Navneet Publications, pp. 10-11.
- Cooper, S., 2003, *Effect of two Breathing Exercises (Buteyko and Pranayama) in Asthma: A Randomised Controlled Trial.* Thorax 2003; 58: 674-679.
- Prakasamma. M., 2007, *A study of Yoga as a nursing intervention in the care of patients with pleural effusion.* Journal of Advanced Nursing .Vol. 9, pp. 127-133.

34

Effects of Yogasana on Motor Fitness

K. Rajendran

Introduction

Globally yoga benefits one and all. Yoga is system of attaining perfect mental and physical health. Yoga was first introduced in second century A.D by the father of yoga—Patanjali. Yoga is a method by which one can remove ignorance and attain union with the supreme self (B.K.S. Iyengar, 1983). Globally, nowadays every individual is conscious about his health and wants to look handsome like their role models heroes. Today, youth spend lot of time in the gymnasium to improve their muscles, to reduce fat and to maintain quality of life. In fact, we know yoga practices helps for improving cardio-vascular system and in reducing fat. Yoga knowledge is essential and very much important for individuals before starting any programme. With a sensible approach, one can be benefited without any side effects. If one goes astray, the wrong footsteps of yoga practices may lead to side effect on the human body. One should always remember to train under the guidance of professional coach which gives him very fast results in safe way.

Yoga was first introduced in second century A.D. by the father of yoga Patanjali. Yoga is a method by which one can remove ignorance and attain union with the supreme self (B.K.S. Iyengar, 1983). BMI is closely related to both percentage body fat and total body fat (Haslam and James 2005). Accumulation of fat deposits in the body tissues results in obesity. Obesity is a condition that arises, when ones body weight exceeds the normal range of BMI, i.e., 19.5 to 25. Flexibility is the ability of an individual to move the body and its parts through as wide a range of motion as possible without undue strain to the articulations and muscle attachments.

A high level of flexibility helps in saving energy during vigorous movement because of the full range of moment of the joint and muscles, the 50 individual may be less prone to injury. Flexibility is the range of motion around a joint, high flexibility helps in lowering the injuries in all stages of life (Uppal, 2004). It is a very important component of sports performance that can be significantly improved if approached correctly. Muscular endurance also plays an important role in the performance of individuals in various sports and games. It is an important fitness component and helps individuals in high performance. Muscular endurance is the ability of muscles to continue performing without fatigue (Hardayal Singh, 1991).

Statement of the Problem

The purpose of this study was to find out the effect of yogasana practices on motor fitness among males.

Methodology

Selection of subjects

The purpose of the study was to find out the effects of yogasana practices on motor fitness. The study, 30 male students in the faculty of arts and science, Annamalai University, Chidamdaram were selected as subjects at random.

Their age ranged between 18 to 24 year. Pre and post-tests were administered on the subjects for B.M.I. flexibility and muscular endurance. Electronic weighing machine was administered in testing body weight (kgs) of the participants and stadiometre in measuring the height, sit and reach test was conducted to find out the flexibility, sit-ups test for 30 seconds for muscular endurance. The yogasana practices were employed for 12 weeks, 6 days in a week, 50 minutes of training session. The subjects of the 30 males were tested on from pre to post test.

Data Analysis

The statistical tools of mean, standard deviation and *'t'*-test were used for the analysis of the data by using statistica software.

Results

Table 1. Body Mass Index (B.M.I.)

S. No	*Body Mass Index*	*No. of Subjects*	*Mean*	*SD*	*t-Value*
1.	Pre-test	30	25.33	5.50	12.9137
2.	Post-test	30	24.06	5.31	

P-value = 0.00,'t'-test for dependent samples marked difference are significant at $p<0.05$.

Table 1 shows that the mean, S.D and t-test of the body mass index of the participants improved from pre to post test. Mean and S.D of the subjects hung on at (25.33, 5.50) and (24.06, 5.31) respectively. The data clearly shows the effect of yogasana practices had profound effect on B.M.I. of subjects, which is significant at ($p<0.05$) and bar diagram shows clear understanding on B.M.I.

Table 2. Flexibility (Sit and reach test)

Sl. No.	*Flexibility (Sit and reach test)*	*No. of Subjects*	*Mean*	*SD*	*t-Value*
1.	Pre-test	30	18.80	7.86	8.22246
2.	Post-test	30	21.90	8.66	

P-value=0.00, 't'-test for dependent samples marked difference are significant at $p<0.05$.

Table 2 shows that the mean, S.D and *t*-test of the body mass index of the participants improved from pre to post test. Mean and S.D of the subjects were (18.80, 7.86) and (21.90, 8.66) respectively. The data clearly shows the effect of yogasana practices had profound effect on flexibility of subjects, which is significant at ($p<0.05$) and bar diagram shows clear understanding on flexibility.

Table 3. Muscular Endurance (Sit-Ups 30 Seconds)

Sl. No.	*Muscular Endurance*	*No. of Subjects*	*Mean*	*SD*	*t-Value*
1.	Pre-test	30	18.50	4.67	7.53367
2.	Post-test	30	23.60	3.74	

P-value=0.00,'t'-test for dependent samples marked difference are significant at $p< 0.05$.

Table 3 shows that the mean, S.D and *t*-test of the body mass index of the participants had improved from pre to post test. Mean and S.D of the subjects were (18.50, 4.67) and (23.60, 3.74) respectively. The data clearly shows the effect of yogasana practices had profound effect on muscular endurance of subjects, which is significant at ($p<0.05$) and bar diagram shows clear understanding on muscular endurance.

Discussion on Finding(s)

From the results of the study, the above tables showed some significant difference in body mass index of participants. Regard to the flexibility (hip and trunk flexibility) of the male subjects, the data clearly speak greater performance from pre to post test. In case of flexibility for sportsmen performed well in various sports and games. Sports men need lot of strength, and muscular endurance, apart from flexibility, to compete in various sports and games.

Athletes need lot of power, strength, speed, muscular endurance apart from flexibility to partake in sports. Playing or training need lot of skills, flexibility, power, speed, and muscular endurance. There is a significant difference on body composition (body mass index) of subjects. The effect of yogasana practices had show improvement from B.M.I, flexibility and muscular endurance, Pre to post-test, which is equally significant. This study is being supported by Holguin (2009) and Backer (1986).

References

- Hayward, Vivian H., *Designs for Fitness: A Guide to Physical Fitness Appraisal and Exercise Prescription,* New York: Macmillan Publishing Company, 1989.
- Holguin F., Fitzpatrick A.M., *Effect of Yoga on Fitness*, Journal of sports 3:1, 15-17, 2009.
- Jackson and Backer, *"The relationship of the sit and reach test to criterion measures of hamstring and back flexibility in young females".* Research quarterly, 57-59, 1986.
- Morehouse, Lawrence E., *Yoga and Health,* New York: McGraw Hill Book Co., 1982.
- Madanmohan, Thombre, D.P., Balakumar, B., Nambinarayanan, T.K., Thakur, S., Krishnamurthy, N. and Chandrabose, A., *"Effect of yoga training on reaction time, respiratory endurance and muscle strength",* Indian Journal of Physiology and Pharmacology, 336, pp. 228-233, 2002.
- P.K., Pradhan, *"Yogic practices for health and sports performance".* Indian Journal of Yoga, Exercise and sports science and physical education, pp. 27-29, Vol. 11, No. 1, 2000.

—

35

Yoga for Women

B. Soundiram and R. Elangovan

Introduction

Woman is the mighty work of God. She is the mysterious mixture of softness, gentleness and gracefulness. She is the compound of service, patience and love. She is an emblem of beauty. She is full of sweetness. She comforts and cheers up husband, children and guests without her. Man is helpless. This world loses all charm without her. There is no creation without her. She creates and sustains a home. Women pray for every child before being born. The child must be prayed for. Such children will glorify the name of the country by noble actions. Only she, who throughout her life continues to gradually build up her own character, can truly build the character of her child. Swami Vivekananda says, "Sita is the ideal of a woman in India and worshipped as God incarnate".

A woman has to undergo different stages of life: childhood, adolescence, motherhood, middle age, and old age. In these stages, physiological changes occur. In each stage, she has to face problems and internal conflicts. This affects her physically, physiologically and mentally. During these periods of change, she loses much of her incoming energy in terms with life. Yogic philosophy and practices in these stages can fill a woman with the divine virtues: energy, virility, power, brightness, courage and fortitude. It is only in the homes of educated and pious mothers that great men are being born. Culture, knowledge, power and devotion will follow in the whole world. Man-made world is crumbling beneath the burden of its own weight. Yoga can make a woman true and authentic. Many will be empowered to rebuild the shattered world in their shakti, the strength of their intuitions, their purity and faith in prayers, their simplicity, sympathy and service, their spiritual aspiration and silent sacrifice. Yoginis, women who have learnt the art of right living, can make their countries and the whole world happy, harmonious and peaceful.

Yoga

Yoga is to live in and to commune with God. Life in God brings eternal bliss. Yoga unites the woman with God and makes her immortal. Yoga is complete life, a method of development on all sides of the human personality. It is a system of integral education of body, mind, intellect and inner spirit. Yoga shows the marvelous method of rising from badness to goodness, and from goodness to godliness, on to eternal divine splendor. Yoga is the art of right living. It is an exact science—a perfect, practical system of self-culture.

A Way of Life

Yoga demands spiritualisation of life. Primarily, it is a way of life. It is an efficient performance of action in the right spirit. It is a process of moulding our attitude to home and society with new understanding.

Yoga is Universal

Yoga is for all. Yoga is purely spiritual and universal. It is way to God. It is an aid to the basic spiritual truths in all religions. To be a Yogini means to live at peace with all. Yoga is union with all.

Yoga is not Physical Exercise

Yogasanas, Pranayamas, Bandhas, Mudras and Kriyas are considered to be aids in Yoga practice. These aids have nothing to do with real Yoga. True yoga needs intense personal discipline coupled with intense thinking under the guidance of an able teacher. Yoga, promises super-physical and spiritual blessing. It becomes unattractive to common man, who clamours for immediate fruits and worldly prosperity.

Prerequisites for Yogic Life

One, who has moral purity, spiritual aspiration, calm mind, faith in the words of Guru and Shastras, moderation in eating and sleeping, and intense longing for deliverance from the sansara-chakra, is a qualified person for the practice of yoga.

An aspirant in the path of Yoga should have faith, energy, cheerfulness, courage, patience, perseverance, sincerity, purity, lack of despondency of mind, dispassion, aspiration, concentration, serenity, self-restraint, truthfulness, non-violence, non-covetousness, etc.

An austere and simple life is indispensable for Yoga. Self-control is its foundation. Discipline of the body and mind is its essence. Steadiness of mind is essential for a reversal of the normal outgoing activity of the mind. The course of the mind can be changed to the opposite direction by making the mind steady and bringing it under complete control.

Spiritual Paths for God-realisation

Karma Yoga (Yoga of Action): Karma Yoga teaches us perform actions without any desire for fruits. In this sadhana, a yogini considers her duty as divine action, performs it with whole hearted dedication, but shuns away from all desires.

Bhakti Yoga (Yoga of Devotion): Bhakti Yoga is a system of intense devotion with emphasis on complete surrender to divine will. The true follower of Bhakti Yoga is free from egoism, humble and unaffected by the dualities of the world.

Jnana Yoga (Yoga of Knowledge and Wisdom): Jnana Yoga teaches us to discriminate between the self and non-self and to acquire the knowledge of one's spiritual entity through the study of scriptures, company of saints and practice of meditation.

Raja Yoga (Yoga of awakening the psychic awareness and faculties through meditation): Raja Yoga, popularly known as Ashtanga Yoga is for all-round development of human personality. These are Yama, Niyama, Asana, Pranayama, Pratyahara, Dharana, Dhyana and Samadhi. The hatha yogic path is primarily concerned with the bodily purification practices which tranquilise the mind and discipline the body, i.e., the balance of idea and pingala nadis. This path is a prerequisite for Raja Yoga. The Table given below gives a list of hatha yogic practices.

Only those practices marked with * can be practiced during pregnancy.

Sl. No.	*Yogic Practices*	*No. of Rounds*	*Time in Minutes*	*Remarks*
1.	Observe silence, chant OM and Pray *		3	
2.	Loosening the joints *		5	
3.	Spin-ups		2	
4.	Arm Circling *		1/2	
5.	Talasana *	3	1/2	
6.	Utkatasana	3	1/2	
7.	Sun Salutation	2	4	
8.	Moon Salutation	1	2	
9.	Parivrtha/ Uthitha Trikonasa	2	2	
10.	Kati Chakrasana		1/2	
11.	Druta Halasana	6	2	
12.	Jathara Parivarthanasana		1 1/2	
13.	Paripoorna Navasana	3	1	
14.	Dwi Padha Pitham	3	1	
15.	Pawana Mukthasana	3	1	
16.	Supta Udhara Akarshanasana	3	1	
17.	Sarvangasana	1	3	
18.	Bhujangasana	3	1/2	
19.	Dhanurasana	2	1/2	
20.	Paschimottanasana	2	1/2	
21.	Ardha Mathsyendrasana	1	1	
22.	Baddha Konasana *	2	1	
23.	Yoga Nidra in Shavasana / lying on left *	1	10	

24.	Kapalabhati 20 strokes + 3 normal breaths	3	2
25.	Nadi Shodhana*/Ujjayi/Bhramari *	10	5
26.	Uddiyana Bandha	3	2
27.	Meditation*	1	20
	Total		**73**

Yoga Applied

A woman in the family will have emotional stability with her practice of Bhakti Yoga. She will have all virtues of Yama and Niyama. She will ask God for a good child, who will be well established in Yama and Niyama, and who will enjoy a long life. She will do all her duties keeping God in her mind, thinking that everything is done through her, by the Almighty. That is her practice of Karma Yoga. As a Yogini, she knows that the whole world is a family. She is Atma, a spark of the Supreme Self. Supreme Self is in all. And all are in the Supreme Self. She will be cheerful, charming and respectful. Until she conceives, she will be regularly practising Loosening Yogic Practices for all joints, Warm Up, Sun and Moon Salutations, Asanas, Pranayama, Mudras, Bandhas, Pranayama, Yoga Nidra in Shavasana and meditation. She will eat satvik food half stomach. She will eat after she gets hungry. She will rest and relax. She will take care of her five sheaths. Throughout her pregnancy, she will enjoy mental serenity.

This will give her the power to give birth to a child in a natural way. Yogic postnatal practice will help her to recuperate. She will be the Guru till the new born child completes seven years. Her life is the Gita, Bible or Koran for the child. This mother, the first Guru and teacher of the child, is thousand times more venerable than the father, according to Manu Shastra. The mother will introduce Surya Namaskar, Chandra Namaskar, Nadi Shodhana pranayama, and Gayatri Mantra from the age of eight. Thus the integral development of the girl is assured from the young age. These practices delay degeneration of the pineal gland and enable the gland, in an adolescent, to hold pituitary hormones responsible for sexual maturity. The adolescent finds a balance between her mental and physical energy.

Average age of menarche is approximately 12 years. Women will continue to menstruate until the age of 45 to 55 years. A woman will approximately have 500 periods in her lifetime. She looses around 40,000 ml of her blood throughout her active life reproductively. By regular practice of yoga, a woman can avoid menstrual disorder, cryptomenorrhoea, oligomenorrhoea, hypomenorrhoea, dysmenorrhoea, pain, metrorragia, aetiology, menorragia, dysfunctional uterine bleeding, premenstrual syndrome, premenstrual dysphoric disorder and menopause.

Conclusion

Yoga is the best way in for women health and wealth, bliss and poise, harmony and efficiency. May all women be in their well-being. Om Shanti Shanti Shanti.

References

- Gharote, (1982). *Guidelines for Yogic Practices,* Lonavala: Medha Publication, 1.
- Gore M.M., (1987). *"Effect of Yogic Training on Neuro Muscular Efficiently in Normal and Stressful Conditions",* Yoga Mimamsa, 26: 3, 4, (24, p. 13).
- www.centeredyoga.com/online
- www.oneyogalove.com/online
- www.yoga.info/www.asanga.org.za/online
- www.books.google.com/online

36

Yoga Education and its Benefits

Kotreshwaraswamy A. Surapuramath

Introduction

The word "yoga" means bringing together two things into a relation. There are many examples of union in yoga, like the union of body and mind, the union of yin and yang, the union of the individual's energy with the cosmic energy—and the union or relation of the teacher and student. Integrating yoga into elementary physical education classes offers more possibilities for a wider group of students than traditional sports and fitness classes (Finger 2000). Children need to experience joy, while participating in physical activity in order to build a foundation for lifelong skills. Since, it has triangular relationship of Body, Mind and Spirit, "Yoga is sophisticated system for achieving radiant physical health, superb mental clarity and therefore peace of mind" (Schiffmann, 1996). Most commonly yoga is regarded as a physical discipline, one that teaches strength, flexibility, and balance of body. A physical yoga practice consists of exercises called postures or asana that strengthen, stretch, and align the body (Finger, 2000). Each posture requires combining the mind, body, and breathing practices. According to Bersma and Visscher (2003), children are natural yogis. Taking moment to breathe, relax, or stretch will leave students calm, alert, and ready to learn. Therefore, yoga can be used as a warm-up or as the class itself. Short yoga exercises are also welcome break or pick-me-up in classroom setting. Yoga makes a difference for kids, when it comes in the class. Interestingly, yoga practice has been a gift even in military classes. Many soldiers are provided regular classes in military camps (Nelson, 2006). Adding yoga to a school's curriculum will help providing a quality physical education. Children love to role play. Moving from poses with music or in some game activity is a fun for tiny tots. Adult and old people get higher level of benefits as a physical exercise from yoga classes, emotional and mental. Today's life is full of stress and pressure for children and adults. Pressure in school, busy parents, competitive sports, and the demands of active participation are contributing to stress foetor. Teaching yoga to children can help them learn to relax, teach self-control, and instil a sense of peace in their daily lives.

Yoga in the Classroom

The system of educating children has to be different. It has to be combined with certain practices which can remove psychological blocks, make them aware of changes that happen in their body and brain, cognising about their own distraction and the ability to focus on the theme they study. The teachers teach pranayama to students. The students were told to breathe in and out in unison with the help of grandfather clock. When the pendulum swung to one side, everybody was supposed to breathe in and when the pendulum swung to the other side, everybody was supposed to breathe out. After a few moments, the breathing pattern had become regular and was coordinated with the swing of the pendulum. The teachers instruct when students were breathing out become silent when breathing in.

Now, you may wonder what this has to do with education. It is very important and relevant because psychologists believe to create psychological, emotional and rational blocks in our mind while we breath in. The energy of the body, brain and mind and withdrawn. When we breathe out, relaxation in the nervous system, the mind had the brain. If you provide information when the physical systems are relaxed, it is retained by the brain and not easily forgotten.

Importance of Yoga

1. Yoga and physical education contribute to not merely the physical development of the child but have a positive impact on psychosocial and mental development.
2. Playing group games have a positive impact on individual self-esteem, promotes better interaction among children, imparts values of co-operation, sharing and to deal with victory and defeat, alike.
3. Yoga practice contributes to the overall development of the child and various studies have shown it contributes to flexibility and muscular fitness and corrects any postural defects among school children.
4. There is a growing realisation that the health needs of adolescents, particularly their reproductive and sexual health needs, require to be addressed. Since these needs predominantly relate to sex and sexuality, which is culturally a very sensitive area, they are deprived of opportunities to get appropriate information.
5. There is a need to provide children accurate and authentic information and help them constructing knowledge and acquire life skills, so that they cope with the concerns related to the process of growing, counter stress and strains and the examination stress.

Benefits of Yoga

The word "yoga" means union. It's an ancient holistic tradition that unites body, mind, and spirit - bringing them into harmony and balance. Yoga is a science that has been practiced for thousands of years. It consists of Ancient

Theories, observations and principles about the mind and body connection, which is now being proven by modern medicine. Substantial research has been conducted to look at the Health Benefits of Yoga - from the Yoga Postures (Asanas), Yoga Breathing (Pranayama), and Meditation. Practicing yoga in a school setting teaches students physical awareness, mental awareness, emotional awareness, community awareness and how to use relaxation techniques to reduce stress. Yoga in the school is a convenient and practical outlet that could improve balance, strength, flexibility, kinesthetic sense, focus and attention.

1. Academic Performance

Yoga not only teaches children techniques to sharpen their focus by quieting the mind, but also creates a subtle motivation to learn.

2. Self-Esteem and Behaviour

Yoga fosters self-acceptance, which is increasingly significant as children approach the peer-pressures during teen years.

3. Yoga Improves Concentration

The meditative practices of yoga will improve the ability of college students to concentrate. Focusing on studying and ignoring distractions such as television, conversations, and loud music, of course will result in better grades. Meditation directly affects the structure and function of the brain - changing it in ways that seem to increase attention span, improve memory, and sharpen focus.

4. Yoga Enhances Mood

Yoga improves the mood and decreases the anxiety.

5. Yoga Strengthens the Body

Another recent yoga study of college-aged men and women (between 18 and 27 years of age) who participated in two yoga sessions every week for eight weeks saw a 19 per cent to 31 per cent increase in arm strength and 28 per cent increase in leg strength.

6. Yoga Relieves Stress

According to some experts, stress is the all trigger of ailments in peoples' physical, emotional, and endocrinal systems. Practicing yoga is splendid to reduce stress caused by academic pressures. Yoga helps college students avoid stress-induced eating, helping them sleep better. It can give students some sense of balance and mental clarity.

By practicing yoga, college students will improve their mood, strengthen their body, relieve stress, and concentrate better. This will help certainly making the most of their college experience!

7. Physical Benefits

Physical Fitness Yoga is calming. It is a wonderful stress reducer. It can be quite helpful for today's generation of over-scheduled, highly stressed children. Yoga promotes physical strength and muscular endurance, encouraging children to use their muscles. It helps to build balance, coordination, flexibility, and body awareness. Almost every position or asana incorporates the use of the core muscles. It ultimately promotes better posture. Yoga teaches a child how to feel them breathe which influences physically on improved posture, coordination, balance, strength, and flexibility.

8. Motor Planning

Yoga positions incorporate using the body in different ways and across all planes of movement. Repetition, an important key in building new motor skills, is being incorporated to help children master new movements. An important part of praxis or motor planning is coming up with novel ideas. Yoga encourages the ideation skills and imagination, as children assist in picking up different asanas and string together on different sequences.

9. Emotional Balance, Reducing Fears

Breathing techniques that children learn through yoga increase and channelise energy, when necessary, and decrease anxiety. Yoga can help to build a child's self esteem, as no positions or ideas can be "wrong". Unlike many physical activities, there is no winning or losing when practicing yoga. It is fun and playful!

10. Behavioural modification

Many of our children with special needs have difficulty in regulating their arousal level, which leads to hyperactive and perceived aggressive behaviours. Yoga incorporates teaching of breathing techniques and poses that require stillness. Yoga teaches the child to become more aware of how their mind and body are being connected and what it feels like to be still and calm.

Conclusion

Yoga offers new learning possibilities to a wider group of students than traditional sports or fitness curricula, making it some valuable addition to any educational programme. Additionally, adding yoga to a school's curricula will help provide the quality oriented physical education programme as some modification of traditional physical education. It can be taught as either a warm-up, or as the fun for entire class. It offers children and adults an opportunity to experience success in physical activity. However, curricula specialists, teachers, trainers and students should know and analyse seriously the real challenges of yoga education in classroom settings and real life as well.

References

- Amidon, E., and Roberts. E. (Eds.) (1996). *Life prayers from around the world,* Y: Harper Collins. Bersma.
- D. and Visscher, M. (2003).*Yoga games for children: Fun and fitness with postures, movements an breaths.* California: Hunter House. Dollan.
- M. (2007). *The Complete Yoga: The lineage of integral education.* International Forum of Teaching and Studies. Marietta: Spring 2007. Vol. 3. Iss 1. pp. 31-38.
- Ferry, J. (July, 2007). *How yoga is changing the classroom.* Independent. Retrieved.
- Finger, A. (2000). *Introduction to yoga: A beginner's guide to health, fitness and relaxation.* New York, NY: Three River Press.
- Gunner, R. (2005). Idol teachings. The Santa Fe New Mexican. Santa Fe N.M. National Association for Sport and Physical Education.

37

Yoga Education in B.Ed. Curriculum

S.D. Subadra

"The very essence of education is concentration of mind".—Swami Vivekananda

Introduction

Yoga is the science by which we stop chitta from assuming, or becoming transformed into several faculties. As the reflection of the moon on the sea is broken or blurred by the waves, so is the reflection of the Atman, the true self, broken by the mental waves. Only when the "mind stuff", the chitta is controlled to absolute calmness is the self to be recognised. Yoga teaches us to make matter our slave, as it ought to be yoga means "yoke", "to join" that is, to join the soul of man with the supreme soul or God. Through practice comes yoga through yoga comes knowledge, through knowledge love and through love bliss. Knowledge is the parent of intuition. Concentration of the mind is the source of knowledge. Knowledge exists eternally. The man who discovers a spiritual truth is what we call inspired and what he brings to the world is revelation. The great saints and teachers were those who had conjured this world of thought within themselves and so spake with power.

According to Swami Vivekananda, "the only true teacher is he who can convert himself as it were into a thousand persons at a moment's notice. The only true teacher is he who can immediately come down to the level of the student, and transfer his soul to the student's soul and see through his mind. Such teacher can really teach and none else. All these negative, breaking-down, destructive teachers that are in the world can never do any good". Teacher taught relationship in his words is to, "Find the (spiritual) teacher, serve him as a child, open your heart to his influence, see in him God manifested. He gives importance to the spirituality which is the prominent yogic concept." Regarding that he says, "I admire you for all that you know, but I dislike the way that you cover what is bad with roses and call it good. Intellectuality is not the highest good. Morality and spirituality are the things for which we strive".

For bringing up spirituality, the teachers must provide Yoga practice to the students. Such practice is possible only when the teachers are trained to practice Yoga in their teacher education course itself. For that teacher education curriculum must give Yoga Education to the prospective teachers. Education is a product of total experience gained by an individual throughout his life. Through education, the whole society can be reformed. Swamiji endorses education in different ways. He upholds, "You cannot teach a child anymore than you can grow a plant. All you can do is on the negative side. You can only help. It is a manifestation from within, it develops its own nature you can only take away obstructions. Education is not filling the mind with a lot of facts. Perfection the instrument and getting complete mastery of my own mind (is ideal of education). If I want to concentrate my mind upon a point, it goes there and the moment I call, it is free (again)". "The practice of meditation leads to concentration".

The saint seeks solution to the social and global evils through education. He wanted a man-making education (Dr. S. Arulsamy-2011) that's why he says, "What I want is muscles of iron and nerves of steel, inside which dwells a mind of the same material as that of which the thunder bolt is made". The function of the teacher is indeed an affair of the transference of something and not one of mere stimulation of the existing intellectual or other facilities in the taught. Something real and appreciable as an influence comes from the teacher and goes to the taught. Therefore, the teacher must be pure. The report of the education commission of 1966, while accepting that there are born teachers who win over the respect of student by the scholarship and dedication, held that the bulk of teachers did not fall into this category and needed some training and orientation to the teaching profession (Padma Satakopachari et.al., 2010)

We have one method of acquiring knowledge from the lowest man to the highest yogi, all have to use the same methods, and that method is what is called concentration (Swami Vivekanda). Such concentration can be gained by yoga.

Need of the Study

The present system of education is all wrong. The mind is crammed with facts before it knows how to think. Control of the mind should be taught first (Swami Vivekananda). The Yogic approach to education arising out of a basic will for progress and improvement of the personality. (Promila Sharma, 2011). One of the main aims of education is to develop one's own personality. On seeing the view of great thinkers' Swami Vivekananda, it is obvious that, concentration of mind through meditation is the best way to acquire knowledge. Meditation is the part of yoga. Today's prospective teachers are future teachers. It is in the hands of teachers to impart the habit of meditation, through yoga. Hence, yoga gains importance and it should be the part of teacher education curriculum. Then only it will be easy for the teachers to impart yoga among students. So teacher education curriculum was analysed in search of yogic education in its core courses and practicum component.

Statement of the Problem

"Yoga Education in Secondary Teacher Education Curriculum"

Limitation of the Study

Only core courses and the practicum components were analysed.

Objectives of the Study

1. To identify the Yoga concepts included in the teacher education curriculum.
2. To pinpoint the units in which Yoga concepts in the teacher education curriculum.

Methodology

This is a qualitative research. This fundamental research is done using the analytical research design. TNTEU B.Ed curriculum was analysed by the investigator.

Tools Used

Tamil Nadu Teacher Education curriculum was the tool used for the investigation.

Finding(s)

There is no concept which gives emphasis on Yoga education in Teacher Education curriculum. Even though there is no direct concept regarding Yoga education, the investigator found the following concepts which can be used by the teacher educator to impart Yogic education.

(i) Core paper-I- Education in the Emerging Indian Society.

- In Unit I on Philosophy and Education in India, the yoga education concept can be added.
- In Unit II on Eastern and Western thinkers on education, in the title Swami Vivekananda and his contribution in developing principles of education with the educational thoughts of Swamiji, his suggestion and ideas in Yoga education were emphasised and spelt out.
- In the title Swami Vivekananda and his contribution to education.

(ii) Core paper-II- Psychology of Learning and Human Development.

- In Unit-IX Mental Health and Hygiene, in the title-promotion of mental health of students and teachers, role of yoga in promoting mental health may be stressed.

- It was understood that the possibility of imparting yogic education lies while analysing the practicum component 17. Camp and 18. Physical education in the following activities:

Educational Implications

The paper reveals the absence of direct inclusion of Yoga education in Teacher Education curriculum.

It suggests the teacher educators to incorporate yoga education in theory and practicum, wherever it is possible.

This paper suggests the curriculum framing board to include Yoga education in the Teacher Education curriculum.

Conclusion

Every region and state has its typical cultural identity. There is a need to utilise the same as a basis for developing meaningful, relevant pedagogies. Birth place or yoga is our country. Certainly, it will be useful for our prosperity. Every one need to be grown by their own self. Nothing needs to be imparted for their development. Just removing the obstacle around them which are the barriers for growth should be done. It is possible by Yoga education. Imparting Yoga education for children makes them pure and spiritually sound. The dream of uniform pattern of education is possible. For that, all teachers must keep themselves ready to give yoga education for children, the prosperity of our country.

References

1. "Mayavati Memorial Edition". 1989. "The complete works of Swami Vivekananda" Advaitha Ashrama, Kolkata.
2. Promila Sharma. 2011. "The aims of education", APH Publishing Corporation, New Delhi.
3. Dr. S. Arulsamy et.al., 2011. "Philosophical and Sociological perspectives on education" Neelkamal Publication, New Delhi.
4. Majumdar R.C. 2004. "Swami Vivekananda – A historical review", Advaitha Ashrama, Kolkata-700014.
5. Padma Satakopachari et. al., 2010. "On education for Teacher Educators", Neelkamal Publication Pvt. Limited, New Delhi.
6. Dr. Kiran Walia – 2008. "My idea of education – Swami Vivekananda" Advaitha Ashrama, Kolkata-700014.
7. Mohammed Sharif Khan. 2010, "Teacher Education in India and aboard". APH Publishing Corporation, New Delhi.

PART–VII: SUBLIMATION OF WORK, LOVE AND SERVICE

38

Realising Youth Potential

V. Usha Sri

Introduction

The purpose of higher education is three-fold for freedom and democracy, for knowledge and innovation and for human kind and environment. The framework of sustainable development encompasses economic and social progress at the service of people, improving living conditions not simply in response to some demand but which is capable of transporting the demand depending upon the goals imposed by the desirable future. Today, we need Higher Education Institutions that will help enhance the capacity of their societies to live together in an interdependent world.

> *"The goal of mankind is knowledge ... Now this knowledge is inherent in man. No knowledge comes from outside: it is all inside. What we say a man 'knows', should, in strict psychological language, be what he 'discovers' or 'unveils'; what man 'learns' is really what he discovers by taking the cover off his own soul, which is a mine of infinite knowledge."* — *Swami Vivekananda.*

Today, higher education breech arrogance of knowledge in place of humility of wisdom, even the arrogance of knowledge is replaced by pride of information. Tolerance has been replaced by hatred—evident from the terror let loose frequently. Time is ripe to replace paternalism in education with partnership for mutual benefit and for the good society at large.

Curricular Issues

The UGC deliberates on the present perplexity in the youth pursuing higher education. The Indian society inhabits simultaneously three eras: traditional, modern and post-modern. Over the last fifty years, our society has become resurgent and our democracy more vibrant; and perhaps a little noisier too. Our economy on the whole is upbeat. Our IT experts have emerged as unique force to reckon across the world. What was earlier viewed as brain drain' has now been transformed as an export asset that gives the Indian Diaspora a forceful voice; besides, it boosts our forex reserves. Even though our education system has expanded, much of what is laudable in our multi-faceted progress is admittedly in spite of our educational system, as it exists today. Our education cannot claim much credit for our progress on various fronts.

Pluralistic Nature of the Indian Society

Our rich social collage should not only strengthen Unity in diversity, but also allow thousand flowers to bloom through socio-emotional unity underlying our social psyche. Revisiting and re-discovering the age old genius of our society in accepting and assimilating diverse cultures and sub-cultures and thereby developing composite culture can truly be our asset today provided Indian education choses to serve and to draw its sustenance.

We now need to harvest the fruits of knowledge generated by science and technology. Education should transform into social experience that enables learners to understand themselves, their social as well as physical environment, to develop skills of living together harmoniously and to make real their mutually shared vision of society—a vision that draws strength from its hoary past and that gives strength to realise their ultimate destiny. The gains of providing education as social experience need to be integrated in educational curricula.

The growing alienation of youth from our cultural heritage, secularism derived from multi-culturism and spiritualism necessitate that curricula in education should enable them discover the best in our culture and also in other cultures. Curricula in education should provide and promote critical insight into our cultural heritage. It helps developing the ability to separate the deadwood from the vital.

The Education Commission (1964-1966) emphasised this imbalance between our outer world and our inner world. The Delors Report (1996) 'Learning – The Treasure Within" reaffirms the view of Education Commission (1964-1966) when it visualises learning as harnessing 'the treasure within'. According to the Delors Report, learning constitutes 'the heartbeat of society' while 'learning to know' 'learning to do'. 'Learning to live together' and 'learning to be' constitutes four pillars of education; mutual understanding, peaceful interchange and harmony can be taken as the social aims of education.

Life Success

Youth life is the active development and fulfillment of processes. This period of youth provides suitable and favourable fields for working out extremely important and most indispensable process in life. This is the special significance, the great importance and supreme value of youth life. It signifies the creation of noble personality. It is Atma-Vikasa. It is Atma -Nirmana. Your success is not measured in terms of what you obtained but in terms of what you become, how you live and what actions you do. Upon this point reflect well and attain great happiness", says Swami Vivekananda.

Let your preparations be wise, correct and of such kind that will lead to your true welfare, supreme good and lasting satisfaction and happiness. This must engage your active, enthusiastic attention throughout the period of your youth life. Our culture refers to this stage as the Brahmacharya Ashram or Vidyarthi Jivan. Here, you acquire knowledge of not only subjects like History, Geography, Mathematics, etc., but also about human nature, correct Vyavahara, science of Self- control, art of developing pure mind, Dharma, the duties of man and the proper relationship between you, your family, your society and the world.

Vivekananda Kendra Manifesting of Swamiji's Message

"An aggregate or a congregation of men does not make a nation, nor do the geographical area and duration of time qualify a society to be known as a nation. A government formed on such basis can be called a state, but not a nation. It is common goal or mission that makes a nation. All the constituents strive collectively for something noble. Service with spiritual orientation results in man-making, which is invariably and inseparably connected with nation building." It is the core of all the thoughts behind Vivekananda Kendra. Vivekananda Kendra is centered on the noble thought service to man is worship of God — and is guided by the national ideals of Renunciation and Service. For actualising vision of Swami Vivekananda, the Kendra has more than 225 branch centers spread over India to work for all stratas (phases) of the society to rebuild the nation. To achieve this, Vivekananda Kendra carries out various service activities through Yoga, Swadhyaya Varga (Study Circle), Samskar Varga, Rural Development, Education, Development of Natural Resources, Organising Youth and Women and Publications based on the life and message of Swami Vivekananda, Indian Culture, Vedic studies. The Kendra urges all to join this task of national regeneration.

150th Birthday Celebration of Swamiji

To commemorate the 150th birth anniversary of Swami Vivekananda, Ramakrishna Mission has been organising a series of service programmes as prelude to the actual birth anniversary celebration. From 2010 itself, certain important service projects which were dear to the heart of Swami Vivekananda. Service to marginalised people (who include the poor, the backward and the tribal has formed the central focus.

"The more we come out and do good to others, the more our hearts will be purified, and God will be in them" — *Swami Vivekananda*

Application of Classroom Learning

Learning is enhanced through direct application in appropriate social contexts of principles and practices taught through formal instruction concurrent with guided reflection of the student's experiences. Service learning offers students immediate opportunities to apply classroom learning to support or enhance the work of local agencies that often exist to effect positive change in the community. The National Youth Leadership Council defines service learning as 'a philosophy, pedagogy, and model for community development that is used as an instructional strategy to meet learning goals and/or content standards'.

> *"Service learning is a method of instruction in which classroom learning is enriched and applied through service to others" (Florida Department of Education in the V.S.A). Key components*
>
> *— Swami Vivekananda*

The Seven Elements

- Integrated Learning
- High Quality Service
- Collaboration
- Student Voice
- Civic Responsibility
- Reflection
- Evaluation

Service Learning, A two-in-one

It can be distinguished as:

- *Curricular connections:* Integrating learning into a service project is the key to successful service learning. Academic ties should be clear and built upon existing disciplinary skills.
- *Student voice:* Being actively engaged in the project, students have the opportunity to select, design, implement, and evaluate their service activity, encouraging relevancy and sustained interest. In community settings, this is alternatively called youth voice.
- *Student's discussion:* Students discuss learning experience during in-class discussions.
- *Reflection:* Structured opportunities are created to think, talk, and write about the service experience. The balance of reflection and action allows student to be constantly aware of the impact of their work.
- *Community partnerships:* Partnerships with community agencies are used to identify genuine needs, provide mentorship, and contribute assets towards completing a project. In a successful partnership, both sides will give to and benefit from the project. For this partnership to be successful, clear guides must be implemented as to how often a student engages in service to a particular community agency.

- *Authentic community needs:* Local community members or service recipients are involved in determining the significance and depth of service activities involved.
- *Assessment:* Well-structured assessment instruments with constructive feedback through reflection provide valuable information regarding the positive 'reciprocal learning' and serving outcome for sustainability and replication.

Service-Learning Plans

The Florida Department of Education has published Standards for Service-Learning in Florida: A Guide for Creating and Sustaining Quality Practice.

1. Direct Mode

Person-to-person, face-to-face projects wherein service impacts individuals who receive direct help from students (tutoring, work with elderly, oral histories, peer mediation, etc.).

2. Indirect Mode

Projects with benefits to a community as opposed to specific individuals (i.e., environmental, construction, restoration, town histories, food and clothing drives).

3. Advocacy Mode

Working, acting, speaking, writing, teaching, presenting, informing, etc., on projects that encourage action or create awareness on issues of public interest (i.e., promoting reading, safety, care for the environment, local history, violence and drug prevention, disaster preparedness).

4. Research Mode

Surveys, studies, evaluations, experiments, data gathering, interviewing, etc., to find, compile, and report information on topics in the public interest (i.e., energy audits of homes or public buildings, water testing, flora and fauna studies, surveys).

Philosophical Bases

It includes Progressivism and Pragmatism. Combining these philosophies, Service-Learning becomes the practice or project combined with learning; or learning while performing. It also encourages students to use their talents, ideas, and gifts to serve, and while performing the service, to learn.

Channelising is Challenging

The Seven Tasks of College Student Development by Rita Landino are: developing competence, managing emotions, becoming autonomous, establishing identity, freeing interpersonal relationships clarifying purposes, and developing integrity or wholeness.

This process involves:

- First, one moves from valuing relation based on need (dependence) to valuing individual differences among people.
- Next, the person learns how to negotiate those differences in relationship.
- Finally, the young person begins to understand the need for interdependence and seeks mutual benefit from relations.

Harnessing the abundant energy and potential of youth is a challenge before the nation. In all earnestness, the youth of today are searching for leaders and capable leaders can be created from among them. The 150th Birth Anniversary of Swami Vivekananda gives us the right occasion to rise up and follow the path shown by him. Higher education with service orientation will make men and women truly humane.

References

- www.divyajivan.org
- Hegde, B.M. bmhegde.com/hedge/articles ssjmar.in/Vol. 1, No. 2 for website /Achana Bhatia.pdf
- Higher Education in India: Issues, concerns and New Direction" Recommendations of UGC Golden Jubilee Seminars 2003, the UGC New Delhi, 2003.
- http://miguelescotet.com/2012/what-is-the-purpose-of-higher-education-knowledge-or-utility.

PART–VIII: CHARACTER AND CULTIVATION OF MIND

39

Character Building and Development of Mind

R. Rajeswari

Swami Vivekananda is one of the famous philosopher as well as educationist in the history of Indian education. He points out the defect of the present education as it has no definite goal to pursue. A sculptor has some clear idea about what he ought to shape out of marble block; similarly, a painter knows what he is going to paint. A teacher, he says, has no clear idea about the goal of teaching. Swamiji attempts to establish, through words and deeds, the end of education is man-making. He prepares the scheme of this man-making education in the light of his philosophy of Vedanta. According to Vedanta, the essence of man lies in his soul, which he possess in addition to his body and mind. Swamiji defines education as 'the manifestation of the perfection already in man.'

In explaining the term 'manifestation' Swamiji quoted one of the yoga aphorisms of Patanjali — tatah kshetrikavat (therefore the obstructions) that is to say, just as a farmer breaks barriers to a course of water, which thereafter flows by its own force to irrigate his fields, so also a person's inherent power will spontaneously manifest when internal and external obstacles, if any, are removed at the appropriate time by teachers or education system.

Swamiji was against the contemporary educational system; it turned men into slaves, capable of slavery and nothing else. Self-development, fulfilment of swadharma, freedom of growth and character formation are the aims of education.

To quote "Education is not the amount of information that is put into your brains and runs riot there undigested, all your life. We must have life building, man-making, character making assimilation of ideas. If you have assimilated five ideas and made them your life and character, you have more education than any man who has got by heart a whole library. If education is identical with information, the libraries are the greatest sages in the world and the encyclopaedias are the rishis".

Education for him means that process by which character is formed, strength of mind is increased and the intellect is sharpened as a result one can stand on one's own feet. The ideal of this type of education would be to produce an integrated person — one who has learned how to improve his intellect, purify his emotions and stand firm on moral virtues and unselfishness.

Real education is that which prepares a man for struggle of existence. It prepares a man for social service and develops his character. Swamiji emphasised that an education which develops character and mental power and intelligence gives self-confidence and self-reliance among individuals.

According to Swami Vivekananda the following are the aims of education:

1. Reaching Perfection

The primary aim is to achieve fullness of perfection already present in child. All material and spiritual knowledge is already present in man covered by a curtain of ignorance.

Education should tear off that veil so that the knowledge shines forth as an illuminating torch to enliven all the corners by and by. This is meant by achieving fullness of the latent perfection.

2. Physical and Mental Development

The child of today, (after studying Gita), is ought to promote national growth and advancement as fearless and physically well developed citizen of tomorrow.

Swamiji, wished education should enable the child to be self-reliant rather than becoming a parasite on others.

3. Moral and Spiritual Development

A nation's greatness is not only measured by parliamentary institutions and activities, but also by the greatness of its citizens. The later is possible only through their moral and spiritual development.

4. Character Development

Swamiji emphasised the practice of Brahamcharya which fosters development of mental, moral and spiritual powers leading to purity of thoughts, words and deeds.

5. Shraddha and a Spirit of Renunciation

Individuals should keep confidence upon their powers. They should inculcate a spirit of self surrender, sacrifice and renunciation of material pleasures for the good of others. Education should foster these qualities in the individual. He gave this call to his countrymen. "Arise, awake and stop not till the goal is achieved."

6. Searching Unity in Diversity

The true aim of education is to develop insight into individuals so that they search out and realise unity in diversity. Swamiji has asserted that physical and spiritual worlds are unique; their distinctness is an illusion (Maya). Education should develop this sense which finds unity in diversity.

7. Religious Development

For Swamiji, religious development is an essential aim of education. Each individual should be search and develop religious seed embedded in a bid to find the absolute truth or reality.

Swamiji advocated the training of feelings and emotions so that the whole life is purified and sublimated. Then only, the capacities of obedience, social service and submission to the teachings and preaching of great saints and saviours will develop in the individual. Education should foster such development.

Swamiji reiterates that religion is the innermost core of education. To be religious for him means leading life in such a way that we manifest our higher nature, truth, goodness and beauty, in our thoughts, words and deeds. All impulses, thoughts and actions which lead one towards this goal are naturally ennobling and harmonising, and are ethical and moral in the truest sense. It is in this context that Swamiji's idea of religion, as the basis of education should be understood. We note, religion and education share the identity of purpose in his interpretation.

Why religion forms the very foundation of education becomes clear in his following words: "In building up character, in making for everything that is good and great, in bringing peace to others, and peace to one's own self, religion is the highest motive power, and, therefore, ought to be studied from that standpoint. Swamiji believes that if education with its religious core can invigorate man's faith in his divine nature and the infinite potentialities of the human soul, it is sure to help man become strong, yet tolerant and sympathetic. It will also help man to extend his love and good will beyond the communal, national and racial barriers".

Swamiji wanted overall development of education to heart and mind, to strengthen character and national consciousness, to help in the cultivation of strength and energy, nurture the brain and intellect and stir feelings of kindness and sympathy.

What is Character?

Swamiji sifts through character as:

- The character of any man is but the aggregate of his tendencies, the sum total of the bent of his mind. We are what our thoughts have made us. Thoughts live; they travel far. Take care of what you think. Every work that we do, every movement of the body, every thought that we think, bears an impression on the mind-stuff. What we are every moment is determined by the sum total of impressions on our mind. Every man's character is determined by the sum total of these impressions. If good impressions prevail, the character becomes good, if bad, it becomes bad.

- As pleasure and pain pass before his soul, they leave upon different pictures, and the result of combined impressions is what is called as man's "character".
- If you take the character of any man, it really is but the aggregate of tendencies, the sum total of the bent of his mind;
- Character is nothing but, repeated habits...
- Never say any man is hopeless, because he only represents a character, a bundle of habits....
- If you really want to judge the character of a man, look not at his great performances. Every fool may become some hero at one time or another. Watch a man do his most common actions; those are indeed the things which will tell you the real character of a great man. Great occasions rouse even the lowest of human beings to some kind of greatness, but he alone is really the great man whose character is always great, the same wherever he may be.

How is Character Formed?

- Every thought that we think, every deed that we do, after a certain time becomes fine, goes into seed form, so to speak, and lives in the fine body in a potential form, and after a time, it emerges again and bears its results. These results condition the life of man. He thus moulds his own life. Man is not bound by any other laws excepting those which he makes for himself.
- If a man continuously hears bad words, thinks bad thoughts, does bad actions, his mind will be full of bad impressions; and they will influence his thought and work without his being conscious of the fact. In fact, these bad impressions are always working, and their resultant must be evil, and that man will be a bad man; he cannot help it. The sum total of these impressions in him will create the strong motive power for doing bad actions. He will be like a machine in the hands of impressions, and they will force him to do evil. Similarly, if a man thinks good thoughts and does good works, the sum total of impressions will be good; and they, in a similar manner, the impression will force him to do good even in spite of himself. When a man has done so much good work and thought so many good thoughts there is an irresistible tendency in him to do good, in spite of himself and even if he wishes to do evil, his mind, as the sum total of his tendencies, will not allow him to do so; the tendencies will turn him back; he is completely under the influence of good tendencies. When such is the case, a man's good character is said to be established.
- We are what our thoughts have made us...
- Every thought is like a little hammer blow on the lump of iron which our bodies are, manufacturing out of it what we want to be.

- Man is, as it were, a centre, and is attracting the powers of universe towards himself, and in this centre is fusing them all and again sending them off in a big current....
- Good and bad, misery and happiness, all are running towards him and clinging round him; and out of them he fashions the mighty stream of tendency called character and throws it outwards. As he has the power of drawing in anything, so has he the power of throwing it out.

Why Character Building?

According to Swami Vivekananda:

- The basis of all system, social or political, rests upon the goodness of men. No nation is great or good because Parliament enacts this or that, but because its men are great and good. Men are more valuable than all the wealth of the world.
- What we want is to see the man who is harmoniously developed...great in heart, great in mind, [great in deed]....We want the man whose heart feels intensely the miseries and sorrows of the world.....And [we want] the man who not only can feel but can find the meanings of things, who delves deeply into the heart of nature and understanding. [We want] the man who will not even stop there, [but] who wants to work out [the feeling and meaning by actual deeds]. Such combination of head, heart, and hand is what we want.
- We have seen that it is the subjective world that rules the objective. Change the subject and the object is bound to change; purify yourself, and the world is bound to be purified. This thing requires to be taught now more than ever before. We are becoming more and more busy about our neighbours, and less and less about ourselves. The world will change if we change; if we are pure, the world will become pure. The question is why I should see evil in others. I cannot see evil unless I am evil. I cannot be miserable unless I am weak. Things that used to make me miserable when I was a child, do not do so now. The subject changed, so the object was bound to change; so says the Vedanta.
- The more we grow in love and virtue and holiness, the more we see love and virtue and holiness outside. All condemnation of others really condemns ourselves. Adjust the microcosm (which is in your power to do) and the macrocosm will adjust itself for you. It is like the hydrostatic paradox, one drop of water can balance the universe. We cannot see outside what we are not inside. The universe is to us what the huge engine is to the miniature engine; and indication of any error in the tiny engine leads us to imagine trouble in the huge one.

- In our families, there are the heads; some of them are successful, others are not. Why? We complain of others in our failures. The moment one is unsuccessful, he/she would say, so-and-so is the cause of the failure. In failure, one does not like to confess one's own faults and weaknesses. Each person tries to hold himself faultless and lay the blame upon somebody else, or even on bad luck. When heads of families fail, they should ask themselves, why is it that some people manage a family so well and others do not. Then you will find that the difference is owing to the man - his presence, his personality.
- A man comes; you know he is very learned, his language is beautiful, and he speaks to you by the hour; but he does not make any impression. Another man comes, and he speaks a few words, not well arranged, ungrammatical perhaps; all the same he makes an immense impression. Many of you have seen that. So it is evident that words alone cannot produce an impression. Words, even thoughts, contribute only one-third of the influence in making an impression, the man, two-thirds. What you call the personal magnetism of the man-that is what goes out and impresses you.
- Coming to great leaders of mankind, we always find that it was the personality of the man that counted. Now, take all the great authors of the past, the great thinkers. Really speaking, how many thoughts have they thought? Take all the writings that have been left to us by the past leaders of mankind; take each one of their books and appraise them. The real thoughts, new and genuine, that have been thought in this world up to this time, amount to only a handful. Read in their books the thoughts they have left to us. The authors do not appear to be giants to us, and yet we know that they were great giants in their days. What made them so? Not simply the thoughts they thought, neither the books they wrote, nor the speeches they made, it was something else that is now gone, that is their personality. It is the real man, the personality of the man, that runs through us. Our actions are but effects. Actions must come when the man is there; the effect is bound to follow the cause.
- The ideal of all education, all training, should be this man-making. But instead of that, we are always trying to polish up the outside. What use is polishing up the outside when there is no inside? The end and aim of all training is to make the man grow. The man who influences, who throws his magic, as it were, upon his fellow-beings, is a dynamo of power, and when that man is ready, he can do anything and everything he likes; that personality put upon anything will make it work.
- What the world wants is character. The world is in need for those whose life is one burning love, selfless. That love will make every word tell like thunderbolt.

- Money does not pay, nor name; fame does not pay, nor learning. It is love that pays; it is character that cleaves its way through adamantine walls of difficulties.
- Perfect sincerity, holiness, gigantic intellect and an all-conquering will-let only a handful of men work with these, and the whole world will be revolutionised.
- Was it ever in the history of the world that any great work was done by the rich? It is the heart and the brain that do it ever and ever and not the purse.

How to Build Character?

- What you want is character, strengthening of the will. Continue to exercise your will and it will take you higher. This will is Almighty. It is character that can cleave through adamantine walls of difficulties.
- Go on doing good, thinking holy thoughts continuously, that is the only way to suppress base impressions....Character is repeated habits, and repeated habits alone can reform character.
- If a man thinks good thoughts and does good works, the sum total of these (his) impressions will be good; and they....will force him to do good even in spite of himself.
- A man plays a tune on a piano; he places each finger on each key consciously. He repeats this process till the movement of the fingers becomes a habit. He then plays a tune without having to pay special attention to each particular key. Similarly, we find in regard to ourselves that our tendencies are the result of past conscious actions...
- Every good thought that we send to the world, without thinking of any return, will be stored up there and break one link in the chain, and make us purer and purer, until we become the purest of mortals.
- Even the least work done for others awakens the power within; even thinking the least good of others gradually instils into the heart the strength of a lion.
- The road to the Good is the roughest and steepest in the universe. It is a wonder that so many succeed but no wonder that so many fall. Character has to be established through thousand stumbles.
- Feel, feel; feel for the poor, the ignorant, the downtrodden; feel till the heart stops and the brain reels and you think you will go mad; then pour the soul out at the feet of the Lord, and then will come power, help and indomitable energy.
- Have fire and spread all over. Work, work. Be the servant while leading. Be unselfish, and never listen to one friend in private accusing another. Have infinite patience, and success is yours.
- Take care! Beware of everything that is untrue; stick to truth, and we shall succeed, maybe slowly, but surely. Work as if on each of you depended the whole work.

Inspiring Thoughts upon Mind

- Take up one idea. Make that one idea your life - think of it, dream of it, live on that idea. Let the brain, muscles, nerves, every part of your body, be full of that idea, and just leave every other idea alone. This is the way to success.
- All the great prophets, saints, and seers of the world - what did they do? In one span of life, they lived the whole life of humanity … In one life, they perfect themselves; they have no thought for anything else … and thus the way is shortened for them. That is what is meant by concentration, intensifying the power of assimilation, thus shortening of the time.
- The more this power of concentration, the more knowledge is acquired, because this is the one and only method of acquiring knowledge.
- How has all the knowledge in the world been gained but by the concentration of the powers of the mind? The world is ready to give up its secrets … There is no limit to the power of the human mind. The more concentrated it is, the more power is brought to bear on one point; that is the secret.
- No force can be created; it can only be directed. … Thus it is clearly seen that chastity is the cornerstone of all morality and of all religion.
- The mind uncontrolled and unguided will drag us down, down, forever - rend us, kill us; and the mind controlled and guided will save us, free us.
- The main difference between the men and the animals is the difference in their power of concentration. The difference in their power of concentration also constitutes the difference between man and man.
- Ninety per cent of thought-force is being wasted by the ordinary human being, and therefore, he is constantly committing blunders; the trained man or mind never makes a mistake.
- Good and evil thoughts are each a potent power, and they fill the universe. As vibration continues, so thought remains in the form of thought until translated into action.
- If we make ourselves pure and the instruments of good thoughts, these will enter us.
- In the history of mankind, you will find that there come the Messengers, … When they speak, each word is direct; it bursts like a bomb-shell. What is in the word, unless it has the Power behind?
- Whatever you do, devote your whole mind, heart, and soul to it.
- It is our mental attitude which makes the world what it is for us. Our thoughts make things beautiful, our thoughts make things ugly. The whole world is in our minds. Learn to see things in the proper light.

Swamiji has explained about thought-transference. He said 'A man here is thinking something, and that thought is manifested in somebody else, in some other place. With preparations — not by chance — a man wants to send a thought to another mind at a distance, and this other mind knows that a thought is coming, and he receives it exactly as it is sent out. Distance makes no difference. The thought goes and reaches the other man, and he understands it. If your mind were an isolated something here, and my mind were an isolated something there, and there were no connection between the two, how would it be possible for my thought to reach you? In the ordinary cases, it is not my thought that is reaching you direct; but my thought has got to be dissolved into ethereal vibrations and those ethereal vibrations go into your brain, and they have to be resolved again into your own thoughts. Here is a dissolution of thought, and there is a resolution of thought. It is a roundabout process. This shows that there is a continuity of mind, as the Yogis call it. The mind is universal. Your mind, my mind, all these little minds, are fragments of that universal mind, little waves in the ocean; and on account of this continuity, we can convey our thoughts directly to one another.

Swamiji says: "There is no limit to the power of the human mind. The more concentrated it is, the more power is brought to bear on one point; that is the secret". All of us have to realise that as parents, teachers and elders we need to garner and embed the seeds of building character in the hearts, minds and souls of the next generation at home, in schools and colleges and society.

If that is not done, then education is only a mass of information and in the words of T.S. Eliot "The Rock" the question before humanity will be:

"Where is the life we have lost in living?
Where is the wisdom we have lost in knowledge
Where is the knowledge we have lost in informations?"

References

- R.C. Majumdar (2004) Swami Vivekananda, Published by Mumukshananda - President, Advaita Asrama Mayavati, Champawat,Uttarakhand from its Publication Department, Kolkata. Email:advaita@vsnl.com; Website: www.advaitaonline.com
- Asim Chaudhuri (2005) Swami Vivekananda in Chicago New Findings, Published by Mumukshananda President, Advaita Asrama Mayavati, Champawat, Uttarakhand from its Publication Department, Kolkata. Email:advaita@vsnl.com; Website: www.advaitaonline.com
- S.C. Sen Gupta (2008) Swami Vivekananda My India and Indian Nationalism, Published by The Secretary The Ramakrishna Mission Institute of Culture, Kolkata -700 029, India.
- Swami Vivekananda (2008) My India the India Eternal, Published by Ramakrishna Mission Institute of Culture Kolkata -700 029, India.

- Swami Vivekananda (2008) My Idea of Education, Published by Swami Bodhasarananda Adhyaksha, Advaita Asrama Mayavati, Champawat, Uttarakhand from its Publication Department, Kolkata. Email: mail@advaitaasrama.org; Website: www.advaitaasrama.org

40

Character and the Cultivation of Mind

M.N. Geetha

Introduction

Come up, O Lions, and shake off the delusion that you are sheep;
You are soul's immortal, spirits free, blest and eternal;
Ye are not matter, ye are not bodies;
Matter is your servant, not you the servant of matter.

— Swami Vivekananda

Swami Vivekananda the supreme monk of India devoted invaluable ideas for self as well as development. He envisioned new educational model for society, evident from speeches.

Aims and objectives

- To emphasis his educational views.
- To impart his spiritual ideas in our existing education system.
- To create awareness of value education among students by his quotes.
- To highlight the power of youth for nation building.

Importance of teaching moral values in higher education:

"Keep the motto before you; Elevation of the masses without injuring their religion.
Education, education, education alone!

Travelling through many cities of Europe and observing the comforts and education of even the poor people, I used to shed tears. What made the difference? Education was the difference I got. Through education comes faith in one's own self the inherent Brahman is waking up in them, while the Brahman in us is gradually becoming dormant" — Swami Vivekananda

In India, we have numerous sectors, caste and creed. There are various practices prevailing among the people. Maintaining one system is highly impossible for us. Even our education system has so many vast differences based on money, caste, religion etc. Even though our government has put forward many valuable programs to develop literacy among people we are unable to reach the destination successfully. To educate the mass is highly a difficult task which needs well accurate and accessible curriculum and proper execution of the curriculum. Swami Vivekananda a foreseer of India; determined well the significance of the education system in advance.

Today, we come across many violence, malpractices, tragedies, treacheries, at our social sectors. An individual suffers by depression, bad companies, addiction, unsociability,... We can therefore easily realise there must be a huge mistake at our present educational system.

So many years ago, Swamiji envisioned the correct education system which is character formation. If every individual gets a self-realisation of their existence, then all the problems will be get over. This self realisation will bloom like a flower within their self without any external compulsion. Here we are going to torch few points of Swamiji for character formation and the functions of mind. If one teacher has a clear vision he will direct his students in the right way. Here, I have highlighted a few of his valuable ideas for better education.

Educational principles of Swamiji are:

- Education must help us manifest the infinite knowledge within.
- Education must result in man-making.
- Education must strengthen faith and pride in ourselves as a nation.
- Education must focus on character-building assimilation of ideas.

Swamiji's principles are countless, but we discuss few stch, on the occasion.

National Education

> *"Mere book - learning won't do. We want that education by which character is formed, strength of mind is increased, the intellect is expanded and by which one can stand on one's own feet."*
>
> *— Swami Vivekananda*

"We must have a hold on the spiritual and secular education of the nation. Do you know that? You must dream it, you must think it, and you must work it. Till then there is no salvation for the race. The education that you are getting now has some good points, but it has a tremendous disadvantage which is so great that the good things are all weighed down. Education is not that amount of information that is put into your brain and runs riot there undigested, all your life. We must have life-building, man-making, character-making, assimilation of ideas. If you have assimilated these ideas and made them your life and character, you have more education than any man who has got by heart a whole library. If education is identical with information the libraries are the greatest sages in the world, and encyclopedias are the Rishis. The ideal, therefore, is that we must have the whole education of our country, spiritual and secular, in our own hands, and it must be on the national lines, through national methods as for as practical."

In this paragraph, he emphasised the importance of education that is character making and not the amount of information but knowledge.

Concept of Shraddha

"We want shraddha; we want faith in our own selves. Strength is life, weakness is death. It is by loosing this idea of shraddha that the country has gone to ruins.... So make men first. Men we want, and how can men we made unless the shraddha is there? We want that education by which character is formed, strength of mind is increased, the intellect is expanded, and by which one can stand on one's own feet. Every boy should be trained to practice absolute Brahmachariya, and then only, faith and shraddha will come. In our country, the imparting of knowledge has always be through men of renunciation. We must compile some books with short stories from the Ramayana, the Mahabharata and the Upanishads, etc.... in very easy and simple language, and these are to be given to our little boys to read".

Self-dedication and involvement is the essential thing for character building. We could know about the noble virtues through the study of epic characters.

Character Building

"Pleasure is not the goal of man, but knowledge is. Pleasure and happiness come to an end. It is a mistake to suppose that pleasure is the goal. Good and evil have an equal share in moulding character, and in some instances misery is a great teacher than happiness. Wisdom is the goal of all life".

"Comfort is no test of truth 'on the contrary truth if often far from being comfortable. If one intends to really find truth, one must not cling to comfort sacrifice is necessary."

"Habit is second nature; it is the first nature also, and whole nature of man, everything that we are is the result of habit. The only remedy for bad habits is counter-habits; all the bad habits that have left their impressions are to be controlled by good habits. Go on doing good, thinking over holy thoughts continuously; that is only way to suppress base impressions. Character is repeated habits, and repeated habits alone can reform character".

"This is the first lesson to learn; be determined not to curse anything outside. Not to lay the blame upon any one outside, but be a man; stand up, lay the blame on you. You will find that it is always true. Get hold on yourself".

"Pleasure is not the goal" this simple line is enough to explain the purpose and goal of our life.

We have to make the students clear about their goal and achievement.

Physical Education

"First you have to build the body by good nutrious food then only the mind will be strong. The mind is but the subtle part of the body. You must retain great strength in your mind and words. You must learn to make the physique very strong, and teach the same to others. Don't you find me exercising every day with dumb-bells even now? Walk in the mornings and evenings, and do physical labour. Body and mind run parallel."

From those lines, we could realise the importance of exercise and fitness of our body.

Teacher-Student Relationship

"The bond between the teacher and the taught—that is peculiar to India. The teacher is not a man who comes just to teach me and I pay him so much and there it ends. In India, it is really like an adoption. The teacher is more than my own father and I am truly his child, his son in every respect. I owe him obedience and reverence first, before my own father even; because they say, the father gave me this body, but he showed me the way to salvation, he is greater than father. And we carry this love, this respect for our teacher all our lives."

Power of Concentration

"Take up one idea. Make that one idea your life; think of it; dream of it; live on that idea. Let the brain, muscles, nerves, every part of your body be full of that idea alone. This is the way to success, and this is the way great spiritual giants are produced."

According to Swamiji, the very essence of education is concentration of mind, not the collecting of facts. There is no limit to the power of human mind. The more concentrated it is, the more power is brought to bear on one point; that is the secret. Breathing exercise is the first step to increase the concentration power.

Leadership Quality

"Have fire and spread all over. Work Work..... Be the servant while leading, be unselfish, and never listen to one friend in private accusing another. Have infinite patience and success is yours. Do not try to 'boss' others. Work; Work for to work only for the good of others is life."

"All the powers in the universe are already ours. It is we who have put our hands before our eyes, and cry that it is dark. Take the hands away and there is the light which was from the beginning. Darkness seldom exist nor weakness. We who are fools cry that we are impure".

All we understand is that leadership quality is to be the boss to others, but Swamiji opposed the view that it is true leader, who is not a boss to others but the servant of others.

Conclusion

"Life is a series of fights and disillusionments…the secret of life is not enjoyment but education through experience".

"Advance like a hero. Don't be thwarted by anything. How many days this body last, with its happiness and misery? I have reached the state of fearlessness!.. and then as long as the body endures, speak unto others this message: " thou art that", "arise, awake, and stop not till the goal is reached!"

One can easily get motivated internally by the reading of Swamiji and retain the vibration throughout life. Instead of blaming darkness we should burn the candle likewise instead of blaming the wrong education system we could provide the books of Swamiji to our students. The cultivation of any system arise from one's own heart with full involvement. There is no doubt about positive results when we implement the ideas of Swamiji in higher education.

References

- Burke, M.L., 1984. Swami Vivekananda in the West: New discoveries, Vol. 6. Calcutta: Advaita Ashrama.
- Dhar, S., 1975. A comprehensive biography of Swami Vivekananda. Vol. 2, Madras: Vivekananda Prakashan Kendra.
- Gnatuk-Danil'chuk, A.P. 1986. Tolstoy and Vivekananda. Calcutta: The Ramakrishna Mission Institute of Culture.
- Hossain, M., 1980. Swami Vivekananda's philosophy of education. Calcutta: Ratna Prakashan.
- Sengupta, S.C., 1984. Swami Vivekananda and Indian nationalism. Calcutta: Shishu Sahitya Samsad.

41

Character and Cultivation of Man

D. S. N. Vimal Kumar

Introduction

A regal, majestic figure of commanding presence, vast learning and deep insight, Swami Vivekananda was barely 30 years old when he created a stir at the World's Parliament of Religious in Chicago in 1893. Three and a half years later, when he returned to India, his homeland, it was a colossus of strength, courage, confidence, love and manliness – the embodiment of the ideal of somewhat 'man-making and character-building' education, he propagated.

Sister Nivedita used to say that those who knew Swami Vivekananda understood that he was one who had experienced in his own life the truths about which he spoke. This is equally valid when he addressed the subject of education. To him, education plays vital role in curing the evils in society, and it is critical in shaping the future of humanity. Although Vivekananda did not write a book on education, he contributed valuable thoughts that are relavant and viable even today. In order to understand his thoughts, we should first consider his oft-quoted definition of education — 'Education is the manifestation of the perfection already in man'.

Education – What it means

Vivekananda's definition of education is one of remarkable insight. First of all, the word 'manifestation' implies that something already exists and is waiting to be expressed. The main focus in learning is to make the hidden ability of a learner manifest. As Vivekananda said, 'what a man "learns" is really what he "discovers"' by taking the cover off his own soul, which is a mine of infinite knowledge.

Next in importance in the Swami's definition of education is the expression 'already in man'. This refers to human being's potential, which is the range of abilities and talents, known or unknown he was born with. "Potential" speaks of the possibility of awakening something that is lying dormant. Israel Scheffler, in his book of human potential, considered three aspects of this: (a) the capacity to acquire a specific characteristic or to become someone who possesses it. For instance, we might say, 'Amal has the capacity to become a

Maradona, the world-famous soccer player'; (b) the propensity—an attribute which indicates what a person is likely to do when the opportunity comes and freedom of choice is available. It suggests something about a person's motivation. For example, Rabindranath Tagore's propensity, expressed in his Gitanjali, indicates his strong aspiration to discover the wonder behind this creation: and (c) the capability — i.e. a person's motivation and efficiency in working towards an intended outcome. It refers to something more than a person's capacity to perform. Rather, it is a person's strength and capacity to rid of obstacles to his learning — such as his lack of motivation or the obstacles encountered.

Thus, three concepts—capacity, propensity and capability — emphasise three aspects of education, respectively: (a) that which makes learning possible; (b) the development of learning; and (c) self-development or self-empowerment.

A child has many potentials of variable worth, and they may create mental conflict within him. Therefore, he has to learn to choose which he should develop, and which he should minimise, counter or ignore. Again, as his chosen potentials he should unfold, supervise in order to achieve harmonious and purposeful development.

Vivekananda also observed that, if education is to serve the entire human race, in all his/her dimensions, the pursuit of knowledge will be lifelong process. Even an illustrious being like Sri Ramakrishna said, from his own experience, "As long as I live, so long do I learn." At the empirical level, today's knowledge explosion can keep people engaged for their entire lives. Therefore, education must be considered somewhat continuous and lifelong process.

So far, our discussion of Vivekananda's ideas on education has been a simplistic analysis centering round his definition of education. However, this fails to do justice to some of his ideas on related issues, such as the relationship between education and society, between education and the teacher, between the professed goals of education and the goals actually achieved, and so forth. It is apparent, therefore, that Vivekananda's deep concern for social justice has not been reflected in our definition.

Training the Mind

Vivekananda concurred with contemporary thinkers when he asserted that the mind - the chief instrument of learning - deserves more attention than it had received earlier. Training the mind should be a student's highest priority, and not simply the accumulation, the memorising and repeating of facts. In the long run, stuffing one's mind with information, technical skills and useless trivia only creates more problems if one's mind in all its aspects is conspicuously absent in today's education.

Learning to concentrate the mind was the focus in the Swamiji's scheme. He said: 'To me, the very essence of education is concentration of mind, not the collecting of facts'. In doing anything—such as thinking, working with the hands, etc., the better the power of concentration.... the better the outcome will be. To concentrate on a specific subject has several stages, the primary one being learning how to collect the mind and preventing it from running hither and thither. The student trains his mind to be more attentive and more 'mindful'.

Culture and Education – The Teacher and the Pupil

A society is forever adding to its learning and culture. To the brilliant mind of T.S. Eliot, education was but a manifestation of culture. He said, 'the purpose of education, it seems, is to transmit culture: so culture is likely to be limited to what can be transmitted by education.'

Similarly, Vivekananda observed that, through education, a child learns a culture and his behaviour is moulded accordingly, and he is thus guided towards his eventual role in society. In this process, several agents — such as his parents, peers and teachers — assist him. But nowadays, as formal; education has become more and more institutionalised, teachers are expected to play a more significant role. A teacher needs to help a student learn how to think, what to think, how to discriminate and how to appreciate things. This is not just a matter of intellectual manipulation. This kind of teaching requires moral conviction and the courage to continuously pursue one's own course at all costs. The teacher must not only possess the knowledge he is to transmit to the student, but he must also know how to transmit it. And, in addition what the teacher gives or transfers, to be truly effective, must possess some other elements. For instance, the teacher should share with the student the conviction that they are both truly one in Spirit - at the same time cultivating in the student a feeling of dignity and self-respect. As Vivekananda said:

Character Education and Universal Values

In order to rectify the defects in the existing system, man's limited view of himself, on which the existing system of education is based, needs to be reconsidered. A human being is not simply a composite of body and mind. He is something more. According to the Vedanta philosophy, a human being has five sheaths, or coveringes: the physical sheath, the vital sheath, the mental sheath, the intellectual sheath, and the blissful sheath. Today's education can at best touch the first four sheaths, but not the last one. Secular knowledge is essential for the fifth. Moreover, it should be noted that the fifth sheath is the reservoir of bliss, knowledge and strength, and the other sheaths are activated by the fifth.

There is no doubt that today's education neglects training of the mind in all aspects, but it also neglects the spiritual side of human beings. People's minds are not directed to higher pursuits of life with the results that their hidden potentials are not revealed. Only when wisdom, peace, strength, unselfishness, loving concern for other and other virtues become evident is a person transformed from a sensuous being to a true human being.

The Education System and the Poor

Vivekananda felt that alienation of any kind from the masses of society, who are mostly poor - whether it be alienation through learning, through wealth or through force of arms - weakens the leadership of a country. Therefore, for a sustainable regeneration of India, if not for anything else, top priority must be given to educating the masses and restoring their lost individuality. They should not only be given education to make them self-reliant, but also ideas, moral training an understanding of their own historical situation so that they can work out their own salvation. Furthermore, they must be given culture, without which there can be no hope for their long-term progress.

The Swami was particularly worried about the degradation of women in India. He was emphatic that women must be educated, for he believed the women mould the next generation, and hence, the density of the country. In Vivekananda's educational scheme for India, the uplift of women and the masses received the highest priority, and his ideas approximated to Paulo Freire's concept of 'Conscientisation'.

Conclusion

There have been many changes in the field of education since Swami Vivekananda passed away one hundred years ago, but not as many changes as in preparing human beings for a new type of society, and it is trying to create a new type of human being for it. Interestingly, Swami Vivekananda had envisioned a society with a new type of human being in whom knowledge, action, work and concentration were harmoniously blended, and he proposed a new type of education for achieving this.

The right to education for everyone, guaranteed by the Constitution of India, was Vivekananda's dream, but it is still a far cry from its goal. His idea of continual, or lifelong, education, however, has been adopted in many countries already. Moreover, because of the adoption of continuous education in these countries, our idea of what constitutes success and failure has altered, raising new hope for the weak, under-privileged section of these societies - the very people who for various reasons cannot complete their education when they are young.

Vivekananda's cry for the uplift of the downtrodden masses, particularly of the long-neglected women, has evoked a favourable response from different quarters, but societies tailor education to meet their own needs, thereby robbing the weak often of their freedom to determine their own density. Unless radical changes are being made in all societies, the poor will never be able to raise themselves. This was a major concern of the Swamiji.

It is remarkable that there are similarities between Vivekananda's thoughts and actions taking place one century ago and the present concerns of UNESCO.

- His commitment towards universal values and tolerance, his active identification with humanity as a whole.
- The struggle in favour of the poor and destitute, to reduce poverty and to eliminate discrimination against women - reaching the unreached.
- His vision of education, science and culture as the essential instruments of human development.
- That education should be a lifelong process.
- And the need to move away from rote learning.

References

- Quotation bearing the reference CW in the text are taken from: The complete works of Swami Vivekananda Vol. I-IX, Calcutta Advaitha Ashrama 1989. Mayavati Memorial Edition.
- Quotation bearing the reference Letter are taken from Letter of Swami Vivekananda 4th ed. Calcutta Advaitha Ashrama, 1976.
- Quotation from Sri Ramakrishna bearing the reference Gospel are taken from: The Gospel of sri Ramakrishna, trans by Swami Nikhilananda Madras Sri Ramakrishnamath, 1981.

Other referances are as follows:

1. Datta, B. 1993. *Swami Vivekananda Patriot-Prophet—A study*. Calautta; Nabaharat Publication.
2. Gambhirananda Swami 1996. *Yuganayak Vivekananda,* Vivekananda the leader of this era.
3. 3 Vols. Calcutta Udbodhan Karyalaya.

42

Guiding Principles of Swamiji on Character Formation

A. Balamallikadevi

We want that education by which character is formed, strength of mind is increased, the intellect is expanded, and by which one can stand on one's own feet. *—Swami Vivekananda*

Introduction

Swami Vivekananda emphasised on Man-making education for human development as well as national development. According to him, man-making education is inherent for character development as well as vocational development. Swami Vivekananda always told one thing that the main purpose of education is to build up such a personality whose character is covered with full of morality. According to him, education without character is like a flower without fragrance. An education system that doesn't recognise this can be self-defeatist at the best. The character of any man is but the aggregate of his tendencies, the sum total of the bent of his mind. Swami Vivekananda realised three things necessary to make every man great, every nation great.

- Conviction of powers of goodness.
- Absence of jealousy and suspicion.
- Helping those who are trying to be and do well.

Swami Vivekananda suggested trying to give up jealousy and conceit and learn to work unitedly for others. He told, purity, patience and perseverance overcome all obstacles. He suggested taking courage and work on. Patience and steady work, according to Swami Vivekananda, this is the only way to get success.

What is Education?

Education isn't mere textbook knowledge. Real education goes beyond that. It should encompass the habits that one imbibes from one's atmosphere and from the friends one keeps. Wisdom would be in maintaining a healthy atmosphere and a healthy friends circle. The more important aspect of education should be to impart humanity to the taught. This is where the teacher plays a prominent role of inculcating these values amongst his/her wards. As Aristotle has said, "Virtue is not learnt by reading big volumes".

True education should impart empathy and social awareness. Education should also impart the fortitude to act righteously upon the knowledge that one has gained. As the Thirukkural says: "Let a man learn thoroughly whatever he may learn and let his conduct be worthy of his learning" (Kural Chapter 40 verse 1). True education would be one that moulds one's character to perform one's duties without fear or favour, and to observe ethics in one's conduct and behaviour. The test would be whether such education lays a strong foundation for a moral path. Gandhiji said "...learning without courage is like a waxen statue, beautiful to look at but bound to melt at the least touch of a hot substance." An unwavering moral standard would liberate the mind from fear. A fearless mind should be the benchmark of good education. What is the use of an education system that doesn't rid the mind of fear? What good is an education that doesn't teach us to follow the path of truth?

Character formation should have priority over knowledge of the alphabet. Education without character is like a flower without fragrance. An education system that doesn't recognise this can be self-defeatist at the best.

Professor Huxley defined education, "That man, I think, has had a liberal education ...whose intellect is a clear, cold, logic engine with all its parts of equal strength and in smooth working order; . . . whose mind is stored with a knowledge of the fundamental truths of nature;...whose passions are trained to come to heel by a vigorous will, the servant of a tender conscience; . . . who has learnt to hate all vileness and to respect others as himself. Such a one and no other, I conceive, has had a liberal education, for he is in harmony with nature. He will make the best of her."

Swamiji on Character

Swami Vivekananda says, "The character of any man is but the aggregate of his tendencies, the sum total of the bent of his mind. We are what our thoughts have made us. Thoughts live; they travel far. And so take care of what you think. Every work that we do, every movement of the body, every thought that we think, bears an impression on the mind-stuff. What we are every moment is determined by the sum total of these impressions on the mind. Every man's character is determined by the sum total of these impressions prevails that the character becomes good, if bad, it becomes bad".

Recently our human civilisation is passing through a dangerous situation. If we observe the present situation of our society sincerely, we can see that very dangerous anti-social activities, immoral activities, corruptions are happening here and there in our society. Not only this, but also a bad effect or impressions of these activities have come into the system of education at school, college and university level. Consequently, we can see that teachers are sleased by their students inside and outside the school. They have no moral values to judge us that what is right or wrong. Lack of morality, their character is also very bad. Sometimes, it is found that the students have forgotten to respect their teachers.

According to Swamiji, it is not a good sign for our society and nation. For this reason, he always told that if we want to develop humanity, morality, honesty, good character among our students, school education is the best way to serve this purpose.

Why Character Building?

The basis of all system, social or political, rests upon the goodness of men. No nation is great or good because Parliament enacts this or that, but because its men are great and good. Men are more valuable than all the wealth of the world. What we want is to see the man who is harmoniously developed...great in heart, great in mind, [great indeed]. We want the man whose heart feels intensely the miseries and sorrows of the world.....And [we want] the man who not only can feel but can find the meanings of things, who delves deeply into the heart of nature and understanding. [We want] the man who will not even stop there, [but] who wants to work out [the feeling and meaning by actual deeds]. Such a combination of head, heart, and hand is what we want.

Coming to great leaders of mankind, we always find that it was the personality of the man that counted. Now, take all the great authors of the past, the great thinkers. Really speaking, how many thoughts have they thought? Take all the writings that have been left to us by the past leaders of mankind; take each one of their books and appraise them. The real thoughts, new and genuine, that have been thought in this world up to this time, amount to only a handful. Read in their books the thoughts they have left to us. The authors do not appear to be giants to us, and yet we know that they were great giants in their days. What made them so? Not simply the thoughts they thought, neither the books they wrote, nor the speeches they made, it was something else that is now gone, that is their personality. As Swamiji remarked, the personality of the man is two-thirds, his intellect, but only one-third, his words. It is the real man, the personality of the man that runs through us. Our actions are but effects. Actions must come when the man is there; the effect is bound to follow the cause.

Swamiji says that the ideal of all education, all training, should be this man-making. But instead of that, we are always trying to polish up the outside. What use is polishing up the outside when there is no inside? The end and aim of all training is to make the man grow. The man who influences, who throws his magic, as it were upon his fellow being is a dynamo of power, and when that man is ready, he can do anything and everything he likes: that personality put upon anything and everything he likes: that personality put upon anything will make it work.

How is Character Formed

If a man continuously hears bad words, thinks bad thoughts, does bad actions, his mind will be full of bad impressions; and they will influence his thought and work without his being conscious of the fact. In fact, these bad impressions are always working, and their resultant must be evil, and that man will be a bad man; he cannot help it. The sum total of these impressions in him will create the strong motive power for doing bad actions. He will be like a machine in the hands of impressions, and they will force him to do evil. Similarly, if a man thinks good thoughts and does good works, the sum total of these impressions will be good; and they, in a similar manner will force him to do good even in spite of himself. When a man has done so much good work and thought so many good thoughts there is an irresistible tendency in him to do good, in spite of himself and even if he wishes to do evil, his mind, as the sum total of his tendencies, will not allow him to do so; the tendencies will turn him back; he is completely under the influence of the good tendencies. When such is the case, a man's good character is said to be established.

Character Qualities Highlighted by Swamiji

The following are the character qualities to be followed:

Character Qualities to Imbibe	
Faith	Diligence
Strength	Love
Unselfishness	Morality
Service	Non-Attachment
Acceptance	Non-Injury
Courage	Obedience
Dedication	Patience
Purity	Perseverance
Self-Restraint	Sincerity
Truthfulness	

Dont's of Character	
Conceit	Want of sympathy
Criticism	Laziness
Jealousy	Partiality
Lack of seriousness	Want of fame

Guidelines for Character Formation

Swamiji has suggested some guidelines for character formation among students, which are:

1. Hard work

Character formation requires hard work. This is not possible by those who wish for enjoyment. Struggle is the best teacher in character building.

2. Moral and Spiritual Values

Purity, thirst for knowledge, perseverance, faith, humanity, submission and veneration, are other values. These qualities may be developed by the teacher's example and the pupil's efforts.

3. Gurukula System

The relationship between the teacher and the taught is possible only in a Gurukula system of education. Swamiji favoured the ancient Indian Gurukula system of education wherein the pupils served the teacher, who in turn helped the pupils everywhere to achieve knowledge.

4. Formation of Good Habits

Habits express character. Good habits owe to for good character.

5. Learning through mistakes

The child should be allowed to mistake in the process of character formation. Errors are the stepping stones to our progress in character. Strong will is the sign of great character.

6. Will make men great

Swamiji was an ideal teacher. His words worked like magic upon men and women. He sought the people build their character and manifest their real nature which is the Effulgent, the Resplendent the Ever Pure.

How to Build Character— Swamiji's View

- What we want is character, strengthening of the will. Continue to exercise our will. It will take us higher. This will is Almighty. It is character that can cleave through adamantine walls of difficulties.
- Go on doing good, thinking holy thoughts continuously, which is the only way to suppress base impressions. Character is repeated habits. Repeated habits alone can reform character.
- If a man thinks good thoughts and does good works, the sum total of these (his) impressions will be good; and they....will force him to do good even in spite of himself.
- Every good thought that we send to the world, without thinking of any return, will be stored up there and break one link in the chain, and make us purer and purer, until we become the purest of mortals.
- Even the least work done for others awakens the power within; even thinking the least good of others gradually instills into the heart the strength of a lion.

- The road to the good is the roughest and steepest in the universe. It is a wonder that so many succeed no wonder, that so many fall. Character has to be established through a thousand stumbles.
- Struggle, struggle, Struggle, when it was all dark, we should say, struggle; when light is breaking in, we should still say, struggle. Be not afraid.
- Have fire and spread all over. Work, work. Be the servant while leading. Be unselfish, and never listen to one friend in private accusing another. Have infinite patience, and success is yours.
- Take care! Beware of everything that is untrue; stick to truth, and we shall succeed, maybe slowly, but surely.

Role of a Teacher in Character Building

A child teaches itself. The teacher can help it to go in its own way. What we can do is not of the positive nature, but of the negative. We can take away the obstacles, but knowledge comes out of its own nature. Loosen the soil a little, so that it may come out easily. Put a hedge around it; see that it is not killed by anything, and there your work stops. We cannot do anything else. The rest is manifestation from within its own nature.

- No one can teach anybody. The teacher spoils everything by thinking that he is teaching. Thus Vedanta says that within man is all knowledge—even in a boy it is so—and it requires only an awakening, and that much is the work of a teacher.
- No one was ever really taught by another; each of us has to teach himself. The external teacher offers only the suggestion which rouses the internal teacher to work to understand things.
- Negative thoughts weaken men. Do we not find where parents are constantly taxing their sons to read and write, telling them they will never learn anything, and calling them fools and so forth, the latter do actually turn out to be so in many cases? If the teacher speak kind words to students and encourage, they are bound to improve in time.
- If the teacher can give them positive ideas, people will grow up to be men and learn to stand on their own legs.
- In language and literature, in poetry and in arts, in everything we must point not the mistakes that people make in their thoughts and actions, but the way in which they will gradually do things better. Pointing mistakes however, wounds a man's feelings.

Disciplines for Building Character-Several disciplines can build character which can be cultivated. These are:

- Acquiring knowledge and training of the physical and mental systems in an integrated manner.

- Practice of three austeries of body, speech and mind. (Bagavat Gita) - worship of God, of the twice born, of teachers, and of the wise, cleanliness, uprightness, continence and nonviolence are austerity of the body, words that do not give offence and that are truthful, pleasant, and beneficial, and the regular recitation of Vedas are austerity of speech, and serenity of mind, gentleness, silence, self control and purity of heart are austerity of the mind.
- Training in acquirement of divine treasure. (Daivi Sampad)
- Practice of Yama and Niyama prescribed by Sage Patanjali (non-killing, truthfulness, continence, and non-receiving are called yama, internal and external purification, contentment, mortification, study and worship of god are the Niyamas).
- Cultivation of approved or ethical conduct and Commitment to higher scheme of values.
- Developing the powers of discrimination, concentration, detachment, and will power.
- Training in developing five powers of the true learner. The power of faith, the power of conscientiousness, the power of fear of the blame that comes from acting wrongly in thought, word or deed, the power of energy to discard wrong thing and adopt the right ones, and the power of insight in to real nature of things and prepare himself to destroy the root cause of sorrow.

Conclusion

Good education is that which will help one in using one's senses positively and creatively. Any education that doesn't achieve this end is no education. Good education would be one that helps the child know right from wrong, make the right choices, stand for truth, and reject the bad and the untrue. Education should impart self-discipline. Good education is one that leads to wholesome development of the body, mind and spirit. True education is one that is successful in opening the eye of reasoning and inquiry.

References

- Swami Budhananda, (2008) How to Build Character, Advaita Ashrama, Kolkata-14.
- Avinasilingam, T.S., (Editor), (2010) Education, Compiled from the Speeches and Writings of Swami Vivekananda, Sri Ramakrishna Math, Madras-04.

43

Character and Cultivation of Mind Among B.Ed Students

Poonum Jahaly

Introduction

The relationship of education and society is multi-faceted. Education is the process by which we prepare children to enter adult life and to shoulder responsibilities that the society entails. No doubt many societies have been successful in preparing individual to be economically, technologically and mentally competent to face the competitive knowledge-based economy. However, it has failed to cater the overall development of students as schools in the twenty-first century incline towards achieving excellence in terms of pass rate at the national and international level examinations.

Moral education with a focus on education for character development and cultivation of mind has always been a perennial aim of education. The function of schools, it was believed, was not only to make people smart but also to make them good. The Gurukulas under the proper guidance of Gurus catered for the holistic development of students. In the present society, we have many students who are cognitively and physically rich, but ironically, morally and emotionally poor. Value education based on character formation and cultivation of the mind is the cry of the day. Swami Vivekananda rightly quoted 'Education is not the amount of information that is put into your brain and runs riot there undigested, all your life.' Education for him means that process by which character is formed, strength of mind is increased, and intellect is sharpened, as a result of which one can stand on one's own feet. Naturally, the school has to play a major role in the process of imparting education for character-building.

Character education, as defined here, is intended to promote student development. The aspects of student development of relevance are those that enable and motivate the individual to be a moral agent (i.e., to engage in systematic, intentional pro-social behaviour). Such developmental outcome include moral values (e.g., pro-social attitudes and motives), socio-moral reasoning competencies (e.g., perspective-taking, moral reasoning), knowledge of ethical issues and considerations, moral emotional competencies (e.g., empathy, sympathy), a pro-social self-system (e.g., moral identity, conscience), relevant behavioural competencies (e.g., ability to disagree respectfully, conflict resolution skills), and a set of characteristics that support the enactment of such pro-social motives and inclinations (e.g., perseverance, courage). In other words, the outcome of effective character education are a complex set of psychological characteristics that motivate and enable one to function as a moral agent (Berkowitz, 1997). Based on above facts, the present study was taken up to find out the role of schools in imparting education for character and cultivation of the mind among B.Ed students.

Methodology

Locale of the study: the present study has been conducted at Mysore among B.Ed students studying at two different B.Ed colleges.

Objectives of the study

- To find the role of school in imparting education for character and cultivation of mind among B.Ed students.
- To compare the level of morality of control and experimental groups of the B.Ed colleges.

Design of the study: An experimental study with experimental and control group was designed.

Selection of the sample

The sample consisted of 130 students of two B.Ed colleges situated in Mysore City, India.

Procedure of the study: the present study has been conducted in three stages:

First stage: Grouping students as experimental group (whereby there is inclusion of moral/spiritual education in the B.Ed college curriculum) and control group (where there is no provision for moral/spiritual program in the B.Ed curriculum programme)

Second stage: The Character Education Quality standard tool was administered to both groups to collect the data which is based on the Eleven Principles of Effective Character Education by Tom Lickona and Matthew Davidson (1996). It is a five point scale inventory.

Third Stage: The data obtained from both colleges were compared and analysed.

Hypothesis

1. There is no significant difference on the role of both schools in imparting education for character and cultivation of the mind among B.Ed students.
2. There is no significant difference between the levels of morality/ spirituality of both control and experimental groups among B.Ed students.

Analysis of data

The table below gives a description of independent *t*-test comparing the mean scores of experimental group and control group in relation to the Character Education Quality standard inventory scores.

S. No.	*Groups*	*N*	*Mean*	*SD*	*df*	*'t' value*
1	Control	60	45.20	10.00	127	4.04
2.	Experimental	70	52.27	13.00		

The table indicates that the difference in mean scores for the two groups, "t" (127) is significant at the 0.01 level. The null hypothesis that the two groups do not differ is rejected. Since the mean of experimental group is larger than that of control group , we may conclude that experimental group has performed better in the Character Education Quality standard test compared to control group.

Discussion

If character is lost everything is lost. A man without character or a nation with such men can never hope to achieve anything great in life. The Kothari commission points out "What we would like to emphasise is the need to pay attention to the inculcation of right values in the students at all stages of education.

However, escalating discipline problems culminating in violent outbursts, alarming rate of drug abuse, family breakdown are indicators of moral values degradation. Leming (1994) rightly points out that the school has a key role to play in perspective building, in equipping the child with necessary intellectual, emotional, social and moral resources to engage in a common process of valuation and decision-taking in a multi-cultural context.

Most of the time, education for character and cultivation of the mind has so far been the concern of those schools with religious and spiritual denomination. The study points out clearly that in the B.Ed College which is part of the experimental group, spiritual and moral education forms part of the core curriculum. Although, this B.Ed College follows the syllabus prescribed as per the requirement of the University of Mysore, it marvelously incorporates value education and spirituality, which helps shaping up the character and mind of the B.Ed students. Self-discipline, sacrifice, service and self-realisation as per the philosophy of Swami Vivekananda and Ramakrishna are propounded among the students through Yoga classes, meditation in the meditation cell, serving food to the needy and personality development sessions.

Conversely, the B.Ed College which forms parts of the Control group also follow the same syllabus as per University of Mysore guidelines yet no special program has been assigned for the provision of value and spiritual education. This B.Ed College's curriculum is geared towards student-centered curriculum with focus on use of innovative technologies: overhead projector, Computer, LCD and slide projector. Additionally, the new methods of teaching are adopted like co-operative learning, brainstorming and discovery method, however somehow the value education program is missing which is crucial for the development of character and cultivation of the mind.

In an era of globalisation, where cultural barriers collapse and with increased mobility of labour, education for character development and cultivation of mind also become a form of multicultural education. Increased interaction of people with different perspectives and different world-views, mobilise students learn to accept other people's beliefs and opinions and learn to question their own. (Mariaye, 2005)

A sound programme of value education should aim at building the cognitive and emotional skills of students necessary to engage in discussion with others and come in terms with their own perceptions. According to Likona (1996), there are three aspects of building character which he perceives as the ultimate end of moral education in schools namely moral knowledge, moral feeling and moral action. All the stakeholders: teachers, students, parents, administrators and the community should make collaborative effort to develop the moral character of the future generation. For the cultivation of mind, the students should be urged towards creative thinking, meditation and critical thinking, which help them discriminate between what is right and what is wrong. To successfully implement character education, schools are encouraged to:

- Take a leadership role to bring the staff, parents and students together to identify and define the elements of character they want to emphasise;
- Provide training for staff on how to integrate character education into the life and culture of the school;
- Form a vital partnership with parents and the community so that students hear a consistent message about character traits essential for success in school and life; and
- Provide opportunities for school leaders, teachers, parents and community partners to model exemplary character traits and social behaviours.

Conclusion

Character education is a learning process that enables students in a school community to understand, care about and acts on core ethical values such as respect, justice, civic virtue and citisenship, and responsibility for self and others. It has been the shared responsibility of parents, teachers and members of the community, who come together to support positive character development and cultivation of the mind. In school, character education must be approached comprehensively to include the emotional, intellectual and moral qualities of a person or group. It must offer multiple opportunities for students to learn about, discuss and enact positive social behaviours. Student leadership and involvement are essential for character education to become a part of a student's beliefs and actions.

References

- Berkowitz, M.W. (1997). The complete moral person: Anatomy and formation. In J. M. Dubois.
- (Ed.), Moral issues in psychology: Personalist contributions to selected problems (pp. 11-41). Lanham, MD: University Press of America.
- Leming, J.S. (1994) Character Education and Multicultural Education: Conflicts and Perspectives, Education Horizons.
- Lickona, T. (1996) Eleven Principles of Effective Character Education, Journal of Moral Education, Vol. 23, pp. 93-100.
- Mariaye, H.S. (2005) Role of the schools in providing Moral Education in a Multicultural society: The case of Mauritius, University of South Africa.

44

Man-Making Education

T.S. Balakrishnan

Introduction

Swamiji defined education as 'the manifestation of the perfection already in man. It was Swamiji's firm belief that nobody teaches the other. The teacher only helps the student to discover things which are latent or inherent in him. The sculptor does not make the idol. He just chisels away the unwanted parts from a rock and brings out the beautiful idol latent within. There is a famous hymn on Guru or teacher as the one who removes the 'cataract of ignorance 'from the eyes of the disciples. Why does Swamiji assume perfection in every human being? It is because every individual is the son of God. That is why the Upanishads call us as 'the children of immortality (Amrutasya putra). Let me quote Swamijis unsubstituted or expressed differently 'All knowledge and all power are within. What we call powers, secrets of Nature, and force are all within. All knowledge comes from the human soul. Man manifests knowledge, discovers that within himself, which is pre-existing, through eternity. Thus, the teacher is only a facilitator.

Character Building

The character of any man, according to Swamiji is the aggregate of his tendencies. 'As pain and pleasure pass before his soul they leave upon it different pictures and the result of these combined impressions is what is called a man's character'. In other words, Swamiji says that each of our experiences leaves an impression on our mind and the sum total of these impressions constitutes a man's character. Further our thoughts also would greatly influence us and shape our character. 'We are what our thoughts have made us, says Swamiji, Thoughts are very powerful. They mould our personality. We should be very careful about our thoughts. Character is repeated habits. Repeated habits alone can reform character. And how these habits are formed? Our thoughts lead to words. Words lead to actions. Action leads to habits. Swamiji says habits form a man's character. Ultimately this character leads to his personality and finally his destiny. Thus a man's rise and fall, success and failure and fame and shame depend upon his character. This is the reason

Swamiji attaches much importance to the formation of character. And he wants such man making, character building education ought to be imparted to the Indian youth. 'We want that education by which character is formed, strength of mind is increased, the intellect is expanded and by which one can stand on one's own feet', proclaims Swamiji.

Man-Making Education

Swamijii is also very clear as to what is not education. He categorically declares 'Education is not the amount of information that is put into your brain and runs riot there, undigested, all your life. We must have life-building, man making, character-making assimilation of ideas. What is happening today in schools and colleges is just 'information overload'. Hour after hour and year after year, the young minds are just stuffed with information and data. There is no freedom given to them to be creative or to think differently. Thus, it is seen that Swamiji's focus is on transformation of youth by way of character building and mind development which he calls as 'man-making'. 'We should give positive ideas. Negative thoughts only weaken men'. 'If you can give them positive ideas people will grow up to men and learn to stand on their own legs. Parents, elders and teachers should always instill hope in the minds of children. Their words should always motivate the youth to become adventurous and bold. That is what Sivaji's mother Jija Bai did to make her son one of the greatest icons in the history of India. It is the same thing which was done by Putli Bai, mother of the father of our nation, which made M.K. Gandhi as Mahatma Gandhi. 'The end of all education, all training should be man making. The end and aim of all training is to make the man grow. It is man making religion that we want. It is man making education all round that we want. Swamiji called upon the youth to become strong. 'Be strong, my young friends, that is my advice to you….you will understand the Gita better with your biceps, your muscles, a little stronger. Swamiji said, 'strength is life and weakness death. Every single word of Swamiji is a dynamo. Even the most timid child will become a hero, if he is exposed to Swamiji's wonderful speeches and writings.

He exhorted the youth of the country to do something heroic. 'We want infinite energy, infinite zeal, infinite courage and infinite patience, only then will great things be achieved. Swamiji does not want the young men and women of India to become fatalists. For him, everything is possible for every man and woman. He thunders 'It is the coward and the fool who says, "This is fate"— so says the Sanskrit proverb. But, it is the strong man who stands up and says," I will make my fate".

Man, the Maker of his Destiny

Swamiji firmly believed that every man writes his own destiny. 'We are responsible for what we are, and whatever we wish ourselves to be, we have the power to make ourselves'. 'Our past created the present and our future is created by our present actions. Therefore, it is within our own hands to shape our destiny. He did not want to us to blame fate or God for the problems we face in our life. We should take responsibility for our life. 'Take the whole responsibility on your own shoulders, and know that you are the creator of your own destiny. The entire success you want is within yourselves'. He felt sad that many of us are groping in the dark without having any fixed goal in life. We are fretting and fuming not realising the fact the power is within us to solve all problems and to grow. Swamiji said 'We can overcome the difficulty by constant practice'. He said 'Purity, patience and perseverance are the three essentials too success and above all-love'. Whether it is Abraham Lincoln or Abdul Kalam, every great man rose to his height of fame and glory only by dint of hard work and perseverance.

How to Achieve Success

Swamiji honestly believed that man is capable of achieving anything in this world; such is the power of human mind. Strong will power, commitment and hard work will enable every man to achieve his goal. "Take up one idea. 'Make that one idea your life- think of it, dream of it, and live on that idea. Let the brain, muscles, nerves, every part of your body, be full of that idea and just leave every other idea alone. That is the way to success" says Swamiji. Knowledge is essential for success in this world and Swamiji says that all the knowledge in the world has been gained only by concentration. According to Swamiji, the main difference between men and the animals is the difference in their power of concentration. And Swamiji also declares that all success in any line of work is the result of this concentration. 'Excellence is a habit,' said a great philosopher. Swamiji echoes the same idea and says that whatever we do we should devote our whole mind, heart and soul to it. In other words success presupposes strong determination, dedication and commitment.

Conclusion

Education is understood today as the process of converting a child into a money making machine. The focus is on information and not transformation of mind. The consequences are a significant rise in white collar crimes, home for the aged, mind boggling psycho-somatic diseases and other social and economic problems. On the contrary, Swami Vivekananda envisaged a man making, mind developing and character building education. Swamiji firmly believed that every man writes of his own destiny. Man is responsible for both his success and failure. Everything is possible for man. To succeed in life, there should be strong will power, perseverance and faith in oneself. Parents, teachers and all those responsible for the welfare of the youth should do their best to facilitate this character building and mind development of the young minds under their care.

Reference

- The Complete Works of Swami Vivekananda, Vol. IV, 1972, p. 358.
- The Complete Works of Swami Vivekananda, Vol. I, 1972, p. 422.
- The Complete Works of Swami Vivekananda, Vol. I, 1972, p. 27.
- The Complete Works of Swami Vivekananda, Vol. VII, 1972, p. 14.
- The Complete Works of Swami Vivekananda, Vol. V, 1972, p. 342.
- The Complete Works of Swami Vivekananda, Vol. III, 1972, p. 302.

45

A Positive Approach to Character and Cultivation of Mind

C. Renuga Devi

Education is not the amount of information that is put into your brain and runs riot there, undigested all your life. We must have life-building, man making, character making and assimilation of ideas. We want that education by which character is formed, strength of mind is increased, the intellect is expanded and by which one can stand on one's own feet. — *Swami Vivekananda*

Introduction

Swami Vivekananda (1863-1902), a great thinker and reformer of India, embraces education, which for him signifies 'man-making', as the very mission of his life. Swamiji belongs to the class of prophets, who appear on our planet from time to time to restate the life giving, eternal values that sustain human progress, societies and civilisations. He was aware of his own stature in history and hence felt no hesitation in making that the highly significant and startling statement: "I have a message to the West as Buddha had a message to the East." — CW, Vol. 5, p. 314" He was not a classroom teacher, but was one of the great teachers of mankind, whose teachings contains the principles and philosophy which are the basis of all good educational systems. Swamiji's fundamental educational ideas are imparting life-building, man-making and character-building education by combining the best elements of the East and the West. He envisioned an educational system wherein the rich cultural and spiritual heritage of our country with its hoary tradition of values like inherent equality, divinity in all beings, unity in diversity, sacredness of knowledge, Shraddha, devotion to truth, chastity, humility, respect for elders, would be blended with modern science, and predominantly western values like scientific temper, rationality of outlook, fearless and objective investigation into the nature of the physical world, technological skill, work efficiency, team work. Swamiji's concept of education is as broad based as life. He pointed that renunciation consists in giving up the lower life for the higher, and that all worthwhile achievements owe to sustained and determined effort. To him education plays vital role in curing the evils in society, and it is critical in shaping the future of humanity. He said, "Educate, educate, than this there is no other way." — CW, Vol. 7, p. 146"

Vivekananda realises that mankind is passing through crisis. The tremendous emphasis on the scientific and mechanical ways of life is fast reducing man to the status of a machine. Moral and ethical values that derive their sanction from spiritual nature of man are being undermined due to materialistic outlook of life. The fundamental principles of civilisation are being ignored. Conflicts of ideals, manners and habits are pervading the atmosphere. Disregard for everything old is the fashion of the day. Vivekananda seeks the solutions of all these social and global evils through education. With this end in view, he feels the dire need of awakening man to his spiritual self, wherein he thinks, lies the very purpose of education. "I look upon religion as the innermost core of education", said Swamiji - CW, Vol. 5, P: 232". Because he knew that "an ethical code, derived from religion and spirituality has the whole of infinite man for its scope. It takes up the individual … and it takes up society … in whatever condition it may be at any given time. Thus we see that there is always the necessity of spiritual religion for mankind… CW, Vol. 2, p. 64"

The Aims

Under the present system, boys and girls go to schools and colleges, and follow a syllabus which has been preset. The teachers, who rarely possess hands-on experience in practical application of what they teach, prepare lessons based on the prescribed syllabus and only act as carrier of convey to the pupils all the information they gather. Since what is conveyed is not based on understanding born out of experience or assimilation, consequently, the purpose of education is confined only for passing examinations and acquiring degrees and diplomas. This, Swamiji termed as "Mere book - learning- CW, Vol. 5, p. 342" The result is the information undigested in their minds and their lives do not reflect any evidence of their learning. Unfortunately, this is true of even practical sciences such as health, hygiene, dietetics, nutrition and engineering, It is not surprising that all progressive thinkers and educationists have condemned this type of education.

While acquisition of knowledge is important, the moulding of our lives on sound lines is a more important purpose of education. Man has created new horizons for himself by expanding the fields of knowledge. Those who have contributed to the widening of his horizon have been men of character and strength, men who could face odds and difficulties, and dare dangers and sufferings for the ideal for which they lived. The quintessence of all education should be to produce such men. This is what Swami Vivekananda called, 'Man-making education - CW, Vol. 3, P 301'. He said, 'Education is not the amount of information that is out into your brain and runs riot there, undigested all your life- CW, Vol. 3, p. 302'. He further said, "We must have life-building, man-making, character-making assimilation of ideas- CW, Vol. 3, p. 301."

Vivekananda points out that the defect of the present-day education is that it has no definite goal to pursue. A sculptor has a clear idea about what he wants to shape out of the marble block; similarly, a painter knows what he is going to paint. But a teacher, he says, has no clear idea about the goal of his teaching.

He prepares the scheme of this man-making education in the light of his over-all philosophy of Vedanta. According to Vedanta, the essence of man lies in his soul, which he possesses in addition to his body and mind. In tune with this philosophy, Swamiji defines "education as 'the manifestation of the perfection already in man. - CW, Vol. 4, p. 358" The aim of education is to manifest in our lives the perfection, which is the very nature of our inner self. For achieving this, one will have to eliminate one's ego, ignorance and all other false identification, which stand in the way. Therefore, man making for him means a harmonious development of the body, mind and soul. (an ideal character that embodies these ideas as ideals to be emulated)

Education for him means that process "by which character is formed, strength of mind is increased, and intellect is expanded, and by which one can stand on one's own feet - CW, Vol. 5, p 342." Consequently, he draws our attention to the fact that "the only duty of the teacher is to remove all obstructions from the way - CW Vol. 4, p. 358." to help the child to manifest its knowledge that is already there. To drive his point home, he refers to the growth of a plant. Just as in the case of a plant, one cannot do anything more than supplying it with water, air and manure while it grows from within its own nature, so is the case with a human child. Vivekananda's method of education resembles the heuristic method of the modern educationists. In this system, the teacher invokes the spirit of inquiry in the pupil who is supposed to find out things for himself under the bias-free guidance of the teacher.

The Positive Approach

In teaching children or in dealing with adults, we should have a positive approach, an approach based on the dignity of and faith in the human personality, Swami Vivekananda said, we should give positive ideas. Negative thoughts only weaken men. If you speak kind words to boys and encourage them, they are bound to improve in time. If you can give positive ideas, people will grow up to be men and learn to stand on their own legs. - CW, Vol. 7, p. 170 (selections)"

The most fruitful approach to life is to have faith and confidence in one's own ability and work. Let every young man and woman be instilled with the great manly thought that he or she is the master of his or her destiny. Hard, intelligent continuous and cooperative work is the gateway to all greatness. When we read the lives of men and women who have contributed towards the progress of human race, we find that they were all indomitable workers, who had refused to accept defeat. It is necessary that our minds are trained to follow this royal road to success. Therefore let us cultivate faith in hard, systematic work.

In the cultivation of these positive qualities, the cooperation of three agencies plays a vital role, namely the family, the school and the community. In the family, first come the mother and the father. The child gets his first ideas and attitudes. If both stress the same qualities and kinds of behaviour, the child gets the strength to follow them without doubt or confusion.

While the influence of parents is supreme during childhood, as the child advances he is open to the influence of school, teacher and his schoolmates. The teacher holds dominant position since he contributes substantially toward the creation of atmosphere in the school. Therefore, all philosophers of education lay the greatest stress on good teacher. The teacher should emphasise by percept as well as by his conduct the value of positive qualities of love, cooperation, hard work and faith.

Character Building

Swami Vivekananda realised three things are necessary to make every man great, every nation great:

- Conviction of the powers of goodness.
- Absence of jealousy and suspicion.
- Helping all who are trying to be and do good

The exposition and analysis of Vivekananda's scheme of education brings to light its constructive, practical and comprehensive character. Swami Vivekananda wanted that we give up jealousy and conceit and learn to work united. He told, purity, patience and perseverance overcome all obstacles. He further suggested that patience and steady work, is the only way to get success. According to Swami Vivekananda "faith, faith, faith in ourselves, faith, faith in God - this is the secret of greatness - CW, Vol. 3, p. 190". He observed "the history of the world is the history of a few men who had faith in themselves. "That faith calls out divinity within. CW, Vol. 8, p. 228"

Swami Vivekananda said: "The character of any man is the aggregate of his tendencies, the sum total of the bent of his mind. As pleasure and pain pass before his soul, they leave upon it different pictures and the result of these combined impressions is what is called a man's character. We are what our thoughts have made us. So take care of what you think. Each thought is a little hammer blow on our minds, manufacturing out of it what we want it to be". Words are secondary but thoughts live, they travel far. - CW, Vol. 1, p. 27; Vol. 7, p. 14 and 20"

In the words of Swamiji, again, in shaping our minds, good and evil have equal share. In moulding character, misery and hardship have been greater teachers than happiness. Comparing the mind to a lake, Swamiji said that every ripple, every wave that rises there, when subsiding, does not die out entirely, but leaves a mark with the possibility of that mark coming out again in the future. Likewise every deed we do, every movement we make, every thought we think, leaves an impression on the mind such that when even it is not obvious on the surface, it is sufficiently strong to work beneath the surface subconsciously. What are at any moment is determined by the sum total of these impressions on the mind. Each man's character is determined by sum total of these impressions. The man ultimately becomes a tool in the hands of these impressions.

High ideals of national life must be held up before our boys and girls. They must be reminded of their duties to the country. This is all the more necessary today when education has come virtually to be interpreted as a means to earning bread. Our educational system should have in it also the elements to inspire higher and nobler qualities in addition to being a means to livelihood. In this age of science and material power, thinkers on education have all agreed on the need for the cultivation or character, since power, unless properly directed, may lead to hatred, jealousy and conflict. Hence, there is need for evolving a system of education which would mould character and further spiritual qualities. Why so? Because "it is religion that has been made a secondary concern, hence those defects have crept in." - CW, Vol. 7, p. 213 in our education system.

Character-building was fundamental in Vivekananda's educational scheme, as against career-orientation, which occupies centre-stage in today's education. A person is what his thoughts have made him. That is why one finds that the focus of the Swami's educational thoughts was on assimilation of man-making, character building ideas. Everything a person does, every thought, every move, leaves an impression on the mind. Even when it is not outwardly apparent, it is strong enough to work beneath the surface. A person's character is determined by the sum total of these impressions.

When a large number of these impressions come together, they form a habit. This then becomes a powerful force, for character is but repeated habits. This is why, through the acquisition and repetition of desirable habits, one's character can be remodelled. The people one associates with, good or bad, contribute much to the development of one's character. In fact, their impact is greater than that of didactic teaching. That is why Swami Vivekananda said: 'Words, even thoughts, contribute only one-third of the influence in making an impression, the man, two-thirds' CW, Vol. 2, p. 14. He therefore desired that the teacher's life and personality should be like a blazing fire could have a positive influence on the pupils in his care. Exposure to exemplary role models, particularly when they are teachers, and also to wholesome curriculum materials that impart culturally-approved values to the young, are critical to character education.

Character-building education might focus on teaching what is right and wrong. But simultaneously, or alternatively, it should teach how to decide what is right and wrong. It has been rightly argued that participation in discussions of morality is more instructive than simply hearing about it. In any case, however, the teachers should be moral exemplars if the classroom and the school are to serve as arenas for the teaching of ethics. The students then have the experience of being part of a group of people who take moral values seriously, and this helps them imbibe moral values spontaneously.

The present education system has overemphasised the cultivation of the intellect at the cost of the general well-being of humanity. To check this dangerous trend, Vivekananda strongly recommended all-round development of human beings. And the Swamiji expected that the education systems would be suitably designed to produce such wholesome human beings. Interestingly, the UNESCO report in 1972, while defining the aim of education, echoed this same idea. It reads: 'The physical, the intellectual, emotional and ethical integration of the individual into a complete man is a broad definition of the fundamental aim of education.'

Cultivation of Mind

Swami Vivekananda says: there is only one method by which to attain knowledge, that which is called concentration. The very essence of education is concentration of mind. The more the power of concentration, the greater the knowledge that is acquired. In doing anything - such as thinking, working with the hands, etc., the better the power of concentration the better the outcome will be. Training the mind to concentrate on a specific subject has several stages:

- The primary one being learning how to collect the mind and preventing it from running hither and thither. The student trains his mind to be more attentive and more 'mindful'.
- Next, the student must learn how to detach his mind from distractions that impose themselves in spite of him.
- Then, simultaneously, he must direct the mind on to the desired subject and focus the full force of his mind on it. To give an example: a convex lens gathers sunlight and focuses it on one point to burn a piece of paper.

Likewise, when a mind becomes concentrated, it acquires tremendous power and unlock the mysteries of subject it is focused upon. Swamiji observes from analysing the external nature, man is led to analyse the internal; the questioning of internal man comes with higher state of civilisation, with deeper insight into nature, with higher state of growth. Then only the true dimension of his personality gets revealed. The personality of the man is two-thirds, and his intellect, his words, are but one-third. It is the real man, the personality of the man, that runs through us. The ideal of all education, all training, should be this man-making. The man who influence, who throws his magic, as it were, upon his fellow-beings, is a dynamo of power, and when that man is ready, he can do anything and everything he likes; that personality put upon anything will make it work.

Sublimation is the process by which man redirects his natural impulses, desires and emotions into higher thinking when activities are raised from lower to higher levels of integration and when there is harmony in that process the resulting behaviour is sublimation. Educationists are familiar with the process through which undesirable traits of children are transformed into desirable qualities. Thus a child who is destructively active may be directed along constructive workmanship. This great sublimation of human mind can be attained through selfless work, (karma-yoga), through love (bhakti-yoga), through spiritual contemplation (Raja-yoga) and through knowledge (Jnana-yoga).

What Can be Learnt?

"What is education? Is it book learning? No. Is it diverse knowledge? Not even that. The training by which the current and expression of will are brought under control and become fruitful is called education. - CW, Vol. 4, p. 490"

Education is regarded as basic infrastructure for an all-round development of a country. Indeed, it is integrally linked with the development process. In the post-Independence era, the Education Policy of the Government of India has been so framed as would provide Free and Compulsory Education to all children at least up to the elementary stage. The National Policy on Education-1986 recognised the need for literate population and provision of elementary education as a crucial input for nation building. The Programme of Action (1992) envisaged the Government of India provide education of satisfactory quality to children up to 14 years of age before the twenty-first century.

In contrast to the contemporary system of education, Vivekananda advocated education that combined eastern and western view. Education according to Western educationalists, aims at man's mastery of external environment. According to the Indian philosophical tradition, true education is mastery of internal nature. Mastery of external nature is confined to a narrow sphere, as an aid to internal enquiry. But Swamiji said that both the views are one-sided. "We talk foolishly against material civilisation. -CW, Vol. 4, p. 368". "A nation that cannot provide for its simple food and clothing, which always depends on others for its subsistence — what is there for it to vaunt about? People of foreign countries are turning out such golden results from the raw materials produced in your country, and you, like asses of burden, are only carrying their load. The people of foreign countries import Indian raw goods, manufacture various commodities by bringing their intelligence to bear upon them, and become great; whereas you have locked up your intelligence, thrown away your inherited wealth to others, and roam about crying piteously for food - CW, Vol. 7, p. 146". But the application of science and technology he talked about imparting to our people was to make them:

- Entrepreneurs, not job seekers: "Give me employment. Trampled under others' feet doing slavery for others, are you men anymore? Within you lies indomitable power - CW, Vol. 7, p. 146
- The knowledge should enrich village level professions. So, he said that, "I do not mean that we should follow this profession (agriculture) as the ignorant farmers of our country do. We have to learn the science of it, and apply that knowledge to the development of our agriculture. We have to work like intelligent people, after acquiring the necessary knowledge." One of anti-nationalistic trend of modern education is the brain drain from villages to cities because the education imparted to students is practical only in cities apart from other benefits that tempts a villager to a city life. Hence, Swamiji was pained to observe that "no sooner do the village boys read a book or two of English than they run to the cities. In the village they may have plenty of land, but they do not feel satisfied. They want to enjoy city-life and enter service……….The inclination to go to the cities is noticeable among the villagers. A farmer's son, after getting a little education, leaves his ancestral profession, goes to the city, and takes a job under the white men- Life, CW, Vol. 1, p. 274"
- Hence Swamiji had given a very practical proposal to strengthen the village guilds that, in his time, were caste bound. "Even with the awakening of knowledge, the potter will remain a potter, the fisherman a fisherman, the peasant a peasant. Why should they leave their hereditary calling?—don't give up the work to which you were born, even if it be attended with defects. If they are taught in this way, why should they give up their respective callings? Rather they will apply their knowledge to the better performance of the work to which they have been born. - CW, Vol. 7, p. 149. He was confident that if the village boys are trained in the use of science and use of technology, "a number of geniuses are sure to arise from among them in the course of time. - CW, Vol. 7, p. 146"

Even today, the vocational training offered in most of organisations are based meant for clientele that lives in dense population and hence, the trainees such programmes, generally seeks jobs in cites or towns. Hence, Swamiji's idea of improving socio-economic status of traditional village guilds can still be implemented by the Government and this will help in arresting the migration of villagers to towns.

The second vital idea of Swamiji yet to see the light of the day is his insistence that students be taught the fundamental truth about the Self.

Knowledge does not come from outside. It is discovered with the individual in the self, which is the source of all knowledge. According to Vivekananda, the function of education is the uncovering of knowledge hidden in our mind. The role of education is to kindle the fire of enquiry so that the latent perfection is manifested. Because, "you can supply the growing seed with the materials for the making up of its body, bringing to it the earth, the water, the air, that it wants. It will take all that it wants by its own nature, it will assimilate and grow by its own nature. - CW, Vol. 3, p. 247". So education should equip them with proper environment to facilitate the process of enquiry leading to self discovery.

The most fundamental component of that environment is religious teaching. Not fundamentalist's concept of religion but the vital, life-giving precepts without which no one can be rationally asked to be moral, ethical and feel the necessity for sacrificing their lives for any worthy cause. True strength, character, self-belief cannot be expected if this vital input is withheld in our education. ... "Never were they allowed to hear of the Atman. Let them hear of the Atman it is a man-making religion that we want. It is man-making theories that we want. It is man-making education all round that we want." CW, Vol. 3, p. 224 (Selections) How to know what should be taught and what not in religion? Swamiji knew that most people identify religion with "occultism and mysticism- these creepy things" that "have nearly destroyed us." So, he said that, "here is the test of truth—anything that makes you weak physically, intellectually, and spiritually, reject as poison; there is no life in it, it cannot be true. Truth is strengthening. Truth is purity, truth is all-knowledge; truth must be strengthening, must be enlightening, must be invigorating. Go back to your Upanishads—the shining, the strengthening, the bright philosophy - and part from all these mysterious things, all these weakening things. Take up this philosophy; the greatest truths are the simplest things in the world, simple as your own existence. The truths of the Upanishads are before you. Take them up, live up to them, and the salvation of India will be at hand." CW, Vol. 3, p. 224 (selections). That is why Swamiji said that, "we must have a hold on the spiritual and secular education of the nation. ..... Till then there is no salvation for the race. - CW, Vol. 3, p. 301"

Unfortunately, in the name of not to offend the sentiments of minority communities in India, we lack the political will to incorporate such religious components in our curriculum. But, it is forgotten that religions do contain elements of these great truths in varying proportions. What is needed is formation of an advisory committee that will contain liberal religious leaders of all denominations to form such a curriculum. This step will be a giant leap in developing inter-faith understanding conducive for national harmony. Whosoever takes this initiative will have his name engraved in golden letters in the history of India is our opinion. Vivekananda supported the idea that everyone has to grow as per their natural propensities. No one has to copy others. External pressure only creates destructive reactions leading to stubbornness and disorderliness. In an atmosphere of freedom, love and sympathy alone, the child will develop courage and self-reliance. He should be talked to stand on his own, to be himself. Each child should be given opportunities to develop according to his own inner nature. Freedom is the first requirement for self development. The child should be given freedom to grow according to his own nature. The teacher should not exert any type of pressure on the child. The child should be helped in solving his problems himself. The teachers should have an attitude of service and worship.

To Swamiji, education plays vital role in curing the evils in society, and it is critical in shaping the future of humanity. Thus, these three concepts - capacity, propensity and capability - emphasise three aspects of education, respectively: (a) that which makes learning possible; (b) the development of learning; and (c) self-development or self-empowerment.

A child has many potentials of variable worth, and they may create mental conflict within him. Therefore, he has to learn to choose which he should try to develop, and which he should minimise, counter or ignore. Then again, as his chosen potentials start to unfold, they should be supervised in order to achieve their harmonious and purposeful development.

A person's inherent power will spontaneously manifest itself when external and internal obstacles, if any, are removed at the proper time by the teachers or the education system. Such obstacles are of various kinds. External obstacles might be in the form of unfair distribution of educational resources and opportunities, inequalities in economic development and socio-political instability; whereas internal obstacles might have to do with the dynamics of the education system, such as the teacher/student relationship, the student's capacity to make personal judgements or to adapt to changes, and the student's mental or physical capacities.

In order to tackle these obstacles, the education system should take on two responsibilities: (i) it should help a person build a healthy and dynamic frame of mind to enable him to meet the challenges of life; and (ii) it should try to prevent, through proper training of its present students, any future evils in people and society which are likely to further complicate the problems of human beings. At the same time, however, the teachers and the designers of education systems must always keep in mind the Vedantic idea that whatsoever good or bad impressions a mind carries, a human being is essentially pure and divine, and a repository of immense possibilities.

In Swami Vivekananda's view, educational concerns related to a person's interaction with society should receive due attention. The purpose of society is to help secure the well-being of human beings. In reality, however, human beings frequently find themselves entrapped in a society that threatens their freedom, a freedom essential for their educational growth. An ideal society, according to Swami Vivekananda, should provide the resources as well as the opportunity for each of its members to develop his or her potential to the maximum. Education must embrace the whole society, with special attention to those who are most in need of it and who, for one reason or another, are unable to avail themselves of the existing facilities. Swami Vivekananda felt that alienation of any kind from the masses of society, who are mostly poor - whether it be alienation through learning, through wealth or through force of arms — weakens the leadership of a country. Therefore, for a sustainable regeneration of India, if not for anything else, top priority must be given to educating the masses and restoring to them their lost individuality. They should not only be given education to make them self-reliant, but also ideas, moral training and an understanding of their own historical situation so that they can work out their own salvation. Furthermore, they must be given culture, without which there can be no hope for their long-term progress.

Swami Vivekananda was the first Indian leader who sought a solution to the problems of the poor and the weak, through education. He argued that a nation was advanced to the extent that education and culture reached the masses. Unless there was uniform circulation of national blood all over the body, the nation could not rise. He insisted that it was the duty of the upper classes, who had received their education at the expense of the poor, to come forward and uplift the poor through education and other means. In fact, the Swami's mission was for the poor. He once said, 'there must be equal chance for all - or if greater for some and for some less - the weaker should be given more chance than the strong'.

Training the mind: Swami Vivekananda concurred with contemporary thinkers when he asserted that the mind-the chief instrument of learning - deserves more attention than it had earlier received.

Similarly, Swami Vivekananda observed that through education, a child learns a culture and his behaviour is moulded accordingly, and he is thus guided towards his eventual role in society. In this process, several agents - such as his parents, peers and teachers - assist him. But nowadays, as formal education has become more and more institutionalised, teachers are expected to play a more significant role. A teacher needs to help a student learn how to think, what to think, how to discriminate and how to appreciate things. This is not just a matter of intellectual manipulation. This kind of teaching requires moral conviction and the courage to continuously pursue one's own course at all costs. The teacher must not only possess the knowledge he is to transmit to the student, but he must also know how to transmit it. And, in addition to the content of teaching, what the teacher gives or transfers, to be truly effective, must possess some other elements. For instance, the teacher should share with the student the conviction that they are both truly one in Spirit—at the same time cultivating in the student a feeling of dignity and self-respect.

As Swami Vivekananda said: "The only true teacher is he who can immediately come down to the level of the student, and transfer his soul to the student's soul and see through the student's eyes and hear through his ears and understand through his mind". Such a teacher can really teach and none else.

In order to rectify the defects in the existing system, man's limited view of himself, on which the existing system of education is based, needs to be reconsidered. A human being is not simply a composite of body and mind. He is something more. People's minds are not directed to higher pursuits of life with the result that their hidden potentials are not revealed. Only when wisdom, peace, strength, unselfishness, loving concern for others and other virtues become evident is a person transformed from a sensuous being to a true human being.

A tremendous explosion of knowledge, without commensurate wisdom, plus immense power not tempered with discrimination, has made education today a potential source of danger. This is a serious problem looming large on humanity's horizon. As Swami Vivekananda observed "Intellect has been cultured with the result that hundreds of sciences have been discovered, and their effect has been that the few have made slaves of the many - that is all the good that has been done. Artificial wants have been created; and every poor man, whether he has money or not, desires to have those wants satisfied, and when he cannot, he struggles, and dies in the struggle (CW, Vol. I, p. 414)."

In order to counterbalance this uneven development, Vivekananda strongly recommended the adoption of a 'spiritual and ethical culture'.

Conclusion

Swami Vivekananda had envisioned a society with a new type of human being in whom knowledge, action, work and concentration were harmoniously blended, and he proposed a new type of education for achieving this. The right to education for everyone, guaranteed by the Constitution of India, was Swami Vivekananda's dream, but it is still a far cry from its goal. His idea of continual, or lifelong, education, however, has been adopted in many countries already. It is remarkable the extent to which there are similarities between Swamiji's thoughts and actions taking place one century ago and the present concerns ofUNESCO.

- His commitment towards universal values and tolerance, his active identification with humanity as a whole.
- The struggle in favour of the poor and destitute, to reduce poverty and to eliminate discrimination against women - reaching the unreached.
- His vision of education, science and culture as the essential instruments of human development.
- That education should be a lifelong process.
- And the need to move away from rote learning.

The lack of basic necessities among the underprivileged all over the world is no less striking than the lack of morality among the educated privileged ones. To squarely meet this great challenge, Vivekananda prescribed 'man-making and character-building education'.

In order to build up a strong nation that will lead the world towards peace and harmony, we have to give serious thought to Swami Vivekananda's philosophy of education and remember his call to everybody, "The infinite strength of the world is yours. Drive out the superstition that has covered your minds. Let us be brave. Know the truth and practice the Truth. The goal may be distant, but awake, arise, and stop not till the goal is reached".

References

- Avinashilinagham, T.S. (1997). Educational Philosophy of Swami Vivekananda. 5th ed. Coimbatore: Sri Ramakrishna Mission Vidyalaya.
- Banga, C. (2011, October 2). CLBANGA EDUCATION. Role of Swami Vivekananda's man making education in present educational system in India http://profchamanlalbanga.blogspot.in/2011/10/role-of-swami-vivekanandas-man-making.html retrieved 12.02.13.
- Prabhananda, Swami (June 2003), "Profiles of famous educators: Swami Vivekananda", Prospects (Netherlands: Springer) XXXIII (2): 235-247 http://www.ibe.unesco.org/fileadmin/user_upload/archive/publications/ThinkersPdf/vivekane.pdf retrieved on 12.02.13.
- Roy, S. (2001) Education in the vision of Swami Vivekananda http://www.esamskriti.com/essay-chapters/Education-in-the-Vision-of-Swami Vivekananda-1.aspx retrieved on 12.02.13.

46

Character and Cultivation of Mind

B. Kalaivani

Introduction

> *"We want that education by which character is formed, strength of mind is increased, the intellect is expanded, and by which one can stand on one's own feet.* — *Swami Vivekananda*

Mother India had given birth to certain glorious sons in her gloomy moments. Swami Vivekananda was one among them. Swamiji was one of the greatest educationalists of India. Swamiji, the great spiritual luminary, thinker, and patriot - prophet of our times, had many deep and insightful ideas on education. His guru, Sri Ramakrishna used to say that manush needs to become man-hush- that is, a man needs to become a true man. 'He alone is a man' he said, whose spiritual consciousness has been awakened. Following his master, Swamiji emphasised that "the ideal of all education, all training, should be this man-making". Lamenting over the prevailing system of education, he said: "But, instead of that, we are always trying to polish up the outside. What use in polishing up the outside when there is no inside? The end and aim of all training is to make the man grow". In this context, M.K. Gandhi said, "the end of all knowledge must be building up character".

Character

Everything a person does, every thought, even more, leaves an impression on the mind. Even when it is not outwardly apparent, it is strong enough to work beneath the surface. A person's character is determined by the sum of total of these impressions. When a large number of impressions come together, they form a habit. This then becomes a powerful force, for character is but repeated habits. This is why, through the acquisition and repetition of desirable habits, one's characters can be recommended.

If you really want to judge the character of a man, look not at his great performances. Every fool may become a hero at one time or another. Watch a man do his most common actions; those are indeed the things which will tell you the real character of a great man. Great occasions rouse even the lowest of human beings to some kind of greatness, but he alone is the really great man whose character is great always, the same whenever he is.

The character of any man, it really is but the aggregate of tendencies, the sum of total of the bent of his mind. As pleasure and pain pass before his soul, they leave upon it different pictures, and the result of these combined impressions is what is called a man's character. It is said, 'Habit is second nature', it is first nature also, and the whole nature of man, everything that we are is the result of habit. That gives us consolation, because, if it is only habit, we can make and unmake it any time. The only remedy for bad habits is counter habits all the bad habits that have left their impressions are to be controlled by good habits. Go on doing good, thinking holy thoughts continuously that is the only way to suppress base impressions. Never say any man is hopeless, because he only represents a character, a bundle of habits, which can be checked by new and better ones. Character is repeated habits, and repeated habits alone can reform character.

Good and evil have an equal share in moulding character and in some cases, misery is a greater teacher than happiness. Every word that we do, every movement of the body, every thought we think leaves such an impression on the mind - stuff, and even when such impressions are not obvious on the surface, they are sufficiently strong to work beneath the surface subconsciously.

Each man's character is determined by the sum total of these impressions. If good impressions prevail, the character becomes good, if bad it comes bad. If a man continuously hears bad words, thinks bad thoughts, does bad actions, his mind will be full of bad impressions, and they will influence his thought and work without his being conscious of the fact.

Similarly, if a man thinks good thoughts and does good work, the sum total of these impressions will be good and they in a similar manner will force him to do good inspite of himself. When a man has done so much good work and thought so many good thoughts, there is irresistible tendency in him to do good. Even if he wishes to do evil, his mind, as the sum total of his tendencies will not allow him to do so.

Education

Education is not the amount of information that is put into your brain and runs riot there, undigested, all your life. We must have life-building, man-making, character-making assimilation of ideas. If you have assimilated five ideas and made them your life and character, you have more education than any man who has got by heart a whole library.

Character Building

Character building was fundamental in Vivekananda's educational scheme, as against career-orientation, which occupies centre - stage in today's education. A person is what his thoughts have made him. Explaining this, the swami said, "Each thought is a little hammer blow on the lump of iron which our bodies are, manufacturing out of it what we want it to be. That is why one finds that the focus of the swami's educational thoughts was on assimilation of man-making, character building ideas.

Character building education might focus on teaching what is right and wrong. But simultaneously, or alternatively, it should teach how to decide what is right and wrong. It has been rightly argued that participation in discussions of morality is more instructive than simply hearing about it. In any case, however, the teachers should be moral examples of the class room, and the schools are to serve as arenas for the teaching of ethics. The students then have the experience of being part of a group of people who take moral values seriously, and this helps them imbibe moral values spontaneously.

The people one associates with—good or bad—contribute much to the development of one's character. In fact, their impact is greater than that of didiactic teaching. That is why Swamiji: words even thoughts, contribute only one - third of the influence in making an impression, the man, two thirds! He therefore desired that the teacher's life and personality should be like a blazing fire which would have a positive influence on the pupils in his care. Exposure to exemplary role models, particularly when they are teachers and also to wholesome curriculum materials that impact culturally - approved values to the young, are critical to character education.

The Present Education System

The present education system has overemphasised the cultivation of the intellect at the cost of the general well-being of humanity. To check this dangerous trend, Swamiji strongly recommended all-around development of human beings. In one of his lectures, he expressed the desire that all men were so constituted that in their minds all these elements of philosophy, mysticism emotion and of work were equally present in full. That is the ideal, my ideal of a perfect man.

Swamiji expected that the education systems would be suitably designed to produce such wholesome human beings. Interestingly. The UNESCO Report-1972, while defining the aim of education, echoed this same idea. It reads "The physical, the intellectual, emotional and ethical integration of the individual into a complete man is a broad definition of the fundamental aim of education (Edger Faure et.al, 1972).

Vivekananda's Aims of Education

Vivekananda wanted all-round development of education to heart and mind, to strengthen character and national consciousness, to help in the cultivation of strength and stir feelings of kindness and sympathy. He emphatically said,

> "We want that education by which character is formed, strength of mind is increased, the intellect is expanded and by which one can

> stand on one's own feet. What our country now wants are muscles of iron and a nerve of steel, gigantic wills which nothing can resists, which can penetrate into the mysteries and secrets of the universe and will accomplish their purpose in any fashion, even if it means going down to the bottom of the ocean, meeting death face to face. It is man-making religion that we want. It is man-making theories that we want. It is man-making education that we want.

The prime aim of education is to achieve the full perfection already present in a child. According to Vivekananda, all the materials and spiritual knowledge are already present in the individuals mind, but it is covered by certain ignorance. The second aim of education is the physical and mental development of the child. "For stressing the mental development of the child, Swamiji, wished education to enable the child to stand on his own legs economically rather than becoming a parasite on others (Singh, 2007). The third aim of education is the character development of the child. In the fourth aim of education, he emphasises the religious development.

Training the Mind

Vivekananda concurred with contemporary thinkers when he asserted that the mind — the chief instrument of learning - deserves more attention than it had earlier received. Training the mind should be a student's highest priority, and not simply the accumulation, the memorising and the repeating facts. In the long run, stuffing one's mind with information, technical skills and useless trivia only creates more problems if one's mind is not nourished and strengthened and made healthy. Yet training of the mind in all its aspects is conspicuously absent in today's education.

Learning to concentrate the mind was the focus in the swami's scheme. He said : "To me the very essence of education is concentration of mind, not the collecting of facts (CW. Vol. VI, p. 38). In doing anything - such as thinking, working with the hands extra. The better the power of concentration the better the outcome will be. And this power of keeping the mind on the task can be improved. Training the mind to concentrate on a specific subject has several stages, the primary one being learning how to collect the mind and preventing it from running hither and thither. The student trains his mind to be more attentive and more mindful.

Next, the student must learn how to detach his mind from distractions that impose themselves in spite of him. Then simultaneously, he must direct the mind on to the desired subject and focus the full force of his mind on it. To give an example: a convex lens gathers sunlight and focusses it on one point to burn a piece of paper. Likewise, when a mind becomes concentrated, it acquires tremendous power and is able to unlock the mysteries of the subject it is focused upon.

Similarly, Swamiji also wanted students to cultivate will power. According to him, will-power is developed when the current and expression of will are brought under control and become fruitful (CW. Vol. IV, p. 490). Will-power is necessary not only to conduct the learning, but also strengthen one's character.

Conclusion

There have been many changes in the field of education since Swamiji passed away one hundred years ago, but not as many changes as in other areas of society. One such noticeable change in education is that it is now engaged in preparing human beings for a new type of society and it is trying to create a new type of human being. Interestingly, Swami Vivekananda had envisioned a society with a new type of human being in whom knowledge, action, work and concentration were harmoniously blended and he proposed a new type of education for achieving this.

"Education is the manifestation of divine
Perfection already existing in man"

— Swami Vivekananda (CW-4.358)

References

- Edgar Faure et al., Learning to be, Paris: UNESCO, 1972, p. 156.
- Singh, Y.K., Philosophical Foundation of Education, New Delhi: APA Publishing Corporation, 2007, p. 233.

47

Education and Character Development

S. Priyadharsini

Introduction

Swami Vivekananda (1863-1902), the great spiritual man, who think creatively ideal indeed can be put into a few words and that is: to preach unto mankind their divinity, and how to make it manifest in every movement of life. According to Swami Vivekananda, "Education is the manifestation of the perfection already in man". The character of any man is but the aggregate of his tendencies, the sum total of the bent of his mind.

Every work that we do, every movement of the body, every thought that we think, bears an impressions on the mind-stuff. What we are every moment is determined by the sum total an impressions on the mind. Every man's character is determined by the sum total of these impressions. If good impressions prevail, the character becomes good, if bad, it becomes bad. If you really want to judge the character of a man, look not at his great performances. Every fool may become a hero at one time or time or another. Watch a man do his most common actions: those are indeed the things which will tell you the real character of a great man. Great occasions rouse even the lowest of human beings to some kind of greatness, but he alone is the really great man whose character is great always, the same wherever he is.

India continues to face stern challenges. Despite growing investment in education, 25 per cent of its population is still illiterate; only 15 per cent of Indian students reach high school, and just seven per cent graduate. The quality of education whether at primary or higher lavel of education is significantly poor as compared with major developing nations.

What Education is?

The training by which the current and expression of will is brought under control and become fruitful is education. Education may be described as a development of faculty, not an accumulation of words, or, as a training of individuals to will rightly and efficiently.

Real education is that which enables one to stand on own one's legs. If you have assimilated five ideas and made them your life and character, you have more education than any man who has got by heart a whole library.

What Education Is Not!

- Is it book-learning? No. Is it diverse knowledge? Not even that.
- Education is not an accumulation of words.
- Education is not the collecting of facts...
- Education is not the amount of information that is put into your brain and runs riot there, undigested all your life.
- If education were identical with information, the libraries would be the greatest sages in the world and encyclopedias the Rishis. Education is not filling the mind with a lot of facts.
- Education as a result of which the will, being continuously choked by force through generations, is now well-nigh killed out; is that education under whose sway even the old ideas, let alone the new ones are disappearing one by one; is that education which is slowly making man a machine?
- The education which does not help the common mass of people to equip themselves for the struggle of life, which does not bring out the strength of character, a spirit of philanthropy, and the courage of a lion—is it worth the name?
- Well, you consider a man as educated, if only he can pass some examinations and deliver good lectures. The present system of education is all wrong. The mind is crammed with facts before it knows how to think. Control of the mind should be taught first.
- The education that you are receiving now in schools and colleges is only making you a race of dyspeptics. You are working like machines merely, and living a jelly-fish existence.
- According to Swamiji, character development is a very important aim of any education. For this, he emphasised the practice of brahmacharya (celebacy) which fosters development of mental, moral and spiritual powers leading to purity of thoughts, words and deeds.

Essence of Education

- Swamiji believed education is the manifestation of perfection already in men. He did not think it a pity that the existing system of education did not enable a person to stand on his own feet, nor did it teach him self-confidence and self-respect.
- To Swamiji, education was not only collection of information, but something more meaningful; he felt education should be man-making, life giving and character-building.
- To him education was an assimilation of noble ideas.
- Education is not the amount of information that we put into your brain and runs riot there, undigested, all your life. We must have life building, man making, and character making assimilation of ideas. If you have assimilated five ideas and made them your life and character,

you have more education than any man who has got by heart a whole library.

Positive Education

Swamiji stressed on giving the public only positive education, because negative thoughts weaken men. He told, if young boys and girls are encouraged and are not unnecessarily criticised all the time, they are bound to improve in time.

In New York, Swamiji used to observe the Irish colonists come - downtrodden, haggard-looking, destitute of possessions at home, penniless, and wooden-headed - with their only belongings, a stick and a bundle of rags hanging at the end, fright in their steps, alarm in their eyes. Swamiji observed a completely different spectacle in next six months-the man walks upright, his attire is changed. In his eyes and steps there is more fright. Swamiji tried to find out the cause, he told, if this incidence is seen by the explanations of Vedanta, that Irishman was kept surrounded by contempt in his own country–the whole of Nature was telling him with one voice — "Pat, you have no more hope, you were born a slave and will remain so". Having been thus told from his birth, Pat started believing in it and hypnotised himself that he is very low. While no sooner had he landed on America than the shout went up on all sided - "Pat, you are a man as we are, it is man who has done all, a man like you and me can do everything; have courage!" Pat raised his head and saw that it was so; the self-confidence within him woke up again. Swamiji feels likewise, the education that young boys and girls receive is very negative. He thinks they do not gain confidence or self-respect from these educations, so according to Swami Vivekananda only positive education should be given to children.

Swamiji's View on: Why Character Building?

- The ideal of all education, all training, should be this man-making. But instead of that, we are always trying to polish up the outside. What use is polishing up the outside when there is no inside? The end and aim of all training is to make the man grow.
- The man who influences, who throws his magic, as it were, upon his fellow-beings, is a dynamo of power, and when that man is ready, he can do anything and everything he likes; that personality put upon anything will make it work.

Swamiji's View On: How to Build Character

- A man plays a tune on a piano; he places each finger on each key consciously. He repeats this process till the movement of fingers becomes a habit.
- He then plays a tune without having to pay special attention to each particular key. Similarly we find in regard to ourselves that our tendencies are the result of past conscious actions.

- Every good thought that we send to the world, without thinking of any return, will be stored up there and break one link in the chain, and make us purer and purer, until we become the purest of mortals.
- Even the least work done for others—awakens the power within; even thinking the least good of others gradually instills (to impress ideas, principles, or teachings gradually on somebody's mind) into the heart the strength of a lion.

Role of a Teacher

- A child teaches itself, but you can help it to go forward in its own way. What you can do is not of the positive nature, but of the negative. You can take away the obstacles, but knowledge comes out of its own nature. Loosen the soil a little, so that it may come out easily. Put a hedge round it; see that it is not killed by anything, and there your work stops. You cannot do anything else. The rest is manifestation from within its own nature.
- No one can teach anybody. The teacher spoils everything by thinking that he is teaching. Thus Vedanta says that within man is all knowledge — even in a boy it is so — and it requires only an awakening, and that much is the work of a teacher.
- No one was ever really taught by another; each of us has to teach himself. The external teacher offers only the suggestion which rouses the internal teacher to work to understand things.
- Negative thoughts weaken men. Do you not find where parents are constantly taxing sons to read and write, telling them they will never learn anything, and calling them fools and so forth, the latter do actually turn out to be so in many cases? If you speak kind words to boys and encourage them, they are bound to improve in time.
- If you can give them positive ideas, people will grow up to be men and learn to stand on their own legs. In language and literature, in poetry and in arts, in everything we must point out not the mistakes that people are making in their thoughts and actions, but the way in which they will gradually be able to do these things better. Pointing out mistakes wounds a man's feelings.

Education and Mind

- To me, the very essence of education is concentration of mind, not the collecting of facts. If I had to do my education over again, and had any voice in the matter, I would not study facts at all. I would develop the power of concentration and detachment, and then with a perfect instrument I could collect facts at will.
- Side by side, should be developed in the child, the power of concentration and detachment.

- Education is not filling the mind with a lot of facts. Perfecting the instrument and getting complete mastery of my own mind [is the ideàl of education]. If I want to concentrate my mind upon a point, it goes there, and the moment I call, it is free [again].

The Character Formation

- We want that education by which character is formed, strength of mind is increased, the intellect is expanded and by which one stands on one's own feet.
- All knowledge is within the individual, it requires only an awakening.
- Take risks in your life. If you win, you can lead; if you lose, you can guide.
- In India, they tell me I ought not to teach Advaita Vedanta to the people at large; but I say, I can make even a child understand it. You cannot begin too early to teach the highest spiritual truths.
- The less you read the better. Read the Gita and other good works on Vedanta. That is all you need. The present system of education is all wrong. The mind is crammed with facts before it knows how to think. Control of the mind should be taught first. If I had my education to get over again and had any voice in the matter, I would learn to master my mind first, and then gather facts if I wanted them. It takes people a long time to learn things because they can't concentrate their minds at will.

Tips to Success

First: Give up the ideas of enjoyment in this world and the next, care only for God and Truth. We are here to know truth, not for enjoyment. Leave that to brutes that enjoy as we never can. Man is a thinking being and must struggle on until he conquers death, until he sees the light. He must not spend himself in vain talking that bears no fruit. Worship of society and popular opinion is idolatry. The soul has no gender, no country, no place, no time.

Second: Intense desire to know Truth and God. Be eager for them, long for them, as a drowning man longs for breath. Want only God, take nothing else, let not "seeming" cheat you any longer. Turn from all and seek only God.

Third: The six trainings: First - Restraining mind from going outward. Second - Restraining senses. Third - Turning mind inward. Fourth - Suffering everything without murmuring. Fifth - Fastening mind to one idea. Take the subject before you and think; never leave. Do not count time. Sixth - Think constantly of your real nature. Get rid of superstition. Do not hypnotise yourself into a belief in your own inferiority. Day and night tell yourself what you really are, until you realise (realise actually) your oneness with God.

Without these disciplines, no results can be gained. We can be conscious of the Absolute, but we could seldom express. The moment we try, we limit, ceases to be Absolute. We have to go beyond sense limit and transcend even reason, and we have the power to do this.

Conclusion

We have to grow from inside out. None can teach us. None can make us spiritual. There is no other teacher other than our own soul. From this, we understand that Vivekananda insist concentration and understanding ourselves enrich student overall personality development is only by education. The education and character development should be judged by what a learner does rather than what he knows.

References

1. Banhatti, G.S. (1995), "Life and Philosophy of Swami Vivekananda", Atlantic Publishers & Distributors, p. 276, retrieved 6 April 2012.
2. Swami Vivekananda on himself. (2nd enl.ed.). Kolkata: Advaita Ashrama. 2006. p. 3.
3. Minor, Robert Neil (1986), "Swami Vivekananda's use of the Bhagavad Gita", Modern Indian Interpreters of the Bhagavad Gita", Albany, New York: SUNY Press.
4. Mukherjee, Dr. Jayasree (May 2004), "Sri Ramakrishna's Impact on Contemporary Indian Society", Prabuddha Bharatha, retrieved 4 September 2008.

Online

1. "Vivekananda Library online". Vivekananda.net. Retrieved 22 March 2012.
2. http://www.belurmath.org/swamivivekananda.htm.
3. http://www.vivekananda.org/books.asp.
4. http://www.vsc.iitm.ac.in/Vivekananda/Complete%20works/Complete_Works_of_Swami_Vivekananda_-_Vol_1.pdf.

48

Education for the Course

Umamaheswari and M. Jayashree

Sound education is never for character — building but always is character.
— Dr. Ordway Tead

Introduction

The topmost concern of every parent today happens to be their child's education. All decisions of their lives are practically based on whether it would fetch their child better education, or sustain an existing good system that they attend at present. They si7ncerely, leave no stone unturned when it is about utilising their resources, finding more and even more ways to make it comfortable for the child to carry on with their studies. A common thing parents carry in their mind is a sense of void which they felt in their childhood, and thus fiercely dedicate themselves to not let their child face similar situations. Character - building has been engaging the attention of educationists and parents. The reasons for deterioration in discipline may be over-crowding in educational institutions, absence of the right quality teachers, lack of proper equipment and facilities, frustration among students, the influences of outside social environment, the type of our examination system etc.

Higher education renovation lies first on the way of thinking / how to recognise problems with the nature of higher education. It always aims to find suitable solutions to improve the effectiveness of training. The social history has confirmed that the change of circumstances requires people to have adequate adaptation. Modern people need to be equipped with necessary knowledge/skills for the integration in information technology, in the globalisation.

According to Swami Vivekananda, "Education is not the amount of information that is put into your brain and runs riot there, undigested all your life. One must have life-building, man- making, character-making, assimilation of ideas". Swami Vivekananda's educational philosophy had two major components of aims-one the individual aims and seconds the social aims. Under individual aims of education, he emphasised total human development including physical, mental, social, cultural and spiritual development of the child. He did not leave out even the vocational development aim.

In a way, he stood as the embodiment of man-making education. Under the social aims of education, he stressed education for citizenship and democracy, education for national integration, education for the poor and education for women, education for strengthening the whole society. In a way he stood for nation- building education. But, these two aspects were not considered by him as separate and independent. He brought a fine synthesis between the individual and the social aims of education when he said "they alone live who live for others; the rest are more dead than alive."

The character of any man is but the aggregate of his tendencies, the sum total of the bent of his mind. Thoughts manifest in the mind. Each thought is a slight hammer-blow on the lump of iron, which our bodies are manufacturing out of it what we want it to be. Thoughts are like seeds from which our feelings, words, actions and habits grow. Thoughts live; they travel far.

And so take care of what you think. The greatest treasure that a student may carry with him is a well-developed character. Character will help to acquire the other good things of life. Thiruvalluvar observes: "Purity of conduct soweth the seed of prosperity; but an evil course is the mother of endless ills."

Swami Vivekananda is of the view that if you really want to judge the character of a man, looks not at his great performances. Watch a man do his most common actions. Those are indeed the things which will tell you the real character of the great man. Great occasions rouse even the lowest of human beings to some kind of greatness, but he alone is really great whose character is great , always the same wherever he be. Three things are necessary to make every man great, every nation great:

- Conviction of the powers of goodness.
- Absence of jealousy and suspicion.
- Helping all who are trying to be and do good. (VIII. 2999)

Thus the students should be helped to acquire responsibility and independence of judgment and action. And the end of all knowledge must be the building up of character.

References

1. Masand Prem. Think belbre you think. Indore.
2. Sharma. Swami Vivekananda's Winning Formulas. Rainbow Offset, Karnataka, 2011.
3. Vivekananda His Call to the Nation. Advita Ashram, Kolkata, 2012.

PART–IX: HYPER VISION OF SWAMI VIVEKANANDA

49

Ancient Educational Ideas

P. Sarvaharana and S. Manikandan

Introduction

The concept of Education is as old as the evolution of mankind itself (1). Presumably every generation, since the beginning of human existence, somehow or the other passed on the values, the traditions, the methods and skills to the next generation (2). While passing on of a cultural value is known as enculturation and the learning of social values and behaviours is known as socialisation. The history of the curricula of such education reflects history itself, the history of knowledge, beliefs, skills and cultures of humanity (3, 4). As the customs and knowledge of ancient civilisations became more complex, many skills were passed down from a person skilled at the job — for example in animal husbandry, farming, fishing, food preparation, construction etc. Oral traditions were central in societies without written texts (5). Literacy in preindustrial societies was associated with civil administration, law, long distance trade or commerce, and religion (6).

But, the bewildering aspect is that in the advent of modernity, people have begun to disregard the very values of culture, which had been carefully inherited from generation to generation. This is a very sorry spectacle and the society is in total chaos. It is not the scope of this paper to discuss the disintegration and chaos of the society, but to point out the ideas of education as enunciated by the greats for a heuristic that will throw light on the objective and scope of contemplated education.

Ancient Indian (Vedic) Education

History of the world proves that Indian Civilisation is the oldest. The terminology Hindu or India came into existence from the syllable "Sindu". In the words of Swami Vivekananda "this word "Hindu" was the name that ancient Persians used to apply to the river Sindhu. Whenever in Sanskrit there is an "s", in ancient Persian, it changes into "h", so that "Sindhu" became "Hindu"; and you are all aware how the Greeks found it hard to pronounce "h" and dropped it altogether, so that we became known as Indians". Therefore, the word Hindu does not exactly reflect great religion we follow from generations to generations that too from time immemorial. This is the reason why Swamiji calls a Hindu as Vedantin (7). F.E Key says, "Throughout long centuries of India's History, educational development was taking place. It began way back in the times when the hymns of Vedas were being composed and has gone on until the present time.

When we talk about the Vedas, the oldest and the richest Veda from which other Vedas formed a position is the "Rigveda" (8). In the initial stages, when the alphabets were not known (the exact dates were not known, it may be thousands of years ago) the mantras of Rigveda was chanted. In those days, they considered chanting or by-hearting the mantras of Rigveda as knowledge or education. Then, every boy from Brahmin community had to compulsorily learn it. Since, every parent knew the mantras, they themselves taught their children. Thus, the technical lore of language and of hymns was handed down from father to son and this was no doubt the beginning of Education in India. Along with the chanting of mantras, they followed strict discipline and regulate their everyday activities so that they remain absorbed in Brahman to attain Moksha (emancipation) which is the absolute focus of Vedic knowledge.

When we talk about the word Moksha, we should not forget about the other words namely Dharma, Artha, Kama. These three precedes Moksha. A sincere seeker of truth should primarily understand these four great words which are otherwise known as "PURUSHARTHAS". Purusharthas literally mean objective of human life. When we say objective of human life, it should not be construed as a mere endeavour just to attain prestige or prime in life, but it should be regarded as the essential practice to be adopted in life so as to achieve the end (9). First let us go to Shanti Parva of the great Mahabharata, wherein King Yudhistra asked many doubts unresolved to his grandfather, the great Bheeshma, who was on the bed of arrows awaiting the arrival of Uttarayanna to depart from his body. Few of the questions are relevant to the subject matter:-

Yudhistra Poses: I want to know about Dharma, Artha and Kama

Bheeshma responds: The three exist together, side by side, when a man amasses wealth always taking care to walk in the path of Dharma. Wealth owes to virtue and pleasure owes to wealth. All of these again are firmly planted in will. Objects exist in this world for gratification of senses and WILL is concerned with these objects. The sum total of the three depends on these. Entire abstraction from objects of pleasure is called emancipation. Virtue is desirable for the protection of the body and wealth for acquiring virtue. Pleasure is after all only for gratifying our senses. All three however, have one quality in common, passion. The pursuit of these three for the sake of themselves with desire to enjoy their fruits makes the rewards remote. However, if the pursuit is spurred by means for an end which is noble, the realisation of self, then the reward is immense "Virtue is to be acquired for the purification of the soul. Wealth should be acquired to be spent without desire for fruits. Pleasure is to be pursued just for supporting the body and not for gratifying. Hence, it is said that all three of them owe to the power of will. Dharma, Artha and Kama are not ends in themselves, but are just means to an end, and that end is Moksha. These three should be abandoned when one has freed oneself by ascetic penance. Emancipation is the only goal of man (10).

Among the Vedas, i.e., Sama, Yajur and Atharva, the Samaveda was initially separated from the 9th book of the Rigveda. In fact, Yajur and Atharva have been separated from Rigveda. Initially, the Rig, Sama and Yajur Vedas alone were originally recognised as canonical collection. But later on there came to be recognised a fourth veda which was known as the "Atharva-Veda". Veda Vyasa made great efforts to integrate Atharva Veda with the rest of the other three Vedas (11).

Methods of Expected Teaching Discipline

Students were admitted into studies at the age of seven. There were regulations for clothing of those who became students. Everyday the students were taught for four to five hours. The teaching begins during full moon period in the month of July-August. When the wind whirls up dust in the day, or audible at night, when the sound of a drum or of a chariot or of a person in pain was heard and when there is barking of dogs and jackals or the chattering of monkeys and during the time when the sky was brilliantly red, chanting or mantras or reading of the texts are disallowed. Gautama says, the students were advised to bathe daily and avoid honey, meat, perfume, garlands, day-time sleep, ointments, a carriage, shoes, a parasol, love, anger, covetousness, perplexity, garrulity, playing musical instruments, bathing for mere pleasure, cleaning teeth, elation, dancing, singing, calumny and terror and taste pungent foods (11).

In the presence of teacher, the student must not cover his throat, cross his legs, or lean against a wall, or stretch his feet out. Tongs, arms and stomach were to be kept in subjection. He was enjoined always to speak the truth and to avoid bitter speeches. They should always speak in respectful manner to superiors. Gambling, low service, taking things which are not offered and injuring animate beings were unlawful for a student. The pupil should not contradict with the teacher at times and should occupy a seat or couch lower than the teacher. The student should always rise in the morning before his teacher wakes up and retire to rest at night after him. If the teacher wished to talk to the student, the student should stand up and should immediately rush when called up. The teacher's name should not be pronounced by the student. Every morning the student should embrace the feet of the teacher. Students had to live with their gurus so long as the course continues. To complete four Vedas, it may take 48 years. It must be noted here that the Vedas are not studied to earn for a living. Vedas were studied to enquire Brahman and realise God within oneself. This is what the scenario in India and it is necessary to know what has happened in Europe in terms of educational advancement (12).

Education in Europe

Philosophers and social thinkers are not lacking in Europe in the ancient past. When we take the history of Greek, the concept of Stoicism comes to our mind. Stoicism is a school of Hellenistic philosophy founded in Athens by Zeno of Citium in the early Third century BC. The Stoics taught that destructive emotions resulted from errors in judgment, and that a sage, or person of "moral and intellectual perfection," would not suffer such emotions (13). As far the sages they point out to Seneca, Epictetus, Socrates and Aristotle who had followed stoicism.

The following table conceptualises educational ideas of eminent social thinkers of Europe right from Socrates. Indeed, Socrates gave importance to Truth, Knowledge, Development of Character and development of mental powers is the testimony as to why he is the staunch believer and the follower of Stoicism and the above "traits" would lead one to become a stoic.

Ideas of Educationists in Europe

Teacher	*Perfection*	*Truth, knowledge*	*Balanced development of all powers*	*Preparation for life*	*Preparation for public service*	*Preparation for eternity*	*Development of character*	*Happiness*	*Development of mental powers*	*Unfolding of innate ability*	*Preparation to earn at living*	*Service to others*	*Culture*	*Control over nature*	*Erudition*	*Elegance*	*Training for leadership*
Socrates (Greece) (469-399 BC)		√					√		√								
Quintilian (Italy) (AD 35-86)																	
Vittorino (Italy) (1378-1446)			√				√										
Loyala (Italy) (1500)							√					√					
Montessori (Italy)			√	√			√		√	√							
Ausonius (France) (310-394)																	
De la Salle (France) (1651-1719)							√				√	√					
Seguin (France)																	

(1812-1880)						
Binet (France)						
(1857-1911)						
Abelard (France)						
(1079-1142)			√			
Origen (Egypt)	√					
Jerome (Palastine)						
Alcuin (Germany)						
(735-804)	√					
Melanchthon (Germany)						
(1497-1560)	√					
Francke (Germany)						
(1663-1721)	√				√	√
Basedow (Germany)						
(1723-1790)			√	√	√	
Herbart (Germany)						
(1776-1852)	√			√		
Froebel (Germany)						
(1782-1852)	√			√	√	
Ascham (England)						
(1515-1568)				√		
Mulcaster (England)						
(1531-1611)	√				√	
Comenius (Poland)	√					
Pestalozzi (Swiss)	√		√	√		√

Source: History of Education-Socrates to Montessori by Dr. Lula Cole.

In the above Table, twenty two eminent personalities' names and their educational ideas were given countrywise. This will give an idea about the objective and scope of learning contemplated and the following inferences are made:

1. Socrates to Montessori i.e., 14 among the 22 eminent teachers of different periods of time from 399 B.C. to 1874 gave importance to development of character. That means the main idea of education according to them has been to inculcate character in the students. During the period of Socrates, no fixed place known as modern day class room were available and Luella Cole says, Socrates taught, but not in a school, it was in the market place, in the gymnasium, and in the streets that Socrates carried on his life-work of teaching young and old Athenians to know themselves, to know what was good, and to know conditions influenced the development of virtue".

2. Eight out of 22 pay attention to Culture. Dr. Luella Cole quotes "through the cultural theory of education is very old. But so far as school work is concerned, it may be thought of as complex of ideas about the world, life, and people that has been passed down from previous generation". Thus cultural education brings an idea of understanding of the cultural heritage of the past generation.
3. Out of 22 in Table 1, 8 had laid importance for development of mental powers. This idea of development of mental powers not only restricted to think, to reason, to memorise and to concentrate alone but also to understand and assimilate the powers of nature and live in harmony with nature.
4. Six out of 22 had emphasised the need for truth and knowledge as the main part of their curriculum.
5. Quintilian, Melanchthon, Loyola, De la Sale and Francke are the persons who laid great importance to prepare students to do public service.
6. Preparing to earn a living: This theory originated only during 16th century. It was propagated by Mulcaster of England and recognised by Dela sale of France, Francke of Germany and Basedow of Germany. All of them belonged to the Sixteenth Century and it is evident that from 16th Century onwards, the educationists turned to pose themselves a question as to what monetary benefit do an individual get out of education? Does it lead to earn for his bread? Does it lead to raise his living standards?

The Emergence of Schools

We notice during the "Renaissance" movement during the Thirteenth century schools were opened in Rome by the Churches with a view to propagate their religion at the same time educate the general public. The greatest educator Alcuin who existed during 8th century, he and his friend Charlemagne were the major source of influence through hard work they laid the foundation for subsequent and more lasting revivals in the Western Europe. However, Alcuins' thoughts mainly were on Preparation for eternity and Development of character. That means from 8 to 13 Century, even in Europe there were no technical or vocational education. Luela Cole notes some Universities in Rome run by the church authorities: the main subjects taught in these universities were Grammer, Rhetoric, Dialetic, Arithmetic, Music, Geometry and Astronomy. "During the entire period of the Middle ages, schools were mainly creations of church. It was not until the 12th Century that a few schools appeared, and the teachers even in these schools drawn were sometimes from priesthood. At the end of the 15th Century, the pressure for secular schools and teachers increased. In Germany, the nobles already had court schools of their own.

The Development of Modern Schools

School system appeared in Germany at an early date and became the world's first public, state-supported, compulsory system. Similarly, in France similar schools were imitated but at a later date. In England similar state-owned compulsory schools were opened much later than France.

That means it is quiet clear that the first state-owned compulsory education was started in Germany in the early Fifteenth Century. "In 1619, the Duchy of Weimar set up a school system in which attendance was compulsory between the ages of six and twelve and some twenty year, later, the duke of tiny Saxe-Gotha established the first modern school system with compulsory education, well-paid teachers, free school book, a system of grading and even pensions for retired teachers or for their widows and children. These schools were controlled jointly by state and church. The religious wars that followed the period of the Reformation halted the growth of Universal education, but by the middle of Seventeenth Century, most of the German states had a system of schools in many of whom, attendance was compulsory. The joint control by church and the state continue to the end of Eighteenth Century, but at some time between 1750 and 1800, various State Governments throughout Germany took over complete responsibility for education. Therefore, it can be concluded that in Europe, education was originated in Greece and slowly spread to Rome, Italy, France, Germany and England.

Conclusion

The conclusion is inescapable that the objective and scope of education in ancient times—in India and Europe has been to inculcate character and virtuous living. But when education on skill development came into existence, the curriculum has been changed to suit the needs of modern day. People have begun to look at the professions with awe and majesty, be that they be a Doctor or Engineer or Scientist. Where are these going to end? I leave it to the learned audience to ponder over.

References

- P. Sarvaharana, "A Study on Higher Education and the Socio-Economic Problems of Scheduled Castes" M.Phil Thesis University of Madras (1991).
- Kendall D., Murray J., Linden R., "Sociology In Our Times" Third Canadian Edition, 2004, Nelson Education Ltd.
- Hailman, W. N. "Twelve lectures on the history of pedagogy, delivered before the Cincinnati teachers' association", 1874, Wilson, Hinkle & Co., Cincinnati, at Chapter 1, page 12 "In its widest sense, the history of education would be the history of the development of the human race."

- Compayre, Gabriel; Payne, W.H., "History of Pedagogy (1899)", translated by W.H. Payne, 2003, Kessinger Publishing; ISBN 0-7661-5486-6; [originally published in French as "Histoire De La Pédagogie", by Gabriel Compayré; first published in English in 1885]; at Introduction, page IX. "What would a complete history of education not include? It would embrace, in its vast developments, the entire record of the intellectual and moral culture of mankind at all periods and in all countries."
- Walter J. Ong. Orality and Literacy, pp. 92-93.

50

Higher Education in India–A Revelation

K.P. Shanmuga Vadivu

Introduction

Swami Vivekananda's inspiring personality was well known both in East and West during the last decade of the nineteenth century and the first decade of the twentieth. The unknown Indian monk suddenly leapt into fame at the Parliament of Religions in Chicago in 1893, at which he represented Hinduism. His vast knowledge of Eastern and Western culture as well as his deep spiritual insight, fervid eloquence, brilliant conversation, broad human sympathy, colourful personality and handsome figure made an irresistible appeal to many types of Americans who came in contact. People who saw or heard him even once still cherish his memory after lapse of over a century. Swamiji's mission was both national and international. A lover of mankind, he strove to promote peace and human brotherhood on the spiritual foundation of the Vedantic Oneness of existence. A mystic of the highest order, Vivekananda had a direct and intuitive experience of reality. He derived his ideas from that unfailing source of wisdom and often presented the soul-stirring language of poetry in them. Amongst the contemporary Indian philosophers of education, Swami Vivekananda is one of those who revolted against the imposition of British system of education in India. He criticised the pattern of education introduced by the British in India. He pointed out that the current system of education only brings about an external change without any reflective inner force. Nowadays, there is a need for renovating the system of higher education, which imbibes the British system of education. Hence, Swamiji's ideas on higher education will be an eye opener for our rejuvenation of higher education. Hence, this paper ornate with the Swamiji's ideas on higher education.

Philosophy of Education

In the Neo-vedanta humanistic tradition of contemporary Indian thought, Vivekananda presented a philosophy of education for man-making. The chief objection raised by Swamiji against the contemporary educational system was that it turned men into slaves, capable of slavery and nothing else. About the prevailing university education, he remarked that it was no better than an efficient machine for rapidly turning out clerks. It deprived people of their faith and belief. Swamiji was very critical about this scheme of education. He compared it to the person who wanted to turn his ass into a horse, was advised to thrash that in order to achieve this transformation and killed his animal in this process. Vivekananda also criticised the contemporary system of education from the humanistic view point.

Aim of Education

According to Swamiji, there are several steps for education. They are as follows:

1. Self-Development
2. Fulfillment of Swadharma
3. Freedom of Growth
4. Character Formation

Self-Development: In contrast to the contemporary system of education, Vivekananda advocated education for self-development. Education according to most of the Western educationalists, aims at man's adjustment with the environment. According to the Indian philosophical tradition, true knowledge does not come from outside. It is discovered with the individual, in the self which is the source of all knowledge. According to Swamiji, the function of education is the uncovering of knowledge hidden in our mind.

Fulfillment of Swadharma: Swamiji supported the idea of Swadharma in education. Every one ought to grow like himself. No one need to copy others. External pressure only creates destructive reactions leading to stubbornness and disorderliness. In an atmosphere of freedom, love and sympathy, the child will develop courage and self-reliance. He should be talked to stand on his own, to be himself. Each child should be given opportunities to develop according to his own inner nature.

Freedom of Growth: Swamiji is a staunch champion in education. Freedom is the first requirement for self-development. The child should be given freedom to grow according to his own nature. The teacher should not exert any type of pressure on the child. The child should be helped in solving his problems. The teachers should have an attitude of service land worship. Education ultimately aims at realisation. It is a means of a sorority of mankind.

Character Formation: Character is the foundation for self-development. The aim of education as self-development, therefore, leads to the aim of education for character. The aim of education is character building. This depends upon the ideals cherished by the individual. The educator should present higher ideals before the educands. The best way to develop a character is the personal example of high character preset by the teacher. In ancient Indian system of education, the teachers used to present higher ideals before the pupils, who in turn imitated these ideals according to their inherent capacities.

Defect in the Present University System

"It is almost wholly one of defects. Why, it is nothing but a perfect machine for turning out clerks. I would even thank my stars if that were all. But no! See how men are becoming destitute of sraddha and faith. They assert the Gita (Sermon of the Lord) as only an interpolation, and that the Vedas are but rustic (elegy)! They like to master every detail concerning things and nations outside India, but if you ask them, they do not know even the name of their own forefathers up to the seventh generation, not to speak of the fourteenth!

According to Swami Vivekananda, we still dream of producing clerks of the computer age—graduates who could handle multiple and diverse information sources and media. But, we forget about our Vedas which is thrust of our journey as good citizen with character and humanity, and we unaware to make secure and to increase the knowledge, skills and values relevant to the nature and practices of participative democracy; also to enhance the awareness of rights and duties, and the sense of responsibilities needed for development of active citizens.

His Interpretation

Does higher education mean mere study of material sciences and turning out things of everyday use by machinery? The use of higher education is how to solve problems of life, and this is what is engaging the profound thought of the modern civilised world, but it was solved in our country thousands of years ago.

Higher Education—An Analysis

Swamiji believed true education as gained by constant living in communion with nature. Knowledge should be acquired in that way, otherwise by educating ourself in the tol of a teacher will be only a human ape all our life. One should live from his very boyhood with whose character is like a blazing fire and should have a living example of the highest teaching before him. Mere reading that it is a sin to tell a lie will be of no use. Every boy should be trained to practice absolute Brahmacharya, and then, and then only, faith - Shraddha - will come. In our country, the imparting of knowledge has always been through men of renunciation. Later, the teachers, by monopolising all knowledge and restricting it to the tols, have only brought the country to the brink of ruin. India had all good prospects so long as Tyâgis (men of renunciation) used to impart knowledge.

Swamiji recapitulated us to have a luminous history, and on the strength of that we know the nation alive. But history has to be rewritten. It should be restated and suited to the understanding and ways of thinking which our men have acquired in the present age through Western education.

Swamiji mentioned that somebody can teach anybody. The teacher spoils everything by thinking that he is in the trade. Thus Vedanta says that within man is all knowledge - even in a boy it is so - and it requires only an awakening, and that much is the work of a teacher. We have to do only so much for the boys that they may learn to apply their own intellect to the proper use of their hands, legs, ears, eyes, etc., and finally everything will become easy. But the root is religion. Religion is as the rice, and everything else, is like the curry. Taking only curries causes indigestion, and so is the case with taking rice alone.

He stated that, "Our pedagogues are making parrots of our boys and ruining their brains by cramming a lot of subjects into them. Looking from one standpoint, you should rather be grateful to the Viceroy for his proposal of reforming the university system, which means practically abolishing higher education; the country will, at least, feel some relief by having breathing time. Goodness gracious! What a fuss and fury about graduating, and after a few days all cools down! And after all that, what it they learn is but that what religion and customs we have are all bad, and what the Westerners have are all good! At last, they cannot keep the wolf from the door! What does it matter if this higher education remains or goes? It would be better if the people got a little technical education, so that they might find work and earn their bread, instead of dawdling about and crying for service."

Swamiji stressed that what we need, we know, is to study, independent of foreign control, different branches of the knowledge that is our own, and with it the English language and Western science; we need technical education and all else that may develop industries so that men, instead of seeking for service, may earn enough to provide for themselves, and save something against a rainy day, and he also pointed that masses and women should be educated for the development of our nation.

Conclusion

The exposition and analysis of Vivekananda'a scheme of education brings light its constructive, practical and comprehensive character. He realises that it is only through education that the uplift of masses is possible. He states it emphatically that if society is to be reformed, education has to reach everyone-high and low, because individuals are the very constituents of society. The sense of dignity rises in man when he becomes conscious of his inner spirit, and that is the very purpose of education. He strives to harmonise the traditional values of India with the new values brought through the progress of science and technology. It is high time that we give serious thought to his philosophy of education and remembers his call to everybody - 'Arise, awake and stop not till the goal is reached'.

References

- Avinashilingam, T.S. (1943): Education - Swami Vivekananda, Sri Ramkrishna Math, Mylapore, Chennai (5th ed.).
- Chandra, S. (1994): Swami Vivekananda's Vision of Education, In: Roy, S. Sivaramkrishnan, M. (Eds), Reflections on Swami Vivekananda: Hundred Years After Chicago, Sterling Publishers Pvt. Ltd, New Delhi.
- Complete Works of Swami Vivekananda (8 Volumes). Advaita Ashrama, Kolkata, 1985.
- Ghosal , S. (2012) : The Educational Thoughts of Swami Vivekananda : A Review, University News, 50 (09), February 27 - March 04, 2012, New Delhi.

51

Swamiji on the Real Man

V. Priya

Introduction

Though the Saint was introduced to western type of education 'he imbibed the best elements on Indian culture and religious tradition and did not deter from mastering some of the difficult philosophers of the west'. He had the opportunity of comparative study of the religious and intellectual heritage of East and West. The meeting of the young turbulent Vivekananda with Ramakrishna Paramahamsa brought far reaching results: Vivekananda relinquished everything and followed Ramakrishna. Although the reforms suggested by Brahma Samaj excited him, Swamiji felt any reform whatsover should come from within. There should be no imposition of western notion from any quarter on Indian beliefs and ideals. He wanted and upheld to some extent Hinduism to recast and emerge as a Universal Religion.

Absolute

It is the Ultimate Reality, only Real, infinite. What is It's nature, how is it related to the universe; how can it be known are the most persistent problems in Advaita Philosophy. In some passages of Upanisads, Brahman is described in tow different way; as the cause of the world and as Absolute, without any characteristics. How were the two views reconciled? Sankara postulates two standpoints; the Absolute, i.e., Paramarthika and Relative, i.e., Vyavakarika. The truth is that Brahman as non-dual, relationless, infinite. It alone is and nothing real exists aside. But from our stand point Brahman appears as God, the cause of the universe. There is no real causation only appearance. Vivekananda tries to balance the two positions.

Vivekananda says that between the Absolute and the universe, one can assume the categories of Time, Space and Causation. The Absolute through Time, Space and Causation forms the universe. These categories are not part of the Absolute, but it is seen or known through them. They are mere foinis not metaphysical realities, not metaphysical in form because they are not independent existences. They are forms and God makes creation possible through them.

The Absolute is not determined by anything, but exists by itself and uncaused. Since, it is a comprehensive whole existing by Itself, no cause can be attributed to it. It is not definable, nor limited by mind. It is unknown, but it is the sum total of all that is known. Knowledge becomes possible through Absolute as It reflect the self of man.

Vivekananda in the line of Advaita asserts that there is One Absolute "All the objects in the universe including man are the very Absolute, the whole of the Absolute and that things are not parts of it." He, after considering the various speculations held by different Indian thinkers about the nature of the Real, tries to shape their conclusion into a harmonic whole. He believed that it is possible to harmonise the divergent views and establish the vedantic theme of unity.

Proofs for the Existence of God

Swamiji has a very deep faith in God. He emphasises the necessity of God concept. God has to be presupposed as the necessary support and ground of the world and soul. If the notion of God is inevitable, then, why every religion tries to prove the existence of God? In fact, Swamiji does not feel to make any effort to prove or demonstrate the existence of God. He asserts to have a direct realisation of God. Any demonstration or proof is not necessary for establishing His existence, he substantiate.

However, it is necessary to give proofs: (1) It is not possible to have the direct realisation of God that requires rigorous practice or sadhana. A few seers had that realisation. So, for ordinary mortals, it is the proof that creates the initial interest and faith. (2) The revelation of those Seers should be communicated to others; they are invariably obscure and needed interpretation in simple language. Hence rational proofs and demonstrations are necessary. It is very difficult to present the demonstration given by Swamiji are unsystematically scattered throughout his writings and speeches.

We find a priori and posterior kinds of proof for the existence of God, from his postulates.

1. In some of his writings, Vivekananda refers similar proof to that traditional telelogy. He says, "The whole of nature at best could teach them only of a personal Being, who is the ruler of the Universe; it could teach nothing further. In short out of the external world, we can only get the idea of an architect, that which is called Design Theory." This clearly shows the grandeur of the world to supposing that there must be an architect and an intelligent designer.

2. On some occasions, we find causal demonstration for the existence of God in Saint's approach. In the world, we come across many things whose origin cannot be accounted for in any naturalistic term. It means that everything in the universe is by turn a cause and an effect. This is called law of causation. This causal series itself leads to a final and ultimate cause — to a cause which,

although is the cause of everything, is itself not caused. That, according to Swamiji, is the Absolute or God. "That which exists by itself alone cannot have a cause. That which is free cannot have any cause; else it would not be free, but bound."

3. God is also sought to be established from the fact of 'oneness of everything'. Swamiji says that the universe expresses an essential unity of everything. One has only to pause and contemplate in order to discover that things that look so very different from each other are really and basically one and the same. He declares, "If you go below the surface, you find that unity between man and man, between races and races, high and low, rich and poor, gods and men, and men and animals. If you go deep enough, all will be seen as only vibrations of the one, and he who has attained to this conception of Oneness has no more delusion." This fact of unity itself is an argument in favour of the One, the supreme God.

4. Swamiji demonstrates the existence of God from the fact of 'love'. He does not have any hesitation in saying that we do not really love and 'other', but love ourselves. Love consists in discovering oneself in the object of love. He says, "None, O beloved, loves the husband for the husband's sake, but it is for the sake of the self who is in the husband, that the husband is love; ..." If love is this type then in the act of love there is no distinction between 'me' and 'thou' and this carried to its ultimate conclusion that reality behind everything is just one supreme principle of love.

5. Swamiji refers the ancient Indian scriptures, the Vedas and the Upanisads as authority in order to justify his assertion regarding the Absolute. As long as one does not have the direct experience one has to believe the scriptures. However this is only for initial knowledge and faith.

6. Using analogical argument Swamiji arrives at the notion of God. He says, "Who enjoys the picture, the seller or seer? The seller is busy with his accounts, computing what his gain will be how much profit he will realise on the picture... That man is enjoying the picture who has gone there without any intention of buying or selling. He looks at the picture and enjoys it. So this whole Universe is a picture, and when these desires have vanished, men will enjoy the world." Swamiji conceives God in the analogy of a painter or a poet or an artist.

7. Further the notion of God cannot be rejected, according to the Saint. God's idea is shown to be necessary on various grounds. It is necessary because it is the Truth and Truth is necessary. It is necessary also because it is freedom. The fact of human freedom presupposes the ideal of absolute freedom which is nothing but Divine Freedom. Swamiji says, "It is the God within your own self that is propelling you to seek for Him, to realise Him... is your own self, the reality of your life, body and soul."

8. Swamiji stresses the intuitional proof for God's existence. There cannot be any better proof than direct realisation, and an intuitional argument stands

on the secure foundation of direct realisation. He is convinced that everybody could realise God provided one should follow the rigorous religious discipline and mediation. In that case any rational proof is redundant.

Swamiji further describes about God as supreme ideal. Man bears the spark of Divinity within himself. This ideal can be reached. The original bond of unity between man and the God is always there. Swamiji accepts both the personal and impersonal aspect of God. This distinction does not affect the nature of God; this in fact helps the ordinary mortal to realise Him through this ladder. He feels that the common man is more inclined towards the personal character of God. But this does not take away his vedantic conviction of Brahman.

The Nature of Man

According to Swamiji, man is the microcosm reflecting the macrocosm. He has unlimited strength and all powerful; son of God; part of bliss; has holiness and perfection. Thinking makes the man what he is. His very thought makes what he is. If, he thinks weak, he becomes so, if he thinks strong enough he is so. Hardwork and efforts bring the man near to his goal. Man should first believe himself, rather others. He should not have any fear; in fact, it should be the slave to him, not the other way. If a man thinks the present position is due to his past karma, then he can plan his future. Man can decide his own destiny. What one sows reap the same. God has created man in order to perform noble and magnificent acts, so he has to live to that expectation.

All the knowledge is within a man. It is the duty of man to awaken it. One should do useful and fruitful acts for the sake of others, i.e., service to others. Serving the needy is serving the God. The divine is from within; himself is divine. The real man is the one Unit Existence, the Divine, and the Infinite, whereas the divergent individual empirical man is apparent. The apparent empirical man undergoes pleasure, pain and all sorts of feeling and dwells in the phenomenal world. Though the Self within him is not very much affected, the apparent main undergoes the cycle of birth and death. Once, the real nature of the Self is realised, the stage is called 'Living Free' or Jivan mukta.

Conclusion

According to him, the real in man is a sort of a 'concentration of spiritual energy'. Man is a spirit. Man is not what he ordinarily appears to be, he represents some aspirations. The picture of man portrayed by the Swamiji is an organised unity of the physical and the spiritual. He gives importance to the physical nature. The presence of brain system in the body distinguishes man from every other being. It has a unique status in the world. This uniqueness is due to the presence of spirituality in him. The real nature of man is to transcend over his physical nature. The true nature of man is Soul Force or Atman.

References

1. Complete Works of Swami Vivekananda, Vol. 1 to 8, Advaita Asram, Calcutta, 1986.
2. Naravane, V.S., Modern Indian Thought, Orient Longman, New Delhi, 1978.
3. Lal, B.K., Contemporary Indian Philosophy, Motilal Banarsidass, New Delhi, 1978.

52

Saintly Reflections on Education

R. Selvamathi Sugirtha

Introduction

The 19th century India produced a galaxy of men, who have enriched our national life by talent and personality. Swami Vivekananda was one among them. Swamiji believed in essential unity of man and God. He was an eclectic educationalist. He tried to unite the Indian spirituality with western materialism. He desired happy mingling or their fusion. He also wanted to unite Para Vidya and Para Vidya. He was revolutionary in the field of education and touched every aspect of it. His ideas on various aspects of education are more relevant and are needed more today than probably during his life time. Although Swamiji did not write a book on education, he contributed valuable thoughts on the relevant and viable subject. He had firm moorings in oriental culture, yet he had the broadness to welcome all that is worth borrowing from the west (Ghosal, 2012). No wonder that today, over a century after his death, we still try to enrich ourselves with the gems of Swamiji's thoughts on education. If we attentively study the writings and lectures of Swamiji, we find that his views on education are products of original reflection. Let us discuss the different aspects of Swamiji's scheme of education.

Defining Education

Swami who describes religion as 'the manifestation of the divinity already in man' defines education as 'the manifestation of the perfection already in man' (1993: 55). First of all, the word 'manifestation' implies that something already exists and is waiting to be expressed. The main focus in learning is to make the hidden ability of learner manifest. According to him, the knowledge is inherent in man, not acquired from external sources. Like sparks in a flint, knowledge is potentially there in human mind. The stimulus of education causes the friction that ignites the fire of knowledge. It is the unfolding of the petals of one's own mind. 'Manifestation' indicates spontaneous growth, provided that the impediments, if any, are removed. Swamiji said "what a man learns is really what he 'discovers', by taking the cover off his own soul, which is a mine of infinite knowledge" (1993: 54).

The Means of Education

According to Swamiji, the means for education is love. Love and character building are the best means for education. Love is the best inspiration in character building. Love in the minds of the educator is the real source of his influence upon the educated. The true education, gives the growth and expansion of personality. He wanted that the education for total human development should be the main vision. "Character, efficiency and humanism should be the aim of all education. Swamiji strongly pleaded that development of character through the service of his fellowmen, the utilisation of his talents for ensuring the happiness and welfare of the millions of his less fortunate fellow-citizens should be the aim of the education." The child should be taught through by love, it makes fellow feelings and love for human beings. Education must help the individual to recognise his cultural heritage and to use it in his struggle of life. Education is a life-long process towards the fullest development of human personality, self-discovery, self-perfection, self-awareness and self manifestation.

Swamiji's Aims of Education

Swamiji wanted all-round development of education to heart and mind, to strengthen character and national consciousness, to help in the cultivation of strength and energy, nurture the brain and intellect and stir feelings of kindness and sympathy. He emphatically said: ion by which character is formed, strength of mind is increased, the intellect is expanded and by which one can stand on one's own feet. What we need is to study, independent of foreign control, different branches of the knowledge that is our own and with it the English language and Western science; we need technical education and all else that will develop industries. So that men, instead of seeking for service, may earn enough to provide for them and save against a rainy day. The end of all education, all training, should be man making. The end and aim of all training is to make the man grow. The training, by which the current and expression of will are brought under control and become fruitful, is called education. What our country now wants are muscles of iron and a nerve of steel, gigantic wills which nothing can resists, which can penetrate into the mysteries and secrets of the universe and will accomplish their purpose in any fashion, even if it means going down to the bottom of the ocean, meeting death face to face. It is a man-making religion that we want. It is man-making theories that we want. It is man making education all round that we want.

According to Swamiji, education is a process in which the young minds, will receive strength, energy and vigorous character. By the way of getting this process, the individual will mould themselves of their life. "All knowledge and all powers are within. What we call power; secrets of nature and force are all within. All knowledge comes from the human soul. Man manifests knowledge, discovers it with himself, which is pre-existing through eternity." Education is a man-making and nation-making process. It is the process which awakens the sleeping soul to self-conscious activity. It will become a powerful instrument to achieve the developmental qualities among the people. The prime aim of education is to achieve the full perfection already present in a child.

According to Swamiji, all the materials and spiritual knowledge are already present in the individuals mind, but it is covered by certain ignorance. The second aim of education is the physical and mental development of the child. "For stressing the mental development of the child, Swami, wished education to enable the child to stand on his own legs economically rather than becoming a parasite on others." The third aim of education is the character development of the child. He emphasises the child should practice Brahmacharya which fosters development of mental, moral and spiritual powers leading to purity of thought, words and deeds. In the fourth aim of education, he emphasises the religious development. Every individual should search out and develop the religious seed and to reach the absolute truth or reality.

Swamiji's aim of education had strong nationalist bias. He was not critical of Western system of education rather; he questioned the suitability of Western Model in India. The system of education in India was based on Indian Foundation that was supported with the broader argument that the every nation should develop a system of education based on his own nature, history and civilisation.

Saintly Principles

Like Rabindranath Tagore, Swamiji prescribed the same ancient spiritual methods of teaching, where Guru and his disciples lived in close association as in a family. The following are the basic principles of education.

- Education is not only for getting information; rather it should develop character, mental aptitude.
- Powers intelligence and inculcate self-confidence together with self-reliance.
- Education should develop the child physically, mentally and spiritually.
- While giving educational qualification, the technical education was necessary for industrial growth which leads to the economic prosperity of the nation.
- Practicing of Brahmacharya is essential for getting knowledge. The concentration is the key to the knowledge trove.
- Religious education should be imparted through sweet impressions and fine conduct in preference to books.

The Saint believed, education deals with physical education, moral and religious education, medium of education, women's education and education for weaker sections of society.

Physical Education

Without the knowledge of physical education, the self-realisation or character building is not possible one must know, how to make our body strong through physical education, for to attain a complete education, it is necessary to develop both the mind and the body. In particular, Swamiji stressed the value of physical education in curriculum. He said, "You will be nearer to Heaven through football than through the study of Gita. You will understand Gita better by your biceps, your muscles a little stronger. You will understand the Upanishads better and the glary of the Atman, when your body stands firm on your feet and you feel yourself as man."

Medium of Education

Like Gandhi and Rabindranath Tagore, Swamiji also emphasised education through the mother tongue. Besides mother tongue, there should be a common language which is necessary to keep the country united. Swamiji appreciated the greatness of Sanskrit that it is the source of all Indian languages and a repository of all inherited knowledge; with the absence of this knowledge, it will be impossible to understand Indian culture. It is like a store house of ancient heritage, to develop our society it is necessary that men and women should know this language, besides the knowledge of the mother tongue.

Moral and Religious Education

Swamiji said, "Religion is the innermost core of education. I do not mean my own or anyone else opinion about religion. Religion is as the rice and everything else, like the curries. Taking only curries causes indigestion and so is the case with taking rice alone." Therefore, religious education is a vital part of a sound curriculum. Swamiji considered Gita, Upanishads and the Vedas are the most important curriculum for religious education. For him, religion is a platform for self realisation and divinisation. It is not only individual's development but also for the transformation of total man. The true religion cannot be limited to a particular place of time. He pleaded for unity of world religion. He realised truth while practicing of religion. The truth is the power, untruth is the weakness. Knowledge is truth, ignorance is untruth. Thus truth increases power, courage and energy. It is light giving, therefore, necessary for the individual as well as collective welfare. In the Vivekananda point of view, ethics and religion are one and the same. God is always on the side of goodness. To fight for goodness is the service to God. The moral and religion education develop the self-confidence among the young men and women.

Education of Masses

The individual development is not a full development of our nation, so he needs to give education to the society or common people. The education is not only confined to the well-to-do persons only but also to the poor people. Swamiji emphasise to improve the conditions of the masses and he advocated mass education. He takes this mass education as an instrument to improve the individual as well as society. By this way, he exhorted to his countrymen to know—"I consider that the great national sin is the neglect of the masses, and that is one of the causes of our downfall. No amount of politics would be of any avail until the masses of India are once more well-educated, well-fed and well cared for.

Man-Making Education

The educational philosophy of Swamiji is a harmonious synthesis between the ancient Indian ideals and modern Western beliefs. He not only stressed on the physical, mental, moral, spiritual and vocational development of the child but also he advocated women education as well as education of the masses. The essential characteristics of his educational philosophy are idealism, naturalism and pragmatism. In a naturalistic view point, he emphasised that real education is possible only through nature and natural propensities. In the form of idealist view point, he insists the aim of education is to develop the child with moral and spiritual qualities. In the pragmatists view point, he emphasised the great stress on the Western education of technology, commerce, industry and science to achieve material prosperity. In short, Swami Vivekananda was an idealist at heart. First of all, he emphasised spiritual development, then the material prosperity, after that safety of life and then solving the problems of fooding and clothing of the masses.

Self-Education

Self-education is the self-knowledge. That is, of our own self is the best guide in the struggle of our life. If we take one example, the childhood stage, the child will face lot of problems or commit mistakes in the process of character formation. The child will learn much by his mistakes. Errors are the stepping stones to our progress in character. This progress will need courage and strong will. The strong will is the sign of great character will makes men great.

Women's Education

Women's education is not in the hands of others. The powers are in the women. Swamiji considered that women to be the incarnation of inspirational power and asked men to respect them everywhere. He rightly pointed out that unless Indian women secure respectable place in this land, the nation can never march forward. The important features of his scheme of female education are to make them strong, fearless, and conscious of their chastity and dignity. He insists that men and women are equally competent not only in the academic matters, but also must have equal companion in the home and family. Vivekananda being a keen observer could distinguish the difference in perception about the status of women in the West and in India. "The ideal women in India is the mother, the mother first, and the mother last. The word woman calls up to the mind of the Hindu, motherhood; and God is called mother.

Education for the Underprivileged

Swamiji pleaded for universal education so that the backward people may fall in with others. To uplift the backward classes he chooses education as powerful instrument for their life process. Thus education should spread to every household in the country, to factories, playing grounds and agricultural fields. If the children do not come to school, the teacher should reach them. Two or three educated men should team up, collect the paraphernalia of education and should go to the village to impart education. Thus, Vivekananda favoured education for different sections of society, rich and poor, young and old, male and female.

Conclusion

From the Swamiji's scheme of education, the uplift of mass is possible only through education. He upholds education bringing a light of its constructive, practical and comprehensive character. By giving education, he tries to materialise the moral and spiritual welfare and the uplift of humanity, irrespective of caste, creed, nationality or time. By the way of his scheme of education, we can get the strong nation with peace and harmony and without caste and creed. He builds a strong nation for our sake.

References

- Avinashilingam, T.S., Education - Swami Vivekananda, Sri Ramakrishna Math, Mylapore, Chennai (5hedt.).
- Prabhananda, Swami (2003): Swami Vivekananda (1863-1902), Prospects, Vol. XXXIII, No. 2, June 2003, pp. 231 - 245, UNESCO, Paris.

53

A Special Dimension on Philosophy of Education

R.R. Madankar

Introduction

"Education is the manifestation of the perfection already in man."

Swami Vivekananda was born in 1863 in Calcutta. His original name was Narendranath Datta. His father was Shri Vishnunath Datta. His father was a lawyer, and an attorney in the Calcutta high court. He provided his son with the best of education. Narendranath Datta was a brilliant student and graduated with honours from Calcutta University. He had an excellent command over languages, Bengali, Sanskrit and English and was a fluent speaker. He was deeply interested in the study of philosophy and studied comparative systems of the religions and philosophies of the east and the west. For some time, he was a classroom teacher. According to him, if education meant information only, then libraries could be the greatest saints of the world and encyclopedias had become seers and rishis. No one was ever really taught by another. Each of us has to teach himself. The external teacher offers only the suggestion which sources the internal teacher to work to understand things. Then things will be made clearer to us by our own power of perception and thought, and we shall realise them in our own souls. The whole of the big banyan tree which covers acres of ground was in the little seed which was perhaps no bigger than one-eighth of mustard seed. All that mass of energy was there confined. The gigantic intellect, we know, lies coiled up in the protoplasmic cell. It may seem like a paradox, but it is true. Each one of us has come out of one protoplasmic cell, and all the powers we possess were coiled up there. You cannot say they came from food, for if you heap up Food Mountains high, what power comes out of it? The energy was there, potentially no doubt, but still there. So is infinite power in the soul of man whether he knows it or not. Its manifestation is only a question of being conscious of it. The Light Divine within is obscured in most people. It is like a lamp in a case of iron: no gleam of light can shine through. Gradually, by purity and Un-selfishness, we can make the obscuring medium less and less dense, until at last it becomes as transparent as glass. Sri Ramakrishna was like the iron cask transformed into a glass cask, through which can be seen the inner light as it is.

- ***Spirit of Humanism:*** Swami Vivekananda revived the spirit of humanism in education. He interpreted Vedantic philosophy to mean that the worship of god is in reality, service to mankind. Education should lead us to the goal of realising god through love of humanity, self-sacrifice and work for the uplift of mankind.
- ***Free and compulsory Mass Education:*** All should reach school regardless of caste, position, wealth of poverty. Education is the birth right of every human being, but we have denied this birth right for centuries to millions of our countrymen, due to discrimination and prejudice against the poorer classes in society.
- ***A National System of Education:*** Should be formulated by schools which include a study of India's heritage of culture arts, poetry, religion, history and languages. The schemes of studies should be built around it.
- ***Women's Education:*** Education has been neglected. All women should receive proper education, training and be prepared to work for socioeconomic and educational reform of the country. They should become leaders and be placed in responsible position in order to function in society effectively.
- ***Attack on Casteism and untouchability:*** Attack on Casteism and untouchability was a very important part of his work. Swamiji believed that there was no scriptural sanction for twin-cancer in Indian society. God created men as equals; individuals determined their own caste, by their character, works and influences in society. All members of the society deserve equal educational opportunities to better their lot through religious study, scientific knowledge, trade, commerce and economics.
- ***The Ramakrishna Mission:*** The yeoman contribution of Vivekananda in the educational and social sphere owes to the magnificent movement in 1899. The famine of 1899 led him to open famine relief centre and establish orphanage. The immense misery caused by floods, plague and cholera were handled by relief measures with the assistance of his disciples. Hospitals, schools and colleges were opened. The Ramakrishna Mission has centres all over India. It is a world famous organisation, which attracts scholars and learned Swamis to its fold from all over.
- ***Vedanta society:*** The Vedanta Society established in San Fransciso by Swami Vivekananda has expanded into several other cities. Lectures, publications and visiting scholars within and outside India spread the message of the Vedanta all over the world.

Knowledge is inherent in man. No knowledge comes from outside; it is all inside. What we say a man 'Knows', should, in strict psychological language, be Knowing is what he 'discovers' or 'unveils'. What a man 'learns' is really what he 'discovers' by taking the cover off his own soul, which is a mine of infinite knowledge. We say Newton discovered gravitation. Was it sitting anywhere in a corner waiting for him? It was in his mind; the time came and he found it out. All knowledge that the world has ever received comes from the mind; the infinite library of the universe is in your own mind. The external world is simply the suggestion, the occasion, which sets you to study your own mind. The falling of an apple gave the suggestion to Newton, and he studied his own mind. He rearranged the previous links of thought in his mind and discovered a new link among them, which we call the law of gravitation. It was neither in the apple nor in anything in the centre of the earth.

All knowledge therefore, secular or spiritual, is in the human mind. In many cases, it is not discovered, but remains covered, and when the covering is being slowly taken off, we say 'we are learning', and the advance of knowledge is made by the advance of this process of covering. The man from whom this veil is being lifted is the more knowing man; the man upon whom it lies thick is ignorant; and the man from whom it has entirely gone is all-knowing, omniscient. Like fire in a piece of flint, knowledge exists in the mind; suggestion is the friction which brings it out. All the knowledge and all power are within.

You cannot teach a child any more than you can grow a plant. The plant develops its own nature. The - child also teaches itself. But you can help it to go forward in its own way. What you can do is not of a positive nature, but negative. You can take away the obstacles, and knowledge comes out of its own nature. Loosen the soil a little, so that it may come out easily. Put a hedge round it; see that it is not killed by anything. You can supply the growing seed with the materials for the making up of its body, bringing to it the earth, the water, the air that it wants. And there your work stops. It will take all that it wants by its own nature. "So with the education of the child. A child educates itself." The teacher spoils everything by thinking that he is teaching. Within man is all knowledge, and it requires only an awakening, and that much is the work of the teacher. We have only to do so much for the boys that they may learn to apply their own intellect to the proper use of their hands, legs, ears and eyes. That system which aims at educating our boys in the same manner as that of the man who battered his ass, being advised that it could thereby be turned into a horse, should be abolished. Owing to undue domination exercised by the parents, our boys do not get free scope for growth. In every one there are infinite tendencies which require proper scope for satisfaction.' Violent attempts at reform always end by retarding reform. If you do not allow one to become a lion, one will become a fox.

Education is not the amount of information that is put into your brain and runs riot there, undigested all your life. We must have life-building, man-making, character-making, assimilation of ideas. If you have assimilated five ideas and made them your life and character, you have more education than any man who has got by heart a whole library. If education were identical with information, the libraries would be the greatest sages in the world and encyclopaedias the rishis.

References

- N.R. Swaroop Saxena, Sikhachaturvedi (2004). Education in emerging India, Surya Publication; Meerut.
- K.K. Bhatia (1997). Principles and Practice of Education, Kalyani Publisher, New Delhi.
- Bhatia and Bhatia (1993). The principles and Methods of Teaching.

54

Reforming the Existing Higher Education System

S. Logeshkumar

Introduction

Education in India is only one between various elements that have captured the attention of the world. The United Nations is quite concerned about the presence of a large number of illiterates, other countries are surprised by the quality of human resources that the Indian education system has shaped. The enlargement of Indian economy in the recent past and the compulsion to sustain force the Indian government speed up the process of developing the branches of Indian education structure. Therefore, it would be very interesting to understand and evaluate the structures of education in India, its present condition and upcoming development. It is known that Indian education system has undergone remarkable changes, particularly the higher education sector due to economic liberalisation. Higher education today is more complex combination of global flows and networks of ideas, knowledge, finance, and inter-institution dealings. All institutional education, socio-political education in a democracy, therefore should be designed to produce citizens who are free, responsible, and politically aware, who feel to belong to the country wherein they live, and are sensitive to what happens around them. Education should produce such enlightened democratic citizens.

Need and the Significance

Recent developments in Indian Education System are generally marks-based. However, some experiments to do away with the system led to cases of depression and suicides among students. A criticism of the system emphasis is laid on passing examinations with higher percentage. Few institutes give importance to developing personality and creativity among students, but not all. Despite efforts to develop the education system in India, access, equity and quality of education in India continue to haunt the policy makers till this date. This has been due to the widespread poverty and various prejudices. This section attempts to discuss the development of Indian education system from ancient India till date. Ancient education system of India was considered one of the best education, which deals directly to get the solution for problems in our daily life. The present education system generally deals with materialism, where an individual faces difficulty in facing the challenges in this competitive world. In addition, tradition and practices starts depreciating in. It is felt that this reforms, our education system with culture and rich heritage through which an individual's character is formed, strength of mind is increased, intellect is expanded and by which an individual can stand in his/her own feet.

Objective

To study the existing Indian higher education practice and its lacuna to reform according to the vision of Swami Vivekananda.

The Background

Indian education system owes to the Gurukul system. The Gurukuls were the traditional Hindu residential schools of learning which were typically run in the teacher's house or a monastery. Even though the education was free, the students from well-to-do families paid the Gurudakshina which was a voluntary contribution after the completion of studies. At the Gurukuls, the teacher imparted knowledge on various aspects of religion, the scriptures, the philosophy, the literature, the warfare, the statecraft, the medicine astrology and the history. This system is being referred as the oldest and the most effective system of education.

In the first millennium and the few centuries preceding, there was a flourishing of higher education at Nalanda, Takshashila University, Ujjain, and Vikramshila Universities. The important subjects were mainly the art, the architecture, the painting, the logic, the grammar, the philosophy, the astronomy, the literature, the Buddhism, the Hinduism, the Arthashastra, the law, and the Medicine. Each university specialised in a particular field of study. For instance, the Takshila has specialised in the study of medicine, while the Ujjain laid emphasis on astronomy.

The System: Present Scenario

The present system of education was introduced and founded by the British in the Twentieth century, by the recommendations of Macaulay. It adapts western style and content. The British government did not recognise the traditional structures and so they have declined. It is said that even Gandhiji has described the traditional educational system as a beautiful tree felled down during the British rule. Different phases of Indian education system comprises the primary education, secondary education, senior secondary education and higher education. Elementary education consists of eight years of education. Each of the secondary and senior secondary education consists of two years of education. Higher education in India starts after passing the higher secondary education or the 12th standard. Depending on the stream any candidate doing graduation in India can take three to five years. Postgraduate courses are generally of two to three years of duration.

After completing post-graduation, the scope for doing research in various educational institutes also remains open.

Global Perspectives

Nowadays, it is a global trend that young brains are being attracted more towards the technological education. There is no doubt that science and technology are complementary in nature and have to grow hand in hand. Besides, the growth of knowledge, the research in fundamental science adds an inevitable input to the advancement of technology. Quick and highly paid job opportunities have been an added advantage for the graduates in technology. In the eighties and nineties of the last century, the best young minds were being attracted more towards basic science courses; howsoever, this situation has undergone a complete change throughout the globe recently.

Even today, there are unlimited mysteries and wonders in the universe, which are to be answered by the scientific communities than the technologists. Hence, the world still expects new path-breaking ideas, originating from intelligent young minds of the science stream. It is a matter of concern that our education system is more inclined towards the textbook exercise. Only a very few of them have developed the habit of thinking over a problem in their own way. The percentage of students taking higher education is hardly about 13 per cent whereas the same is varying between 28 to 90 per cent, across the world. The lowest percentage being 28 per cent and the same is as high as 90 per cent in developed countries. It is necessary to find out the lacuna in the present education system to meet and overcome the challenges existing around us.

Lacuna in Present Phase

The current system of teaching and evaluation does not provide any opportunity to find solution for the problems which we face today. Further, they are not encouraged to have crazy ideas. Starting from the primary to the higher education, the present emphasis is on maximisation of the quantity of information instead of leaving room for imagination or recreation of minds. We forget that the creative mind has no problem in acquiring information on its own. The complete division between the cultures of science and humanities and deviation of science from philosophy has reduced the sphere of scientific thought. Science educators may ponder over this problem and provide an opportunity to enlarge the sphere of scientific thoughts. Now-a-days, it is very frequently observed that students sign up for higher studies with less interest or take it casually. Mostly institutions in India make the citizens employable rather liveable. There are very few institutions who are give quality inputs so as to inculcate the learning skills amongst students.

Character among the individual has disappeared. Our English education has taken away many things which are considered to be very essential. Our children have lost their politeness. To talk nicely is degrading. To be reverential to one's elders is degrading. Irreverence has been the sign of liberty. It is high time that we go back to our old politeness. The reformers have nothing to give in place of what they have taken away. Swami Vivekananda pointed out that it is almost wholly one of the imperfections. It is nothing but a perfect machine for turning out clerks; men are becoming destitute of Shraddha and faith. They assert that the Gita was only an interpolation, and that the Vedas were but rustic songs. They like to master every detail concerning things and nations outside India, but if we ask them they do not know even the names of their own forefathers up to the seventh generation.

The Need to Reform

Our present higher education is mere study of material sciences and turning out things of everyday use by machinery. The use of higher education is to solve the problems of life, and this is what has been engaging the profound thought of modern civilised world, but it was solved in our country, some thousands of years ago. The masses in our country are alike the sleeping leviathan. The education imparted in the present university system reaches one or two percent of the masses. And even those who get that do not succeed in their endeavour of doing any good to the country. In order to drive the existing deficits out, there must be a reform in the higher education.

Education that India Needs

From the day when education and culture began to spread gradually from patricians to plebeians, there is a distinction between the ancient civilisation as of western countries and civilisation of India, Egypt and Rome. Swamiji visualised any nation advanced in proportion as education and intelligence spread among the masses. The chief cause of India's ruin has been monopolising the whole education and intelligence of the land, by dint of pride and royal authority, among a handful of men.

"Old institution of living with the Guru" and similar systems of imparting education are needed. What we want are western science coupled with Vedanta, Bharmacharya as the guiding motto, and also Shraddha and faith in one's own self. Another thing that we want is the abolition of that system which aims at educating our boys in the same manner as that of man who battered his ass, being advised that it could thereby be turned into a horse.

According to Swamiji, the prime aim of education is spiritual growth and development. This does not mean that he did not advocate material prosperity and physical well-being. His feelings have advocated the inclusion of those subjects and activities, in the curricula, which foster material welfare with spiritual advancement.

For spiritual perfection he prescribed Religions, Philosophy, Puranic lore, Upanishads, Company of saints and their preaching's and for material advancement and prosperity he recommended Languages, Geography, Science,

Political Science, Economics, Psychology, Art, Agriculture, Industrial and Technical subjects together with Games, sports and other Physical exercises.

He also prescribed the same ancient spiritual methods of teaching wherein the Guru and his disciples lived in close association as in a family. The essential characteristics of those religious and spiritual methods were as under:

- To control the fleeting mental faculties by the practice of Yoga.
- To develop the mind by concentration and deep meditation.
- To gain the knowledge through lectures, discussions, self-experience and creative activities.
- To imitate the qualities and character of teacher intelligent and clear understanding.
- To lead the child on the right path by means of individual guidance by the teacher.

Place of Child

Swamiji emphasised the education to be child-centered. According to him, the child is the store and repository of all learning material and spiritual. Like a plant, a child grows by his/her own inner power naturally. Hence, advising the child to grow naturally and spontaneously, Vivekananda asserted Go into your own and get the Upanishads out of your own self. You are the greatest book that ever was or will be. Until the inner teacher opens, all outside teaching is in vain.

Place of Teacher

Swamiji believed in self-education. According to him, each of us is his own teacher. The external teacher only guides and inspires the inner teacher (soul) to rise up and start working to develop the child. Hence discussing the role of teacher Swami Vivekananda said- "Teacher is a philosopher, friend and guide helping the educand to go forward in this own way."

Education of Masses

Previously education was not available to the common people. It was confined to the well-to-do persons. The poor, the miserable and the lowly placed used to starve and die for hunger. Swamiji yearned to improve the condition of the masses and thus advocated mass education as the only way to achieve any improvement in individual as well as society.

Technical Education

Technical education should be implemented to study the independent of foreign control, different branches of knowledge with the English language and Western science. He also quoted that getting some unmarried graduates, where they may send over to Japan for technical education, so that when they come back, they may turn their knowledge to the best account of India. In Japan, we find assimilation of knowledge and not its digestion as we have here.

They have taken everything from Europeans, but they remain Japanese all the same, and have not turned European; while in our country, the terrible mania of becoming Westernised has seized upon us like a plague.

Inference

This is the time to remove the defects in present higher education system to bring back our ancient culture, traditions and practices to make an individual self-dependent, great thinker and bring innovations in all fields. Swamiji has rightly pointed out that education for individual should be: Reaching perfection, Physical and mental development, Moral and spiritual development, Character building, Development of faith in oneself and Shraddha, Spirit of renunciation, Aim of searching unity in diversity and Religious development. Imparting this kind of higher education for every child in our country, Swamiji visualised the glorious and wonderful future for our nation.

Conclusion

Positive education should be given to common mass. All the members of a society ought to have same opportunity for obtaining wealth, education or knowledge. We must awake the knowledge of an individual with modern science. Teaching subjects like history, geography, science, literature, and along with truths of religion must be given importance so that the growth of the nation will be high. Higher education plays vital role in promoting individual as well nation.

References

- Arnold, David (2004), The New Cambridge History of India: Science, Technology and Medicine in Colonial India, Cambridge University Press, ISBN: 0-521-56319-4.
- Ahluwalia, B. 1983. Vivekananda and the Indian Renaissance. New Delhi: Associated Publishing Co.
- Avinashalingam, T.S. 1974. Educational Philosophy of Swami Vivekananda. 3rd ed. Coimbatore: Sri Ramakrishna Mission Vidyalaya.
- Blackwell, Fritz (2004), India: A Global Studies Handbook, ABC-CLIO, Inc., ISBN: 1-57607-348-3.
- Burke, M.L. 1984. Swami Vivekananda in the West: new discoveries, 6 Vols. Calcutta: Mission Institute of Culture.

55

Swamiji's Aims of Education

A.V. Karabasanagoudra

Biography

Swami Vivekananda was born in an orthodox family, in Bengal, on the Twelfth of January 1863. Narendranath, as he was named by his parents, was a naughty child, subject to fits of restlessness during which he was beyond control. He was a gay youth taking part in many kinds of activities like boxing, wrestling, swimming and riding, at the same time he was very eager for all kinds of knowledge. He was an earnest student of philosophy and poetry. He studied all systems of Western philosophy and became very well acquainted with Herbert Spencer and John Stuart Mill. Wordsworth and Shelly were his favourite poets. As a student, Narendranath Dutta was very well known and popular with the students and the teachers, alike for his genius and extraordinary talents. Narendra's association with Sri Rama Krishna Paramahamsa brought a change not only in him, but it began a new chapter in the history of Hinduism.

Swami Vivekananda broadcasted the truths of Vedanta in India, Europe and America. He demonstrated to the world that the great Indian spiritual tradition was still alive and vigorous. He showed by precept and by example that if the ancient Vedanta were reinterpreted in the light of Sri Ramakrishna's spiritual experiences and applied to modern life. India would rise again to deliver a message to humanity. He asked his countrymen to put those truths into practice while he has explaining the philosophy of Vedanta to the puplic in America and later in Europe. Vivekananda taught theoretical Vedanta in the West and practical Vedanta in India. He declared the most practical form of Vedanta was the uplift of masses. He was not a politician, but he wanted to make the Indian mass strong and self-reliant. He was not a professional teacher, but observed that "education alone made the people in the West comfortable, there was brought to my mind the state of our own poor people, and I used to shed tears. What made the difference? Education was the answer I got". To Swami Vivekananda, an ideal society should combine the spiritual culture of India and the secular culture of America and England. According to him, the strength was the crying need of the hour. He was never tired of asserting that India needs strength giving religion and a man-making education.

Vivekananda's association with Ramakrishna Paramhamsa resulted in his becoming a 'wandering monk' after the death of his master. After wandering throughout the country and a few parts of the world, Vivekananda established a monastic order called the Ramakrishna Mission and thus began the educational activities of this philosopher. The Ramakrishna Mission today has more than hundred and twenty five centres all over the world. Swamiji's activities as a 'sanyasee' brought his end a little too soon. He died at a very a tender age of just 39 years on July 4th, 1902.

His Philosophy of Life

Vivekananda was a true Vedantist. He regarded Vedanta as eternal and believed in Advaita (monotheism) and Dwaita (dualism) concept. According to Swamiji, God is all powerful and without attributes (personal qualities). He saw God in three forms, viz., Being (sat), Awareness (chit) and Bliss (Ananda). He believes that the force of God prevails in all things of this universe. He emphasises the universalness of soul and brotherhood.

Vivekananda's faith in man is tremendous. He believed that man is the highest creation of God. He believed that religion is progressive. The purpose of life is to experience God within one's own self. Once he does that he begins to experience himself in all other creatures. Then he applies himself to the service of each and every living being. The philosophy of life of Swami Vivekananda is based on universal oneness and spiritual brotherhood.

Vivekananda believed that perfection is inherent in man, which ought to be manifested. Service to man is the greatest worship of God.

His Concept of Education

Swamiji educational philosophy emanated from his philosophy of eternal values and eternal religion. In the true idealistic spirit, he considered the highest goal of human life to be unfoldment of the divinity within. Vivekananda believed every soul to be divine, education has to manifest this divinity by controlling nature, external and internal. For Vivekananda, knowledge, alone is not the only factor for individual good; physical strength, moral strength and character are equally important to any system of education. Education according to Vivekananda is acquiring knowledge formation of character and development of social traits.

His Aims of Education

About the aims of education Swamiji has summed up his ideas in one sentence. "The end of all education, all training should be man-making". He recommended several aims of education.

Faith in One's Own Self

This is first step towards advancement and the first prerequisite to attain education and perfection. The main function of education is to make a person conscious of his latent powers. This will lead him to a life is sublime and divine is all respects. Education must create self-reliance through shradha (concentration-self regarding sentiment).

Man devoid of sentiment runs to ruin. This was strongly felt by Swamiji. Education, must, therefore provide self-knowledge which brings material prosperity and freedom from the bondage of worldly existence. Though self analysis and self insight, a man can attain perfection and achieve the glory of life. Swamiji's call was "be strong and have this shradha. Education must aim at this kind of knowledge of the 'self' and at creation of self-confidence and self-reliance.

Education Must Develop Moral Character

Swamiji clearly said "Education is not the amount of information that is put into your brain and runs riot there, undigested in your life. We must have life-building, man-making, character making assimilation of ideas". All the time he spoke of formation of character through education. The beauty and glory of life lies in character-making. (Complete Works of Swami Vivekananda, Vol. III, P. 302).

Practical Side of Life

Swamiji was very much concerned with the wretched poverty of his countrymen. He was anxious to see millions of starving and poverty stricken Indians properly fed. He considered a system of education worthless, which ignores the practical side of life. By the practical of life, he means that every one must be able to get his primary needs satisfied. Everyone must stand on his own legs. Here, he suggested the establishment of workshops and other centres to solve the problems of hunger and unemployment in the country. He equally favoured the study of western technology and engineering, for the economic prosperity.

Promotion of Universal Brotherhood

Education must promote the feeling that the Atman (soul) is the same in all—from the ant to the perfect man—the difference being only in its manifestation. He asserts that "from the highest God to the meanest grass the same power is potent in all-whether manifested or not". Education must call forth this power in every man. This spirit will certainly mean annihilation of all misery from this earth. Vivekananda stood for internationalism, unity of mankind and transformation of the world society into a compact union of hearts and souls.

Rote Learning

Swamiji was against bookish knowledge. True education is that which develops the will and enables one realise the divinity latent in him. In the words of Dr. Chaube, "education must aim at the development of infinite energy, infinite zeal, infinite courage and infinite patience in man".

Spirit of Renunciation

Swamiji has said that education must generate the spirit of renunciation in man. This renunciation means the inculcation of feeling that we should work for others and it is a great privilege to be able to do something for the world.

Immense Faith in Man

Swamiji's faith in man was immense. To him, "man is higher than all animals and angels, none is greater than man. Even the Gods will have to come down again to attain salvation through a human body". The teacher has to make the pupil conscious that he has to reach his perfection. (Complete works of swami Vivekananda, Vol. I, p. 142).

With the above aims, the Swamiji has established glorious traditions of India, which formed a basis for building modern India.

Conclusion

One cannot have an effective educational system without clear philosophy of education that takes into account the many factors which go to make up such complex structures as human personality, human society and the influence of environment and conditions of all sorts, on both society and the individual. Though today's education is supposed to be child-centered, in practice it is not so. The modern academics do not cultivate overall the child's personality, i.e., physical, intellectual, aesthetic, social and spiritual power of the child. All are interested in getting or giving degrees. Neither the individual nor the nation profits from such type of education being organised and imparted today. In the present condition, where lack of national solidarity, regionalism, communalism, casteism, terrorism, violence, mindless and unabated killings, omnipotent corruption are prevalent, it ought to have good system of education to uplift the people from childhood onwards, physically, intellectually, economically, socially, morally as well as spiritually.

References

- Admirers, Eastern and Western (1964). Reminiscences of Swami Vivekananda. II Edition, Rama Krishna Vedanta Matt. Calcutta.
- Advaita Ashrama (1966) The Message of Swami Vivekananda, Advaita Ashrama, Calcutta.
- Aggarwal, J.C. (1967) Thoughts on Education, Arya Book Depot. New Delhi.
- Avinashilingam, T.S. Education-Complied from the Speeches and Writings of Swami Vivekananda, Sri R.K. Mission Vidyalaya.
- Biswas, A. and Aggarwal, J.C. (1968) Some Indian Educationists, Asha Prakashan Griha, New Delhi.

56

The Philosophy and Method of Education

P. Ranganayaki

Introduction

Swami Vivekananda (1863-1902), a great thinker and reformer of India, embraced education, which for him signifies 'man-making', as the very mission of his life. Swamiji realised that mankind pass through a crisis. The tremendous emphasis on the scientific and mechanical ways of life is fast reducing man to the status of a machine. Moral and religious values are being undermined. The fundamental principles of civilisation are being ignored. The conflicts of ideals, manners and habits are pervading the atmosphere. Disregard for everything old is the fashion of the day. Swamiji sought solutions for social and global evils through education. He feels the dire need of awakening man to his spiritual self, wherein he thinks, lies the very purpose of education.

The Objectives

Swami Vivekananda prepares the scheme of this man-making education in the light of his over-all philosophy of Vedanta. According to Vedanta, the essence of man lies in his soul, which he possess in addition to his body and mind. In true sense with this philosophy, Swamiji defines education as 'the manifestation of the perfection already in man.' The aim of education is to manifest in our lives the perfection, which is the very nature of our inner self. This perfection is the realisation of infinite power, which resides in everything and every-where-existence, consciousness and bliss (satchidananda). After understanding the essential nature of this perfection, we should identify it with our inner self. For achieving this, one will have to eliminate one's ego, ignorance and all other false identification, which stand in the way. Meditation, fortified by moral purity and passion for truth, helps man to leave behind the body, the senses, the ego and all other non-self elements, which are perishable. He thus realises his immortal divine self, which is of the nature of infinite existence, infinite knowledge and infinite bliss.

At this stage, man becomes aware of his self as identical with other selves of the universe, i.e., different selves as manifestations of the same self. Hence, the education, in Swamiji's sense, enables one to comprehend one's self within as the self everywhere. The essential unity of the entire universe is realised through education. Accordingly, man making for Swamiji stands for rousing man to the awareness of his true self. However, education thus signified does not point towards the development of the soul in isolation from body and mind. We ought to remember that basis of Swamiji's philosophy is Advaita which preaches unity in diversity. Therefore, man making for him means a harmonious development of the body, mind and soul.

Philosophy of Education

Education is not the amount of information put into our brain and runs riot there, undigested all our life. We must have life-building, man-making, character-making, assimilation of ideas. If we have assimilated five ideas and made them our life and character, we have more education than any man who has got by heart a whole library. First, his definition of education and his concern about the need to strengthen spiritual and secular values in education; second, his appeal for spreading moral and ethical education; third, his ideas of women's education; fourth, his call for education of the masses; and fifthly, his idea about the need for an interface between science and religion in the present-day world. If education were identical with information, the libraries would be the greatest sages in the world and encyclopedias the Rishis. 'The training by which the current and expression of will are brought under control and become fruitful is called education'.

The education that does not help the common mass of people to equip themselves for the struggle for life, which does not bring out strength of character, a sprit of philanthropy and the courage of a lion. Is it worth the name?

Swami Vivekananda wanted that education by which character is formed, strength of mind is increased, the intellect is expanded and by which one can stand on one's own feet. What we need is to study, independent of foreign control, different branches of the knowledge that is our own, and with it the English language and Western science; we need technical education and all else that will develop industries, so that men instead of seeking for service may earn enough to provide for themselves and save against a rainy day.

Swamiji propounds his philosophy of education which mainly emphasise on man-making. It constitutes as one of the very missions of his life. Swamiji finds mankind gradually being reduced to the status of machine due to the tremendous emphasis on the scientific as well as mechanical ways of life. In his vision, this mainly is leading mankind to pass through the stage of a crisis. It results into the ignorance of the fundamental principles of civilisation. The atmosphere is being pervaded by the constant conflict of ideals, manners and habits. There is only constant attempt to disregard and discard everything that is old which has become a fashion of the day. Swamiji finds education as the major weapon to fight against social as well as global evils. He realises that solution lies in education, enlightenment. In his vision, the spiritual awakening of mankind is mainly needed. This constitutes as the main purpose of his philosophy of education.

Method of Education

There is only one method by which to attain knowledge, that which is called concentration. From the lowest man to the highest yogi, all have to use the same method to attain knowledge. The more the power of concentration, the greater the knowledge acquired. Even lowest shoeblack, if he gives more concentration, will black shoes better. The cook with concentration will cook a meal all the better. In making money, or in work-shipping God, or in doing anything, the stronger the power of concentration the better will that thing be done. This is the one call, the one knock, which opens the gates of Nature, and lets out floods of light.

The trained man or mind never makes a mistake. Compare the lowest with the highest man. The difference hangs on in the degree of concentration. All success in any line of work is the result of this. High achievements in art, music, etc., are the result of concentration. When the mind is concentrated and turned back, all within us will be our servants, not our masters.

The power or concentration is the only key to the treasure house of knowledge. The practice of meditation leads to mental concentration. To Swami Vivekananda, the very essence of education is concentration of mind, not the collection of facts. He wanted to develop the power of concentration and detachment, and then with a perfect instrument, collect facts at will.

Faith is one of the potent factors of humanity. First, we should have faith in ourselves. One may be a little bubble and another may be a mountain-high wave, yet behind both the bubble and the wave, there is the infinite ocean. The infinite ocean is the background of all.

Fields of Study

Swami Vivekananda in his scheme of education, meticulously includes those studies, which are necessary for the all-around development of the body, mind and soul of the individual. These studies can be brought under the broad heads of physical culture, aesthetics, classics, language, religion, science and technology. According to Swamiji, the culture values of the country should form an integral part of the curriculum of education. The culture of India owes to her spiritual values. The time-tested values are to be imbibed in the thoughts and lives of the students through the study of the classics like Ramayana, Mahabharata, Gita, Vedas and Upanishads. This will keep the perennial flow of our spiritual values into the world culture.

Education, according to Swamiji, remains incomplete without the teaching of aesthetics or fine art. He cites Japan as an example of how the combination of art and utility can make a nation great. Swamiji reiterates religion as the innermost core of education. However, by religion, he does not mean any particular kind but its essential character, which is the realisation of divinity already in man. Swami Vivekananda reminds us time and again that religion does not consist in dogmas or creeds or any set of rituals. To be religious for him means leading life in such a way that we manifest our higher nature, truth, goodness and beauty, in our thoughts, words and deeds. All impulses, thoughts and actions which lead one towards this goal are naturally ennobling and harmonising, and are ethical and moral in the truest sense. It is in this context that Swamiji's idea of religion, as the basis of education should be understood. We note that in his interpretation, religion and education share the identity of purpose.

Conclusion

The exposition and analysis of Vivekananda's scheme of education brings to light its constructive, practical and comprehensive character. He realises it as only through education that the uplift of masses is possible. Swami Vivekananda states it emphatically that if society had to be reformed, education ought to reach everyone-high and low, because individuals are the very constituents of society. The sense of dignity rises in man, when he becomes conscious of his inner spirit, and that is the very purpose of education. He strives to harmonise the traditional values of India with the new values brought through the progress of science and technology. It is in the transformation of man through moral and spiritual education that he finds the solution for social evils. Founding education on the firm ground of our own philosophy and culture, he shows the best of remedies for today's social and global illness. Through his scheme of education, he tries to materialise the moral and spiritual welfare and uplift of humanity, irrespective of caste, creed, nationality or time. However, Swami Vivekananda's scheme of education, through which he wanted to build up a strong nation that will lead the world towards peace and harmony, is still a far cry. It is high time that we give serious thought to his philosophy of education and remembers his call to everybody—"Arise, awake, and stop not till the goal is reached".

57

Swamiji on Philosophy of Education

V. Pradeepa

Introduction

Swami Vivekananda views that education is not information of knowledge which will insert into the mind of a child by force. In his own words—"Education is the manifestation of perfection already reached in man." He describes that the libraries could be the greatest saints of the world and encyclopedias have become seers and rishis. Vivekananda's concept of education was that, "it is the manifestation of the perfection already in man. He further said that the education was not of getting huge amount of information; it would be an undigested material of our brain. The good quality education must have the life building, man-making, character building, and assimilation of ideas. This would help to the common people to equip themselves for the struggle of life.

Swamiji's Philosophy of Life

The main essence of his philosophy of life is to become fearless through struggle and serve humanity with peace. He wants to make a individual without fear from enemies, face all the challenges boldly and confidently without any suppression. By synthesising the idealistic philosophy of the west and creative philosophy of the ancient Hindu Dharm, he got a glory and greatness to the Hindu way of living.

Swamiji's Philosophy of Education

The real education according to Swami Vivekananda is that which prepares the individual for struggle for existence. Education prepares a man for social service, to develop his character and finally iambuses him with the spirit and courage of a lion. For getting degree is not an education, the proper education must be viewed on the basis of character, mental powers, intelligence and inculcates. Self-confidence and self-reliance should be in the individuals. Swamiji has emphasised that the knowledge which we get from worldly or spiritual lies embedded in the human mind. It was covered with a veil of darkness and ignorance. Education is a tool for opening from the darkness and ignorance, after getting of education, the knowledge will shine out dazzlingly.

The teaching and learning are the one way of process. The teacher only guides, suggests, points out and helps the student. Self-learning and self-getting knowledge is the real education. The teacher only motivates and encourages the students to find out the hidden treasure of knowledge that lies dormant within him. He condemned and refused the bookish learning and rote memory education. Condemning the theoretical and academic education, he spoke emphatically for practical and experimental education. He warned his countrymen saying "you will have to be practical in all spheres of work. The whole country has been ruined by mass theories."

Swamiji's Means of Education

According to Vivekananda, the means for education is love. Love and character building are the best means for education. Love is the best inspiration in character building. Love in the minds of the educator is the real source of his influence upon the educated. The true education, gives the growth and expansion of personality. He wanted that the education for total human development was the main vision. "Character, efficiency and humanism should be the aim of all education. Swamiji strongly pleaded that development of character through the service of his fellowmen, the utilisation of his talents for ensuring the happiness and welfare of the millions of his less fortunate fellow-citizens should be the aim of the education." The child should be taught through by love, it makes fellow feelings and love for human beings. Education must help the individual to recognise his cultural heritage and to use it in his struggle of life. Education is a life-long process towards the fullest development of human personality, self-discovery, self-perfection, self-awareness and self-manifestation.

Swamiji's Aims of Education

Swamiji wanted all-round development of education to heart and mind, to strengthen character and national consciousness, to help in the cultivation of strength and energy, nurture the brain and intellect and stir feelings of kindness and sympathy. He emphatically said:

> "We want that education by which character is formed, strength of mind is increased, the intellect is expanded and by which one can stand on one's own feet. What we need is to study, independent of foreign control, different branches of the knowledge that is our own and with it the English language and Western science; we need technical education and all else that will develop industries. So that men, instead of seeking for service, may earn enough to provide for them and save against a rainy day. The end of all education, all training, should be man-making. The end and aim of all training is to make the man grow. The training, by which the current and expression of will are brought under control and become fruitful, is

> called education. What our country now wants are muscles of iron and a nerve of steel, gigantic wills which nothing can resists, which can penetrate into the mysteries and secrets of the universe and will accomplish their purpose in any fashion, even if it means going down to the bottom of the ocean, meeting death face to face. It is a man-making religion that we want. It is man-making theories that we want. It is man-making education all round that we want.

According to Swamiji, education is a process in which the young minds, will receive strength, energy and vigorous character. By the way of getting this process, the individual will mould themselves of their life. "All knowledge and all powers are within. What we call power; secrets of nature and force are all within. All knowledge comes from the human soul. Man manifests knowledge, discovers it with himself, which is pre-existing through eternity. Education is a man-making and nation-making process. It is the process which awakens the sleeping soul to self-conscious activity. It will become a powerful instrument to achieve the developmental qualities among the people. The prime aim of education is to achieve the full perfection already present in a child. According to Vivekananda, all the materials and spiritual knowledge are already present in the individuals mind, but it is covered by certain ignorance.

The second aim of education is the physical and mental development of the child. "For stressing the mental development of the child, Swamiji, wished education to enable the child to stand on his own legs economically rather than becoming a parasite on others. The third aim of education is the character development of the child. He emphasises the child should practice Brahmacharya which fosters development of mental, moral and spiritual powers leading to purity of thought, words and deeds. In the fourth aim of education, he emphasises the religious development. Every individual should search out and develop the religious seed and to reach the absolute truth or reality.

Vivekananda's ideas on education had a democratic angle. He expressed deep concern for the mass, "The education which does not help the common mass of people to equip themselves for the struggle for life, which does not bring out strength of character, a spirit of philanthropy, and the courage of a lion - is it worth the name? Real education is that which enables one to stand on one's own legs. The education that you are receiving now in schools and colleges is only making you a race of dyspeptics. You are working like machines merely, and living a jelly-fish existence. Swamiji's aim of education had strong nationalist bias. He was not critical of Western system of education rather; he questioned the suitability of Western Model in India. The system of education in India was based on Indian Foundation that was supported with the broader argument that the every nation should develop a system of education based on his own nature, history and civilisation.

Swamiji's Principles of Education

Like Rabindranath Tagore, Vivekananda also prescribed the same ancient spiritual methods of teaching, where Guru and his disciples lived in close association as in a family. The following are the basic principles of education.

(i) Education is not only for getting information; rather it should develop character, mental powers, intelligence and inculcate self-confidence together with self-reliance.

(ii) Education should develop the child physically, mentally and spiritually.

(iii) While giving educational qualification, the technical education was necessary for the industrial growth which would lead to the economic prosperity of the nation.

(iv) Practicing of Brahmacharya is very essential for getting knowledge. The concentration is the key to all the knowledge.

(v) Religious education should be imparted through sweet impressions and fine conduct in preference to books.

(vi) Education should be foster spiritual faith, devotion and self-surrender in the individual and full development through service and sacrifice.

(vii) Education should develop character, mental powers, intelligence and inculcate self-confidence together with self-reliance.

(viii) All the subjects must be included in the curriculum which promotes the material and spiritual advancement of a child.

Swamiji's Views on Education

Vivekananda's views on education deals with physical education, moral and religious education, medium of education, women education and education for weaker sections of society.

Physical Education: without the knowledge of physical education, the self-realisation or character building is not possible one must know, how to make our body strong through physical education, for to attain a complete education, it is necessary to develop both the mind and the body. In particular, Swamiji stressed the value of physical education in curriculum. He said, "You will be nearer to Heaven through football than through the study of Gita. You will understand Gita better by your biceps, your muscles a little stronger. You will understand the Upanishads better and the glary of the Atman, when your body stands firm on your feet and you feel yourself as man.

Medium of Education: Like Gandhi and Rabindranath Tagore, Swamiji also emphasised education through the mother tongue. Besides mother tongue, there should be a common language which is necessary to keep the country united. Swamiji appreciated the greatness of Sanskrit that it is the source of all Indian languages and a repository of all inherited knowledge; with the absence of this knowledge, it will be impossible to understand Indian culture. It is like a store house of ancient heritage, to develop our society it is necessary that men and women should know this language, besides the knowledge of the mother tongue.

Moral and Religious Education: Swamiji said, "Religion is the innermost core of education. I do not mean my own or anyone else opinion about religion. Religion is as the rice and everything else, like the curries. Taking only curries causes indigestion and so is the case with taking rice alone." Therefore, religious education is a vital part of a sound curriculum.

Vivekananda considered Gita, Upanishads and the Vedas are the most important curriculum for religious education. For him, religion is a self-realisation and divinisation. It is not only individual's development but also for the transformation of total man. The true religion cannot be limited to a particular place of time. He pleaded for unity of world religion. He realised truth while practicing of religion. The truth is the power, untruth is the weakness. Knowledge is truth, ignorance is untruth. Thus, the truth increases power, courage and energy. It is light giving, therefore, necessary for the individual as well as collective welfare. In the Swamiji's point of view, ethics and religion are one and the same. God is always on the side of goodness. To fight for goodness is the service to God. The moral and religion education develop the self-confidence among the young men and women.

Education of Masses: The individual development is not a full development of our nation. He needs to give education to the society or common people. The education is not only confined to the well-to-do persons only but also to the poor people. Swamiji emphasised to improve the conditions of masses advocating mass education. He takes this mass education as an instrument to improve the individual as well as society. By this way, he exhorted his countrymen to know—"I consider that the great national sin is the neglect of masses, and that is one of the causes of our downfall. No amount of politics would be of avail until the masses of India are well-educated, well-fed and well-cared for.

Man-Making Education: The educational philosophy of Swamiji is a harmonious synthesis between the ancient Indian ideals and modern Western beliefs. He not only stressed on the physical, mental, moral, spiritual and vocational development of the child but also he advocated women education as well as education of the masses. The essential characteristics of his educational philosophy of Swamiji are idealism, naturalism and pragmatism. In a naturalistic view, he emphasised that real education is possible only through nature and natural propensities. In the form of idealist view point, he insists that the aim of education is to develop the child with moral and spiritual qualities. In his pragmatists view, he emphasised the great stress on the Western education of technology, commerce, industry and science to achieve material prosperity. In short, Swamiji remained an idealist at heart. First of all, he emphasised spiritual development, then the material prosperity, after that safety of life and solving the problems of fooding and clothing of masses.

Self-Education: Self-education is the self-knowledge. That is, of our own self is the best guide in the struggle of our life. If we take one example, the childhood stage, the child will face lot of problems or commit mistakes in the process of character formation. The child will learn much by his mistakes. Errors are the stepping stones to our progress in character. This progress will need courage and strong will. The strong will is the sign of great character will makes men great.

Women's Education: Women's education is not in the hands of others, the powers are in the women. Vivekananda considered that women to be the incarnation of power and asked men to respect them in everywhere. He rightly pointed out that unless Indian women secure a respectable place in this country, the nation can never march forward. The important features of his scheme of female education are to make them strong, fearless, and conscious of their chastity and dignity. He insists that men and women are equally competent not only in the academic matters, but also must have equal companion in the home and family. Swamiji, on being a keen observer could distinguish the difference in perception about the status of women in the West and in India.

Education of the under privileged: Swamiji pleaded for universal education so that the backward people man not fall in with others. To uplift the backward classes, he chooses education as a powerful instrument for their life process. Thus education should spread to every household in the country, to factories, playing grounds and agricultural fields. If the children do not come to the school the teacher should reach them. Two or three educated men should team up, collect the paraphernalia of education and should go to the village to impart education to the children. Thus, Swamiji favoured education for different sections of society, rich and poor, young and old, male and female.

Conclusion

From the analysis of Swamiji's scheme of education, the uplift of masses is possible only through education. He views on education brings a light of its constructive, practical and comprehensive character. By giving education, he tries to materialise the moral and spiritual welfare and upliftment of humanity, irrespective of caste, creed, nationality or time. By the way of his scheme of education, we can get the strong nation with peace and harmony and without caste and creed. He builds a strong nation for our sake.

References

- Nagarajan, K., (2010). Philosophical and sociological foundation in education.
- http://vivekananda@amazon.com
- Avinashalingam, T.S., (1974). Educational philosophy of Swami Vivekananda. 3rd ed. Coimbatore.

58

The Scheme of Education

P. Vasantha

Introduction

Swami Vivekananda, the spiritual luminary, great thinker, patriot-prophet of our times and the educationist par excellence is a pioneering figure in the cultural and the spiritual history of Indian people. He enlightened not only India, but also the whole world by his outstanding personality and intellectuals. He tried to revive and reshape the ancient culture and wisdom at a crucial period. He had great faith in education. He believed that it is the basic means for achieving human excellence and solving national problems. He had envisioned a society with the type of human being in whom knowledge, action, work and concentration are harmoniously blended and he proposed a new scheme of education for making this a reality. This was revealed in his numerous lectures delivered at various places in India and abroad. He was revolutionary in his thoughts on education and touched every aspect of it. He emphasised that education must provide life-building, man-making, character-moulding assimilation of ideas.

Goals of Education

Swami Vivekananda's scheme of education is based on the overall philosophy of Vedanta. Vedanta emphasises the essence of man lies in his soul which he possess in addition to his body and mind. Having understood this well, Swamiji defined education as the manifestation of perfection already in man.

According to him, manifestation indicates a spontaneous growth provided that the impediments are removed. He elucidated the term perfection as the goal of actualising the highest human potential. However, the goal varies from society to society and in the context of the vast Indian civilisation. Perfection may be viewed from two levels. First is the metaphysical level where perfection means the realisation of the soul's own ever-perfect nature. Second is the empirical level. There, according to Swamiji, perfection means achieving the stage where one stands on one's legs, well-equipped to face the challenges of life with a spirit of philanthropy and the courage of a lion.

Swami Prabhananda, the present General Secretary and a senior monk of Sri Ramakrishna Order has interpreted 'perfection' that is mentioned in Swamiji's definition of education as the human beings' potential which has again three aspects. The first is capacity which means the acquisition of a specific characteristic or competence that makes learning possible. The second is the propensity of doing something when the opportunity comes, implying the development of learning. And the third aspect is capability, the competence of working towards an intended outcome with the strength of getting rid of obstacles to learning. It implies self-development or self-empowerment. Swamiji wanted education by which character is formed, strength of mind is enhanced, intellect is expanded and self-reliance is developed. Then he went on to say, "The training by which the current and expression of will are brought under control and become fruitful is called education."

Curriculum of Education

Swami Vivekananda, in his scheme of education, meticulously illustrated to include those studies, necessary for the all-around development of the body, the mind and the soul of the individual. These studies can be brought under the broad heads of physical culture, classics, language, religion, science and technology. According to Swamiji, the cultural values of the country should form an integral part of the curriculum. The culture of India has its roots in her spiritual values. The time-tested values are to be imbibed in the thoughts and lives of the students through the study of the classics like the Ramayana, the Mahabharata, the Gita, the Vedas and the Upanishads. This will keep the perennial flow of our spiritual values into the world culture. According to Swamiji, remains incomplete without the teaching of aesthetics or fine arts. He cited Japan as an example of how the combination of art and utility can make a nation great. He wanted to include technical education and all else which will develop industries. He reiterated that religion is the innermost core of education. In building up character, in making for everything that is good and great and in bringing peace to others and peace to one's own self, religion is the highest motive power, and, therefore, ought to be studied from that standpoint.

Medium of Instruction

Every man is capable of receiving knowledge, if it imparted in his own language. With regard to the medium of instruction, Swamiji strongly advocated for mother-tongue. Being a true nationalist and a champion of national education, he favoured instruction through mother-tongue. He visualised for providing education in the national context. He also wanted to spread mass education through mother-tongue so that it will reach everyone. Though Swamiji is of the opinion that mother tongue is the right medium for social or mass education, he prescribed the learning of English and Sanskrit also. While English is necessary for mastering Western science and technology, Sanskrit leads one into the depths of our vast store of classics. The implication is that if language does not remain the privilege of a small class of people, social unity will march forward unhampered.

The Teacher

Swami Vivekananda asserted that a good teacher can register a positive impact and everlasting impression in his students. He listed out a number of essential qualities of the teacher. In his views, the teacher must know the spirit of the scriptures. The teacher who deals too much in words and allows the mind to be carried away by the force of words loses the spirit. It is the knowledge of the spirit of the scriptures alone that constitutes the true religious teacher. The second condition necessary in the teacher is that he must be perfectly pure, and then alone comes the value of his words. The function of the teacher is indeed an affair of the transference of something, and not one of mere stimulation of the existing intellectual or other faculties in the taught. Something real and appreciable as an influence comes from the teacher and goes to the taught. Therefore, the teacher must be pure. The teacher should have sound knowledge of his subjects and he should desire to learn more and more. He alone teaches who has something to give for teaching is not talking, teaching is not imparting doctrines, and it is communicating.

The only true teacher is he who can convert himself, as it were into a thousand persons at a moment's notice. The only true teacher is he who can immediately come down to the level of the student, and transfer his soul to the student's soul, see through the student's eyes, hear through his ears and understand through his mind. Such a teacher can really teach and none else. A good teacher is a source of creativity and innovations. He finds the ways to put the learner into new avenues of knowledge. Swamiji wanted the teacher to provide freedom and opportunities to the student to develop according to his own nature. The teacher should be sympathetic to his students. He should be like a father who gives his children their emotional, social, intellectual and spiritual birth and shows them the way to eternal life.

The Student

The student has a significant place in the system of education. The conditions necessary in the taught are purity, a real thirst after knowledge and perseverance. Purity in thought, speech and action is absolutely necessary. As to the thirst after knowledge, there must be a continuous struggle, a constant fight and an unremitting grappling with his lower nature till the higher want is actually felt and victory is achieved. The student who sets out with such a spirit of perseverance will surely find success and realisation at last.

Concentration of mind is the royal road for acquisition of all knowledge. So, Swamiji wanted the student to practise meditation and observe brahmacharya. He should have faith in the teacher and should open his heart to his influences. He should feel that his relationship with the teacher is the greatest in life. In order to facilitate manifestation of his inner strength and knowledge, he should cultivate the spirit of 'shraddha'- faith in himself, humility, submission and veneration for the teacher. He should carry this love and respect for his teacher throughout his life. The righteous living of the teacher is sure to inspire and stir value consciousness of the student and facilitate internalisation of values by him. Hence, he must live in close contact with the teacher and interact with him to promote his learning as in the old Gurukula system of education.

Methods of Teaching

Vedanta says that within man is all knowledge - even in a child, it is so and it requires only an awakening, and that much is the work of a teacher. Swami Vivekananda affirmed that the teacher has to do only so much for the children that they may learn to apply their own intellect to the proper use of their hands, legs, ears, etc., and finally everything will become easy. The teacher only motivates and encourages the students to find out the hidden treasure of knowledge that lies dormant within them. Here, he suggested that the teacher should act as a guide on the side.

This method of education resembles the heuristic method of education of the modern educationists in which the teacher invokes the spirit in the student who is supposed to find out things for himself under the bias-free guidance of the teacher. He wanted learner-centered education and this is clear from his statement: "The teaching must be modified according to the needs of the taught. ... Fire a mass of bird-shots, one at least will strike; give a man whole museum of truths, he will at once take what is suited to him. Past lives have moulded our tendencies; give the taught in accordance with his tendency. Intellectual, mystical, devotional, practical - make one the basis, but teach the others with it."

He condemned the bookish learning and rote memory education. He is skeptical about the system of education where the learner's mind gets jam-packed with information without having any space for independent thinking. Condemning the theoretical and academic education, he spoke emphatically for practical and experimental education. He warned his countrymen saying "You will have to be practical in all spheres of work. The whole country has been ruined by mass theories." Swamiji accepted learning through activities as an ideal method of teaching. It can provide direct experience to the learner. He suggested that activities like singing, story telling, drama and dancing should be performed by the students in the spirit of the Ramayana and the Mahabharata. He recommended for the introduction of other activities like excursion, camps, first aid programmes, etc., to help them understand the value of social service. He also advocated Question and Answer session and Deductive and Inductive methods in his educational philosophy.

Conclusion

Education is regarded as the catalyst for social, cultural, economic, scientific and technical developments. In this era of information technology, moral values are getting eroded. Social fiber is getting weakened. Corruption, pollution, violence, suicides, etc., increase day by day. It is in the transformation of man through moral and spiritual education that we can find solution for all these social evils. Swami Vivekananda's ideas on various aspects of education are more relevant and are needed more today than during his life time. He strived to harmonise the traditional values of India with the new values emerging through the progress of science and technology. His scheme of education brings a light of its constructive, practical and comprehensive character and also ensures emotional intelligence in man which will certainly pave the way for peace and harmony in the world. Recognising his contribution, UNESCO has acknowledged Swami Vivekananda as one of the eminent educationists of the world. In the words of E.P. Chelishev, "I think that Vivekananda's greatest service is the development in his teaching of the lofty ideals of humanism which incorporate the finest features of Indian culture. …. Many years will pass, many generations will come and go, Vivekananda and his time will become the distant past, but never will fade the memory of the man who all his life dreamed of a better future for his people, who did so much to awaken his compatriots and move India forward." As long as human civilisation exists, Swamiji's prolific views on education will have much relevance and great significance.

References

- Ajit Mondal and Dr. Jayata Mete (2012), Swami Vivekananda: Some Reflections on Education, International Journal of Multidisciplinary Educational Research, Volume 1, Issue 3, August 2012.
- Bicas C. Sanyal (2012), Revisiting Educational Thoughts and Actions of Swami Vivekananda, Bulletin of the Ramakrishna Institute of Culture, 2012.
- Nithya P. (2012), Swami Vivekananda's Views on Philosophy of Education, Asian Journal of Multidimensional Research, Vol. 1, Issue 6, November 2012.
- Santosh kumar Behera, S.K. (2012), Educational Ideas of Swami Vivekananda: Perception of the Essential Nature of a Teacher, the Taught, Methods of Teaching and the Discipline, Samwaad: *e*-Journal, Vol. 1, No. 1, 2012.
- Swami Vivekananda (2011), (Kiran Walla, Comd.), My Idea of Education, Advaita Ashram, Kolkata.

59

Swamiji's Mission of Life

A. Selvalakshmi

Introduction

> *"If you read Swami Vivekananda's writings and speeches, the curious thing you will find is that they are not old... They are fresh today... .And I think that our younger generation will take advantage of this fountain of wisdom of spirit and fire."* —*Jawaharlal Nehru*

In recent years, the renovation of higher education has particularly attracted a number of educators all over the world. In many countries across all regions, regardless of socio-economic and cultural context, recognition of the need to revive, renew and strengthen higher education systems and structures is manifest. This recognition confirms that higher education should contribute more effectively to meeting both the objectives of development policies and educational and training needs. Generally to celebrate means to rejoice, to observe a feast or a holiday. But an extended meaning of the term is to pay homage or pay tribute. The point is to honour and give expression to our appreciation of the works of a great person's personality and teachings. Spirituality grows only where spiritual men and women are honoured and respected. For spirituality is not an academic subject, but a living force, transforming a person from a brute to a divine personality. Swami Vivekananda has reached splendid heights in his spiritual journey, should be respected and honoured.

Swami Vivekananda (1863-1902), a great thinker and reformer of India, embraces education, which for him signifies 'man-making', as the very mission of his life.

In this paper, which purports to expound and analyse Vivekananda's views on education for national service, an endeavour has been made to focus on the basic theme of his philosophy, viz, the spiritual unity of the universe. Whether it concerns the goal or aim of education, or its method of approach or its component parts, all his thoughts, we shall observe, stern from this dormant theme of his philosophy which has its moorings in Vedanta.

The current dynamic to renew the higher education sector has created two particular imperatives:

(a) The need to widen the understanding of, to enhance access to research on systems and structures of higher education, research and knowledge—that is, to follow trends in these areas, and to analyse and advise on aspects of national and institutional policy on the basis of up to date information and research. Both efforts aimed at reinforcing higher education as an academic discipline, and at providing enhanced advisory services to policy-makers should be undertaken.

(b) The need to collate and make available data and analysis of the research mission in higher education. Through research, the sector has traditionally contributed to the generation and dissemination of advanced knowledge. Research is considered the necessary part of academic higher education. However, due to major changes in knowledge production, research function needs to be analysed and adjustments considered ensuring its quality.

It is thus essential to reaffirm the importance of research development in all countries, industrialised and developing, and to secure wide support and improve conditions for strengthening the development of research.

Swamiji points out that the defect of the present-day education is that it has no definite goal to pursue. A sculptor has a clear idea about what he wants to shape out of the marble block; similarly, a painter knows what he is going to paint. But a teacher, he says, has no clear idea about the goal of his teaching. Swamiji attempts to establish, through his words and deeds, that the end of all education is man making. He prepares the scheme of this man-making education in the light of his over-all philosophy of Vedanta. According to Vedanta, the essence of man lies in his soul, which he possesses in addition to his body and mind. In true with this philosophy, Swamiji defines education as 'the manifestation of the perfection already in man.'

The aim of education is to manifest in our lives the perfection, which is the very nature of our inner self. This perfection is the realisation of the infinite power which resides in everything and every-where-existence, consciousness and bliss. After understanding the essential nature of this perfection, we should identify it with our inner self. For achieving this, one will have to eliminate one's ego, ignorance and all other false identification, which stand in the way. Meditation, fortified by moral purity and passion for truth, helps man to leave behind the body, the senses, the ego and all other non-self elements, which are perishable. He thus realises his immortal divine self, which is of the nature of infinite existence, infinite knowledge and infinite bliss.

According to Swamiji, the prime aim of education is spiritual growth and development. But this does not mean that he did not advocate material prosperity and physical well-being. He feelingly advocated the inclusion of those subjects and activities, in the curriculum, which foster material welfare with spiritual advancement. For spiritual perfection, Swamiji prescribed Religions, Philosophy, Puranic lore, Upanishads, Company of saints and their preaching's and for material advancement and prosperity he recommended Languages, Geography, Science, Political Science, Economics, Psychology, Art, Agriculture, Industrial and Technical subjects together with Games, sports and other Physical exercises. He prescribed the same ancient spiritual methods of teaching wherein the Guru and his disciples lived in close association as in a family. The essential characteristics of those religious and spiritual methods were as under:

- To control fleeting mental faculties by the practice of Yoga.
- To develop the mind by concentration and deep meditation.
- To gain knowledge through lectures, discussions, self- experience and creative activities.
- To imitate the qualities and character of teacher intelligent and clear understanding.
- To lead the child on the right path by means of individual 21.1 idance by the teacher

Hence education, in Vivekananda's sense, enables one to comprehend one's self within as the self everywhere. The essential unity of the entire universe is realised through education. Accordingly, man making for Swamiji stands for rousing rnen to the awareness of his true self. However, education thus signified does not point towards the development of the soul in isolation from body and mind. He was an embodiment of love and strength. Humility and self-confidence, spirituality and service. He himself observed during his stay at the Thousand Island Parks in 1896: "Those who give themselves up to the Lord do more for the world than all the so called workers. One man who has purified himself thoroughly accomplishes more than a regiment of preachers. Out of purity and silence comes the word of power.

According to Swamiji, the culture values of the country should form an integral part of the curriculum of education. The culture of India has its roots in her spiritual values. The time-tested values are to be imbibed in the thoughts and lives of the students through the study of the classics like Ramayana, Mahabharata, Gita, Vedas and Upanishads. This will keep the perennial flow of our spiritual values into the world culture. Hence in Swamiji's view, for the development of a balanced nation, we have to combine the dynamism and scientific attitude of the West with the spirituality of our country.

The entire educational program should be so planned that it equips the youth to contribute to the material progress of the country as well as to maintaining the supreme worth of India's spiritual heritage. Another important aspect of Swamiji's scheme of education is women's education. He realises that it if the women of our country get the right type of education, then they will be able to solve their own problems in their own way. The main objective of his scheme of female education is to make them strong, fear-less, and conscious of their chastity and dignity. It is in the transformation of man through moral and spiritual education that he finds the solution for all social evils. Swamiji had thus a holistic and complete picture of the human situation and needs. What he upheld was the ideal of the renunciation and service to others. To celebrate Swamiji, means to follow him.

References

- Masand Prem. Think befare you think. Indore.
- Sharma. Swami Vivekananda's Winning Formulas. Rainbow Offset, Karnataka, 2011.
- Vivekananda His Call to the Nation. Advita Ashram , Kolkata, 2012.
- Life of swami Vivekananda by his Eastern and Western Disciples. Advita Ashram, Kolkata, 2012.

Swamiji's Views on Education

P. Suseela and M. Nala

Introduction

Education is indispensable for the progress and growth of an individual. Education makes a man what he is. Swamiji knew that education plays a vital role in curing the evils in society, and as critical in shaping the future of humanity. Although Swamiji did not write a book on education, he contributed valuable thoughts relevant and viable even today. With an urgent need of an hour and concern for the nation, everyone likes to spread his message particularly among the youth of our country. This article attempts to focus on Swamiji's views of education.

What is Education?

Swamiji quotes of education as: "Education is the manifestation of the perfection already in man'. The word 'manifestation' implies that something already exists and is waiting to be expressed. The main focus in learning is to make the hidden ability of a learner manifest. Next importance in the Swamiji's definition as the expression 'already in man'. This refers to a human beings potential, which is the range of the abilities and talents, known or unknown that he is born with. 'Perfection' in the metaphysical sense implies the realisation of the soul's own ever-perfect nature. At the empirical level, the concept of 'perfection' has to address the various problems, human beings encounter in society. What Swamiji said long ago is found in the pronouncement of Rogers. Carl Rogers said,

> "The individual has within himself the capacity and tendency, latent if not evident, to move forward towards maturity. In a suitable psychological ultimate this tendency is released. This tendency may become deeply buried under layer after layer of entrusted psychological defenses. It may be hidden behind elaborate facades which deny its existence. But, it is my belief that it exists in every individual and awaits only the proper condition to be released and expressed".

As Swamiji has said: 'The education which does not helps the common mass of people to equip themselves for the struggle for life, which does not bring out strength of character, a spirit of philanthropy and the courage of a lion - is it worth the name? Real education is that which enables one to stand on one's own legs. Education he said must provide 'life building, man making, character-making assimilation of ideas'. The ideal of this type of education would be to produce an integrated person - one who has learned how to improve his intellect, purify his emotions, and stand firm in moral virtues and usefulness.

The Purpose of Education

Unfortunately, the formal education is often restricted only to career - making and acquisition of working skills for earning a livelihood. This approach leads to schools and colleges where the purpose of all activity is only to make the students score high marks or grades overlooking other aspects of life. The real purpose of education should be to create right type of human being. Men and women are skilled in work and strong in character is what is wanted. Through man making or personality development, they can achieve it. Swamiji said, "There is only one purpose in whole life-education, otherwise what is the use of men and women, land and wealth?

Education and Development

While nation may be rich in natural resources, it is the human resources that are most important. To have human resource management, therefore is vial for nation's growth and development. Competition, co-operation and self dedication are three motive forces that drive a nation to growth and prosperity. Taking care of education given to an individual, it is the key nation building.

Learning or education starts right when one is in mother's womb. Mother thoughts and activists shape in growing child. A child learns by watching and observing parents, relatives and others around. He learns to co-relate the things that are observes, right or wrong, and thus his personality begins to develop. As he grows, he passes through different stages until he reaches the development of his race. Only he does it swiftly and quickly. When the basic physiological needs are met, a baby craves for physical and psychological security. Only mother can provide this need. Interpersonal relationships among this need interpersonal relationship among the family members create an atmosphere of belongings.

Essence of Education

There is only one method by which to attain knowledge which is called concentration. To Swamiji, the very essence of education is concentration of mind, not the collecting of facts. From the lowest to the highest all have to use the same method to attain knowledge. The power of concentration and detachment, and then a perfect instrument he could collect facts at will. Further formal education and interaction with other certainly will develop the individuals personality. Education, however, is much more than formal education. Swamiji observed that if education is to serve the entire human being, in all his or her dimensions the pursuit of knowledge will be a life long process. A learned person learns as along as he lives. To-days knowledge explosion can keep people engaged for the entire lives. Therefore education must be considered a continuous and life long process. Education must provide 'life-building, man making or personality development, character making assimilation of ideas. If they have assimilated these ideas and made them their life and character, they have more education than any man who has got by heart a whole library. Swamiji said, "We want that education by which character is formed strength of mind is increased, the intellect is expanded and by which one can stand on one's own feet".

Culture and Education

Every society has its outer aspect called 'civilisation' and also its inner aspect called 'culture'. In both of these a child is moulded and educated so that the beliefs and practices of his forefathers are carried on and not forgotten. Vivekananda observed that through education, a child learns a culture and his behaviour are moulded accordingly, and he is thus guided towards his eventual role in society. The teacher must not only possess the cultural knowledge he is to transmit it. And in addition to the content of the teaching, what the teacher gives or transfer to be truly effective, must posses some elements. For instance the teacher should share with the students the conviction that they are both truly in one spirit at the same time cultivating in the student a feeling of dignity and self respect. As Vivekananda said: “The true teacher is he who can immediately come down to the level of the student and transfer his soul to the students soul and see through and understand through his mind, such a teacher can really teach and none else”.

Personality Development

Human personality has three dimensions — physical, intellectual, and moral. Education deals with all the three. As Swami Vivekananda has remarked the personality of the man is two-thirds and his intellect, his words are but one-third. It is the real man, the personality of the man, that runs through them. Their actions are but effects. Actions must come when the man is there; the effect is bound to follow the cause.

Physical Dimension

The first dimension of man's personality is his body. It is the physical dimension. It refers to man's physical needs and growth. One should learn how to be physically strong and healthy. Right education should help in developing a strong stamina and healthy habits. Strong physical constitution helps one accept and face challenges of life. One should also learn the importance of right eating habits. Food is source of energy for physical growth. One should also learn the importance of physical exercises and games. They should become part of one's life. Walking and simple forms of exercise are much value in this context. Sound mind in a sound body helps man's physical and psychological development. Vivekananda said, "Strength is life, weakness is death".

Intellectual Dimension

Intellectual growth refers to a person's thinking, logical and memory skills. Reading books and articles, watching Television, visiting places and interacting with men of intellectual eminence — all these go a long way in one's intellectual growth. A good atmosphere also both inside and outside the house may be the primary reason to become an intellectual growth. Exposure to healthy literature and a proper approach to learning help develop intellectual faculty. Self discipline plays a vital role in developing one's intellect. Strength of mind and steadiness of character can be developed along with intellectual development. Those who choose the intellectual path strive to explore the meaning of truth, justice and so on. Philosophers, scientists and mathematician belong to this category. They are always in search of New Truth. Swamiji said, "Societies should be moulded upon truth, and truth has not to adjust itself to society".

Moral Dimension

Morality is the basis of character building. The training in moral principles begins at home, early in life, while the growing child observes and interacts with his parents, sibling, friends and other. Today the world has become small and so students can get communication and information through computer. While it has a bright side, there are many darker aspects of it. Easy access to internet and entertainment has exposed the young minds to all kinds of low, absence and negative thoughts and they become prey to many wrong things at an early age. One of the best ways to check this is that the parents and elders should spend quality time with children and also make them aware of the life building ideas of great personalities including Swami Vivekananda. The students should be encouraged to read and discuss Swamiji's life and teachings through forming Vivekananda study circles. The young minds can easily understand Swamiji's teachings through interactions with knowledgeable persons. Moral education can not be given by books only. One needs an example in order to develop faith in moral principles. Hence teacher should themselves practice what they preach. With the teacher their relationship is same as that between an ancestor and his descendant. Without faith the humility, submission and veneration in their hearts towards the teacher there can not be any growth in the. Swamiji placed the ideal of such education thus: "We want the man whose heart feel intensely the miseries and sorrows of the world .... And (We want) the man who not only can feel but can find the meaning of things, who delves deeply into the heart of nature and understanding. We want the man who will not even stop there, but who wants to work out the feeling and meaning by actual deeds. Such a combination of head heart and hand is what we want".

References

- Swami Vivekananda, My Idea of Education, Ramakrishna Mission, West Bengal - Novcmber, 2011.
- Swami Vivekananda, Arise, Awake! Call of the Saviour Prophet, Ramakrishna Ashrama, Rajkot.
- Swami Bodhasarananda Adhyaksha, Vivekananda His call to the Nation, Uttarkhand, 1969.
- Swami Vivekananda, Awakening India, New Delhi, 2011.
- Swami Vivekananda, My India - The India Eternal, Kolkata, 1993.

61

Education in His Vision

P. Perumal and S. Rajaguru

Introduction

Swami Vivekananda (1863-1902), a great thinker and reformer of India, embraces education, which for him signifies 'man-making', as the very mission of his life. In this paper, which purports to expound and analyse Swamiji's views on education, an endeavour has been made to focus on the basic theme of his philosophy, viz. the spiritual unity of the universe. Whether it concerns the goal or aim of education, or its method of approach or its component parts, all his thoughts, we shall observe, stem from this dormant theme of his philosophy which has its moorings in Vedanta.

Swamiji realised that mankind is passing through a crisis. The tremendous emphasis on the scientific and mechanical ways of life is fast reducing man to the status of a machine. Moral and religious values are being undermined. The fundamental principles of civilisation are being ignored. Conflicts of ideals, manners and habits are pervading the atmosphere. Disregard for everything old is the fashion of the day. He seeks the solutions of all these social and global evils through education. With this end in view, he feels the dire need of awakening man to his spiritual self wherein, he thinks, lies the very purpose of education.

Here is an interesting perspective of what education is, and what it is not, in the vision of Swamiji.

What is Education?

- Education is the manifestation of the perfection already in man.
- The training by which the current and expression of will is brought under control and become fruitful is called education.
- [Education] may be described as a development of faculty, not an accumulation of words, or, as a training of individuals to will rightly and efficiently.
- Real education is that which enables one to stand on his own legs.
- If you have assimilated five ideas and made them your life and character, you have more education than any man who has got by heart a whole library.

- We must have life building, man making, and character making assimilation of ideas.

What Education is not?

- Is it book-learning? No. Is it diverse knowledge? Not even that..
- [Education is] not an accumulation of words….
- [Education is] not the collecting of facts…
- Education is not the amount of information that is put into your brain and runs riot there, undigested all your life.
- If education were identical with information, the libraries would be the greatest sages in the world and encyclopedias would be the Rishis.
- Education is not filling the mind with a lot of facts.
- …is that education as a result of which the will, being continuously choked by force through generations, is now well-nigh killed out; is that education under whose sway even the old ideas, let alone the new ones are disappearing one by one; is that education which is slowly making man a machine?
- Well, you consider a man as educated if only he can pass some examinations and deliver good lectures…

The Objective of Education

Swamiji points out that the defect of present-day education has no definite goal to pursue. A sculptor has a clear idea about what he wants to shape out of the marble block; similarly, a painter knows what he is going to paint. But a teacher, he says, has no clear idea about the goal of his teaching. Swamiji attempts to establish, through his words and deeds, that the end of all education is man making. He prepares the scheme of this man-making education in the light of his over-all philosophy of Vedanta. According to Vedanta, the essence of man lies in his soul, which he possesses in addition to his body and mind. In true with this philosophy, Swamiji defines education as 'the manifestation of the perfection already in man.' The aim of education is to manifest in our lives the perfection, which is the very nature of our inner self. This perfection is the realisation of the infinite power which resides in everything and every-where-existence, consciousness and bliss. After understanding the essential nature of this perfection, we should identify it with our inner self. For achieving this, one will have to eliminate one's ego, ignorance and all other false identification, which stand in the way. Meditation, fortified by moral purity and passion for truth, helps man to leave behind the body, the senses, the ego and all other non-self elements, which are perishable. He thus realises his immortal divine self, which is of the nature of infinite existence, infinite knowledge and infinite bliss.

At this stage, man becomes aware of his self as identical with all other selves of the universe, i.e., different selves as manifestations of the same self. Hence education, in Swamiji's sense, enables one to comprehend one's self within as the self everywhere. The essential unity of the entire universe is realised through education. Accordingly, man making for Swamiji stands for rousing mans to the awareness of his true self. However, education thus signified does not point towards the development of the soul in isolation from body and mind. We have to remember that basis of Swamiji's philosophy is Advaita which preaches unity in diversity. Therefor, man making for him means a harmonious development of the body, mind and soul. In his scheme of education, Swamiji lays great stress on physical health because a sound mind resides in a sound body. He often quotes the Upanishadic dictum 'nayamatma balahinena labhyah'; i.e., the self cannot be realised by the physically weak. However, along with physical culture, he harps on the need of paying special attention to the culture of the mind. According to Swamiji, the mind of the students has to be controlled and trained through meditation, concentration and practice of ethical purity. All success in any line of work, he emphasises, is the result of the power of concentration. By way of illustration, he mentions that the chemist in the laboratory concentrates all the powers of his mind and brings them into one focus-the elements to be analysed-and finds out their secrets.

Concentration, which necessarily implies detachment from other things, constitutes a part of Brahmacharya, which is one of the guiding mottos of his scheme of education. Brahmacharya, in a nutshell, stands for the practice of self-control for securing harmony of the impulses. By his philosophy of education, Swamiji thus brings it home that education is not a mere accumulation of information but a comprehensive training for life. To quote him: 'Education is not the amount of information that is put into your brain and runs riot there undigested, all your life.' Education for him means that process by which character is formed, strength of mind is increased, and intellect is sharpened, as a result of which one can stand on one's own feet.

Procedure of Education

Having analysed the goal or objective of education, the next question that naturally arises is about the method of imparting education. Here again, we note the Vedantic foundation of Swamiji's theory. According to him, knowledge is inherent in every man's soul. What we mean when we say that a man 'knows' is only what he 'discovers' by taking the cover off his own soul. Consequently, he draws our attention to the fact that the task of the teacher is only to help the child to manifest its knowledge by removing the obstacles in its way. In his words: 'Thus Vedanta says that within man is all knowledge even in a boy it is so and it requires only an awakening and that much is the work of a teacher.' To drive his point home, he refers to the growth of a plant. Just as in the case of a plant, one cannot do anything more than supplying it with water, air and manure while it grows from within its own nature, so is the case with a human child. Swamiji's method of education resembles the heuristic method of the modern educationists. In this system, the teacher invokes the spirit of inquiry in the pupil who is supposed to find out things for himself under the bias-free guidance of the teacher.

Swamiji plays a lot of emphasis on the environment at home and school for the proper growth of the child. The parents as well as the teachers should inspire the child by the way they live their lives. Swamiji recommends the old institution of gurukula (living with the preceptor) and similar systems for the purpose. In such systems, the students can have the ideal character of the teacher constantly before them, which serves as the role model to follow.

Although Swamiji is of the opinion that mother tongue is the right medium for social or mass education, he prescribes the learning of English and Sanskrit also. While English is necessary for mastering Western science and technology, Sanskrit leads one into the depths of our vast store of classics. The implication is that if language does not remain the privilege of a small class of people, social unity will march forward unhampered.

Fields of Study

Vivekananda, in his scheme of education, meticulously includes all those studies, which are necessary for the all-around development of the body, mind and soul of the individual. These studies can be brought under the broad heads of physical culture, aesthetics, classics, language, religion, science and technology. According to Swamiji, the culture values of the country should form an integral part of the curriculum of education. The culture of India has its roots in her spiritual values. The time-tested values are to be imbibed in the thoughts and lives of the students through the study of the classics like Ramayana, Mahabharata, Gita, Vedas and Upanishads. This will keep the perennial flow of our spiritual values into the world culture.

Education, according to Swamiji, remains incomplete without the teaching of aesthetics or fine arts. He cites Japan as an example of how the combination of art and utility can make a nation great.

Swamiji reiterates that religion is the innermost core of education. However, by religion, he does not mean any particular kind of it but its essential character, which is the realisation of the divinity already in man. He reminds us time and again that religion does not consist in dogmas or creeds or any set of rituals. To be religious for him means leading life in such a way that we manifest our higher nature, truth, goodness and beauty, in our thoughts, words and deeds. All impulses, thoughts and actions which lead one towards this goal are naturally ennobling and harmonising, and are ethical and moral in the truest sense. It is in this context that Swamiji's idea of religion, as the basis of education should be understood. We note that in his interpretation, religion and education share the identity of purpose.

Why religion forms the very foundation of education becomes clear in his following words: 'In building up character, in making for everything that is good and great, in bringing peace to others, and peace to one's own self, religion is the highest motive power, and, therefore, ought to be studied from that standpoint. Swamiji believes that if education with its religious core can invigorate man's faith in his divine nature and the infinite potentialities of the human soul, it is sure to help man become strong, yet tolerant and sympathetic. It will also help man to extend his love and good will beyond the communal, national and racial barriers.

It is a misinterpretation of Swamiji's philosophy of education to think that he has overemphasised the role of spiritual development to the utter neglect of the material side. Vivekananda, in his plan for the regeneration of India, repeatedly presses the need for the eradication of poverty, unemployment and ignorance. He says, We need technical education and all else which may develop industries, so that men, instead of seeking for service, may earn enough to provide for themselves, and save something against a rainy day. He feels it necessary that India should take from the Western nations all that are good in their civilisation. However, just like a person, every nation has its individuality, which should not be destroyed. The individuality of India lies in her spiritual culture. Hence in Swamiji's view, for the development of a balanced nation, we have to combine the dynamism and scientific attitude of the West with the spirituality of our country. The entire educational programme should be so planned that it equips the youth to contribute to the material progress of the country as well as to maintaining the supreme worth of India's spiritual heritage.

Another important aspect of Swamiji's scheme of education is women's education. He realises that it if the women of our country get the right type of education, then they will be able to solve their own problems in their own way. The main objective of his scheme of female education is to make them strong, fear-less, and conscious of their chastity and dignity. He observes that although men and women are equally competent in academic matters, yet women have a special aptitude and competence for studies relating to home and family. Hence he recommends the introduction of subjects like sewing, nursing, domestic science, culinary art, etc., which were not parts of education at his time.

Conclusion

The exposition and analysis of Swamiji's scheme of education brings to light its constructive, practical and comprehensive character. He realises that it is only through education that the uplift of masses is possible. To refer to his own words: Traveling through many cities of Europe and observing in them the comforts and education of even the poor people, there was brought to my mind the state of our own poor people and I used to shed tears. When made the difference? "Education" was the answer I got.'

He states it emphatically that if society is to be reformed, education has to reach everyone-high and low, because individuals are the very constituents of society. The sense of dignity rises in man when he becomes conscious of his inner spirit, and that is the very purpose of education. He strives to harmonise the traditional values of India with the new values brought through the progress of science and technology.

It is in the transformation of man through moral and spiritual education that he finds the solution for all social evils. Founding education on the firm ground of our own philosophy and culture, he shows the best of remedies for today's social and global illness. Through his scheme of education, he tries to materialise the moral and spiritual welfare and upliftment of humanity, irrespective of caste, creed, nationality or time. However, Swami Vivekananda's scheme of education, through which he wanted to build up a strong nation that will lead the world towards peace and harmony, is still a far cry. It is high time that we give serious thought to his philosophy of education and remembers his call to every-body— 'Arise, awake, and stop not till the goal is reached.'

References

- http://en.wikipedia.org/Dr. Sudipa dutta Roy, July 2001
- Harini, R. (1991). An evaluation of teacher's attitude towards tenth standard English.
- Textbook. Unpublished M.Phil. Dissertation, Bharathiar University, Coimbatore.
- http://en.wikipedia.org/wiki/ Vivekananda _education
- http://history-world.org/ Vivekananda _of_education.htm
- http://www.education.nic.in/
- http://en.wikipedia.org/wiki/Education_in_India

62

Saintly Thoughts on Education

P. S. Ashwini

Introduction

Swami Vivekananda also defines education as "life-building, man-making, character-making assimilation of ideas", and not a certain "amount of information that is put into your brain and runs riot there, undigested all your life. Education is not mere book-learning or passing examinations, not even delivering impressive lectures. It is an ability to think originally, to stand on your own feet mentally as well as practically, interacting with people successfully. Importance in Swamiji's definition of education is the expression 'already in man'. This refers to a human being's potential, which is the range of the abilities and talents, known or unknown that is born with. 'Potential' speaks of the possibility of awakening something that is laying dormant (Prabhananda, 2003). The word 'perfection' in Vivekananda's definition of education is also very significant. This calls for a right and pragmatic approach.

Education for men means that process by which character is formed, strength of mind is increased, and intellect is sharpened, as a result of which one can stand on one's own feet. Thus, according to Swamiji, education is the discovery of the inner self, i.e., self revelation. It is not an imposition on the individual of certain borrowed ideas from the external sources, but a natural process of enfoldment of all the inherent powers which lie in dormant condition in an individual. Education is development from within. His thoughts on education ought to be seriously re-examined today.

Saintly Precepts

Swamiji points out that the defect of the present-day education is that, it has no definite goal to pursue. A sculpture has a clear idea about what he wants to shape out of the marble block; similarly, painter knows what he is going to paint. But a teacher, he says, has no clear idea about the goal of his teaching. Swamiji attempts to establish, through his words and deeds, that the end of all education is man-making.

Education that he maintains should help people to build up self-confidence and self reliance, based on balanced human relationships. The ultimate goal of all educational effort is to strive towards character development that is characterised by the development of will-power, leading to courage, stamina and fearlessness. Through education the individual should develop adaptability and able to meet the challenge of a changing society and this can be able through education and training that he or she receives from his parents and teachers. Education should lead to a feeling of brotherhood and the unity of mankind.

(a) Method of Teaching

Vivekananda's method of education resembles the heuristic method of modern Educationists.

- In this system, the teacher invokes the spirit of inquiry in the pupil who is supposed to find out things for himself under the bias-free guidance of the teacher.
- Anticipating the much acclaimed modern with student centered method of learning where the teacher plays the role of a facilitator.
- Vivekananda asks the teacher to come down to the level of the learner and 'give them a push upwards'.
- There should be least intervention and the ideal teacher should consciously under-teach so that the learners get ample scope for learning themselves 'No one can teach anybody. The teacher spoils everything by thinking that he is teacher'.

(b) As a Teacher

It is true that today's education does not produce properly developed personalities having faith, hope, confidence, motivating power, balanced outlook in life, conscious of their rights as well as their duties. The reason does not lie with the youth or with their mind as such as but with the agencies responsible for moulding a person's character, i.e., parents, teachers, social conditions in which he/she grows, and the system of education to which we trust his/ her future.

- The teacher should share with the student the conviction that they are both truly one in Spirit, i.e., at the same time cultivating in the student a feeling of dignity and self-respect".
- "The only true teacher is he, who can immediately come down to the level of the student, and transfer his soul to the student's soul and see through the student's eyes and hear through his ears and understand through his mind. Such a teacher can really teach and none else".
- "Education is the manifestation of the perfection already in man", therefore, a teacher's job is only to remove obstruction from the pupil's path. What we call learning is actually 'unfolding' or 'unveiling'.

(c) All Round Development

Although Swamiji believed education lays extreme emphasis on the training of mind, it seldom undermine the importance of an all-round development of human personality.

- It aims at the untrammeled development of the personality in all spheres, i.e., physical, mental and spiritual. In this scheme of education, Swamiji lays great stress on physical health because 'a sound mind resides in a sound body'. He often quotes the Upanishadic dictum 'nayamatma balahinena labhyah'; the self cannot be realised by the physically weak.
- Accordingly, he recommends that physical exercise of some kind or the other must form part of an educational training. The mind acts on the body and the body acts on the mind. They run parallel to each other.
- Along with physical culture, he also stressed on the need of paying special attention to the culture of the mind. According to Vivekananda, the mind of students has to be controlled and trained through meditation, concentration and practice of ethical purity. All success in any line of work, he emphasises, is the result of the power of concentration.
- Concentration, which necessarily implies detachment from other things, constitutes a part of Brahmacharya, which is one of the guiding mottos of his scheme of education. Brahmacharya, in a nutshell, stands for the practice of self-control for securing harmony of the impulses.

(d) Medium of Instruction

As regards to medium of instruction, Vivekananda strongly advocated for mother-tongue.

- As a true nationalist and a champion of national education he argued instruction through mother-tongue.
- He visualised to Indianise Indian education.
- He also wanted to spread mass education through mother-tongue so that it will reach to everyone.
- Swamiji believes that mother tongue is the right medium for social or mass education, he prescribes the learning of English and Sanskrit also.

Conclusion

Swami Vivekananda's views of education, through which he wanted to build up a strong nation that will lead the world towards peace and harmony, is still a far cry. It is high time that we give serious thought to his philosophy of education and remembers his call to everybody - 'Arise, awake and stop not till the goal is reached'.

References

- Chandra, S. (1994): Swami Vivekananda's Vision of Education, In: Roy, S. and Sivaramkrishnan, M. (Eds), Reflections on Swami Vivekananda: Hundred Years After Chicago, Sterling Publishers Pvt. Ltd., New Delhi. Complete Works of Swami Vivekananda (8 Volumes). Advaita Ashrama, Kolkata, 1985.
- Ghosal, S. (2012) : The Educational Thoughts of Swami Vivekananda : A Review, University News, 50 (09), Feb. 27 - March 04, 2012, New Delhi.
- Vivekananda, Swami (1993): My India: The India Eternal, Ramkrishna Mission Institute of Culture, Kolkata.
- Websites
- www.ijmer.in/pdf/volume1-issue3-2012/79-85.pdf
- www.stanford.edu/group/hsc/vivekananda.html

63

Swami Vivekananda: The Unparalled Preceptor

R. Sheela Banu

"Education is the manifestation of the perfection already in man"

Introduction

Modern education has myriad maladies. It is myopic and crippled. The burgeoning evils in the human society testify to the inherent deficiency in our education system. Higher education has not reduced the miseries of this world; it seems to have contributed more to it. The divide between the rich and the poor is ever increasing. In spite of being educated, people have been fighting and killing themselves like animals. This is because our education has not taught us to cope with the social, physical, emotional, and professional pressures. It gives us knowledge but it does not emphasise on application of this knowledge. Marring the innate creativity of man, modern education has deformed humans as formidable intellectual demons instead of transforming them as refined humans. It is hightime we realised the deplorable state of our education and devise new strategies to impart quality education for the youth.

In modern days, a plethora of knowledge is available from the internet. It is, indeed a welcome boon for knowledge seekers. Those who crave for knowledge need not necessarily step into colleges and universities. They can very well gather a heap of knowledge from their own drawing rooms in their houses at the click of the mouse, and get very many degrees online. But the sad fact is that the internet which is considered a boon has already proved a bane for man. The alarming rise of cyber crimes speak of the lethal impact of internet on the current generation.

We have accomplished many a feat through science and technology. Modern methods of communication and travel have shrunk our vast world into a tiny village. But as man has dared to probe the space, his moral degradation has also been going on apace. Our mad materialistic pursuits has augmented the erosion of human values. Our love of luxury has resulted in an enormous increase in natural calamities too. We have become nothing but robots, incapable of thinking about the future.

Swami Vivekananda says, "All knowledge that the world has ever received comes from the mind; the infinite library of the universe is in our own mind" (//greathumancapital//). Lack of spiritual education is the salient reason for the present day moral crisis. Among the many preceptors of our timeless past, Swami Vivekananda's teachings best suit the needs of the modern society. One finds in his teachings, a fine and judicious blend of Indian spiritualism and Western humanism. He has laid the foundation for 'spiritual humanism'. His concept of potential divinity of the soul prevents gross degradation of human society, divinizes human relationships, and makes life meaningful and worth living.

William James called the Swami the "paragon of Vedantists." Max Muller and Paul Deussen, the famous Orientalists of the nineteenth century, held him in genuine respect and affection. "His words," writes Romain Rolland, "are great music, phrases in the style of Beethoven, stirring rhythms like the march of Handel choruses". Several eminent leaders of India's freedom movement have acknowledged their indebtedness to Swamiji. Jawaharlal Nehru wrote: "Rooted in the past, full of pride in India's prestige, Vivekananda was yet modern in his approach to life's problems, and was a kind of bridge between the past of India and her present ... he came as a tonic to the depressed and demoralised Hindu mind and gave it self-reliance and some roots in the past." Netaji Subhash Chandra Bose wrote: "Swamiji harmonised the East and the West, religion and science, past and present. And that is why he is great. Our countrymen have gained unprecedented self-respect, self-reliance and self-assertion from his teachings."

Swami Vivekananda was India's first great cultural ambassador to the West. He bridged the wide chasm between the East and the West with his supreme teachings. He made the Westerners realise the profundity of Indian spirituality and its potential for the universal well-being. While advocating Indian spirituality, he never blindly opposed Western culture. He wanted Indians to master Western science and technology, adapt Western ideas of individual freedom, social equality and justice and respect for women to Indian ethos and simultaneously develop spiritually. He gave Indians proper understanding of their country's great spiritual heritage and thus inculcated in them a pride in their pristine past. He revealed the true foundations of our glorious culture and clearly defined and strengthened the unity among Indians.

Long before the ideas of Karl Marx were known in India, Swamiji spoke about the role of the labouring classes in the production of the country's wealth. He was the first religious leader in India to speak for the masses and formulate a definite philosophy of service, and organise large-scale social service. Swamiji's most unique contribution to the creation of new India was to open the minds of Indians to their duty to the downtrodden masses.

Swamiji preached that knowledge alone is not the only factor for individual good; physical strength, moral strength, and character are equally important to any system of education. He emphasised that the youth need to build their character more than knowledge. According to him, "Education is not the amount of information that is put into your brain and run riot there undigested all your life. We must have life-building, man-making, character assimilation of ideas" (Complete Works Vol. IV, p. 302).

According to Swamiji, education should allow one to explore oneself from different perspectives. The essence of education is concentration of mind, not mere collection of facts. "The treasure of knowledge can be opened only with the key of concentration" (Complete Works Vol. VII, pp. 147-148). True education should equip the youth for the many struggles of life.

Swamiji has given a new theory of ethics and new principle of morality based on the intrinsic purity and oneness of the Atman. His teachings emphasise purity of human mind because purity is our real nature. He urged his followers to love and serve fellow humans because we are all one in the Supreme Spirit known as Paramatman or Brahman.

Education should enable youth to pursue their goals and steer forward in their life. It should lead the learner to nationalism and wider internationalism. It should create faith in one's own self. It should make the learner conscious of his own talents and potentials. It should instill Self-knowledge, Self-confidence and Self-reliance. It should develop moral character. It should promote universal brotherhood and must enable learners realise the inherent divinity in themselves. Education should "develop infinite energy, infinite zeal, infinite courage, and infinite patience" (Bharathy S.V. 37). It should show that religion and science are not contradictory but complementary to each other and make the youth follow the global religion of supreme freedom, supreme knowledge, and supreme happiness.

In this stress-filled world, Swamiji's teachings possess the ability to mould learners, increase their strength of mind, expand their intellect, and enable them to stand on their own feet. His teachings are a panacea for the infesting ills of our society. Our learners should be trained in Value education, Meditation, Traditional music, dance and Physical education to develop a healthy body and mind.

Classroom activities, hobby clubs, cultural and literary activities, discourses on values, competitions, classroom projects on meaningful topics should be encouraged. Scientific knowledge should combine humanism too. Hence, students should be taught about the life-giving, ennobling principles of the Swami Vivekananda and find suitable ways to apply them in practical life. As Vivekananda said, students should be taught to have faith in themselves and God in order to lead a happy and peaceful life.

References

- Bharathi S.V. Educational Philosophy of Swami Vivekananda. New Delhi: Discovery, 2005.
- Vivekananda, Swami. Complete Works of Swami Vivekananda Vol. IV. Advaita Ashram, 1989.
- Vivekananda, Swami. Complete Works of Swami Vivekananda Vol. VII. Advaita Ashram, 1989.
- http //greathumancapital.wordpress.com//16.03.13

64

Education in the Vision of Swamiji

S. S. Jayanthi Devi

We want that education by which character is formed, strength of mind is increased, the intellect is expanded and by which one can stand on one's own feet." — *Swami Vivekananda*

Introduction

Education is necessarily a process of inculcating values to equip the learner lead a life—a kind of life that is satisfying to the individual in accordance with the cherished values and ideals of the society. Philosophers, spiritual leaders and educationists of our country, all in various ways, have emphasised the role of education for 'character development', 'bringing out the latent potentialities and inherent qualities' and developing an 'integrated personality' for the well being of the individual and the society at large. The concern for value education is reflected in our key policy documents from time to time.

Swami Vivekananda signifies 'man-making', as the very mission of his life. Vivekananda realises that mankind is passing through a crisis. The tremendous emphasis on the scientific and mechanical ways of life is fast reducing man to the status of a machine. Moral and religious values are being undermined. The fundamental principles of civilisation are being ignored. Conflicts of ideals, manners and habits are pervading the atmosphere. Disregard for everything old is the fashion of the day. Vivekananda seeks the solutions of all these social and global evils through education.

The Education of Character

- School should hone psychological skills called executive functions that are needed to plan and carry out goal-directed activity.
- Learning issues afflict large numbers of children not because they are unintelligent but because they have trouble focusing or following through in the face of frustration.
- A dispassionate focus on the present-mindfulness-helps to ward off stress and can improve brain function.

- Thinking about thinking, known as metacognition, may give kids better control over how they think and feel in ways that could enhance learning.

The Goals of Education

'Education is the manifestation of the perfection already in man.'
— Swami Vivekananda

Swamiji points out that the defect of the present-day education is that it has no definite goal to pursue. A sculptor has a clear idea about what he wants to shape out of the marble block; similarly, a painter knows what he is going to paint. But a teacher has no clear idea about the goal of his teaching. Swamiji attempts to establish, through his words and deeds, that the end of all education is man making. According to Vedanta, the essence of man lies in his soul, which he possesses in addition to his body and mind. With this philosophy, Swamiji defines education as 'the manifestation of the perfection already in man.' The aim of education is to manifest in our lives the perfection, which is the very nature of our inner self. After understanding the essential nature of this perfection, we should identify it with our inner self. For achieving this, one will have to eliminate one's ego, ignorance and all other false identification, which stand in the way. Meditation, fortified by moral purity and passion for truth, helps man to leave behind the body, the senses, the ego and all other non-self elements, which are perishable. He thus realises his immortal divine self, which is of the nature of infinite existence, infinite knowledge and infinite bliss.

At this stage, man becomes aware of his self as identical with all other selves of the universe, i.e., different selves as manifestations of the same self. Hence education, in Vivekananda's sense, enables one to comprehend one's self within as the self everywhere. The essential unity of the entire universe is realised through education. Accordingly, man making for Swamiji stands for rousing mans to the awareness of his true self. However, education thus signified does not point towards the development of the soul in isolation from body and mind. Therefore, man making for him means a harmonious development of the body, mind and soul.

In his scheme of education, Swamiji lays great stress on physical health because a sound mind resides in a sound body. He often quotes the Upanishadic dictum 'nayamatma balahinena labhyah'; i.e., the self cannot be realised by the physically weak. However, along with physical culture, he harps on the need of paying special attention to the culture of the mind. According to Swamiji, the mind of the students has to be controlled and trained through meditation, concentration and practice of ethical purity. All success in any line of work, he emphasises, is the result of the power of concentration. He also mentions that the chemist in the laboratory concentrates all the powers of his mind and brings them into one focus-the elements to be analysed-and finds out their secrets. Concentration, which necessarily implies detachment from other things, constitutes a part of Brahmacharya, which is one of the guiding mottos of his scheme of education. Brahmacharya, in a nutshell, stands for the practice of self-control for securing harmony of the impulses. Swamiji in his philosophys thus says that education is not a mere accumulation of information but a comprehensive training for life. He also quoted that, 'Education is not the amount of information that is put into the brain and runs riot there undigested, all through our life.' Education for him means that process by which character is formed, strength of mind is increased, and intellect is sharpened, as a result of which one can stand on one's own feet.

Religion Owes to the Character

In building up character, in making for everything that is good and great, in bringing peace to others and peace to one's own self, religion is the highest motive power, and, therefore, ought to be studied from that standpoint. Swamiji believes that if education with its religious core can invigorate man's faith in his divine nature and the infinite potentialities of the human soul, it is sure to help man become strong, yet tolerant and sympathetic. It will also help man to extend his love and good will beyond the communal, national and racial barriers.

Swamiji says, We need technical education and all else which may develop industries, so that men, instead of seeking for service, may earn enough to provide for themselves, and save something against a rainy day. He feels it necessary that India should take from the Western nations all that are good in their civilisation. However, just like a person, every nation has its individuality, which should not be destroyed. The individuality of India lies in her spiritual culture. Hence in Swamiji's view, for the development of a balanced nation, we have to combine the dynamism and scientific attitude of the West with the spirituality of our country. The entire educational programme should be so planned that it equips the youth to contribute to the material progress of the country as well as to maintaining the supreme worth of India's spiritual heritage.

Another important aspect of Swamiji's scheme of education is women's education. He realises that it if the women of our country get the right type of education, then they will be able to solve their own problems in their own way. The main objective of his scheme of female education is to make them strong, fear-less, and conscious of their chastity and dignity. He observes that although men and women are equally competent in academic matters, yet women have a special aptitude and competence for studies relating to home and family. Hence he recommends the introduction of subjects like sewing, nursing, domestic science, culinary art, etc., which was not part of education at his time.

Conclusion

The exposition and analysis of Vivekananda's scheme of education brings to light its constructive, practical and comprehensive character. He realises that it is only through education that the uplift of masses is possible. He states it emphatically that if society is to be reformed, education has to reach everyone-high and low, because individuals are the very constituents of society. The sense of dignity rises in man when he becomes conscious of his inner spirit, and that is the very purpose of education. He strives to harmonise the traditional values of India with the new values brought through the progress of science and technology. It is in the transformation of man through moral and spiritual education that he finds the solution for all social evils. Founding education on the firm ground of our own philosophy and culture, he shows the best of remedies for today's social and global illness. Through his scheme of education, he tries to materialise the moral and spiritual welfare and upliftment of humanity, irrespective of caste, creed, nationality or time. However, Swami Vivekananda's scheme of education, through which he wanted to build up a strong nation that will lead the world towards peace and harmony, is still a far cry. It is high time that we give serious thought to his philosophy of education and remember his call to everybody "Arise, awake, and stop not till the goal is reached".

References

- Sudipa Dutta Roy (2001), Education in the Vision of Swami Vivekananda, E-sanskriti - The Essence of Indian Culture.
- Suma Mary, (2013), Role of value education in schools Swami Vivekananda, papyrus club, online campus.
- www.google.com www.yahoo.com

65

Spiritual Values of Swamiji in Higher Education

P. Rajalakshmi and J. Vincent Thaninayagam

Definition

Swami Vivekananda describes religion as "The Mainfestation of the divinity already in man" and also defines education as the mainfestation of the perfection already in man. First of all, the word 'Mainfestation' implies that something already exists and is waiting to be expressed. The main focus in learning is to make the hidden ability of learner manifest. According to him, knowledge is inherent in man, not acquired from external sources like sparks in flint; knowledge is potentially there in the human mind. The stimulus of education causes the friction that ignites the fire of knowledge. It is the unfolding of the petals of one's own mind. 'Mainfestation' indicates spontaneous growth provided that the impediments, if any, are removed. Vivekananda said "What a man learns is really what he 'discovers' by taking the cover off his own soul, which is a mine of infinite knowledge" (1993: 54).

Aims

1. Reaching Perfection

The prime aim of education is to achieve fullness of perfection already present in a child. According to Swamiji all material and spiritual knowledge is already present in man covered by a curtain of ignorance. Education should tear off that veil so that the knowledge shines forth as an illuminating torch to enliven all the corners by and by. This is meant by achieving fullness of the latent perfection.

2. Physical and Mental Development

The second aim of education is the physical and mental development of the child so that the child of today, after studying the Gita, is able to promote national growth and advancement as a fearless and physically well developed citizen of tomorrow. Stressing the mental development of the child, Swamiji, wished education to enable the child to stand on his own legs economically rather than becoming a parasite on others.

3. Moral and Spiritual Development

According to Swami Vivekananda, a nation's greatness is not only measured by its parliamentary institutions and activities, but also by the greatness of its citizens. But the greatness of citizens is possible only through their moral and spiritual development which education must foster.

4. Character Development

According to Swamiji, character development is a very important aim of any education. For this, he emphasised the practice of *Brahmacharya* which fosters development of mental, moral and spiritual powers leading to purity of thoughts, words and deeds.

5. Shraddha and Spirit of Renunciation

All through his life Swamiji exhorted the individuals to keep full confidence upon their powers. They should inculcate a spirit of self surrender, sacrifice and renunciation of material pleasures for the good of others. Education should bring in, all these qualities in the individual. He gave this call to his countrymen. "Arise, awake and stop not till the goal is achieved."

6. Unity in Diversity

The true aim of education is to develop an insight into the individuals so that they are able to search out and realise unity in diversity. Swami Vivekananda has further asserted that physical and spiritual worlds are one; their distinctness is an illusion (Maya). Education should develop this sense which finds unity in diversity.

7. Religious Development

To Swamiji, religious development is an essential aim of education. To him, each individual should be able to search out and develop the religious seed embedded in him and thus find the absolute truth or reality.

He hence, advocated the training of feelings and emotions so that the whole life is purified and sublimated. Then only, the capacities of obedience, social service and submission to the teachings and preaching's of great saints and saviours will develop in the individual. Education should foster this development.

Objectives of the study:

1. To study the spiritual values in Higher Education
2. To identify the higher education students who feel any difficulty
3. To analyse the students in the area of Problem Solving
4. To study the higher education level of different variables.

Medium of Instruction

As regards to medium of instruction, Vivekananda strongly advocated for the use of mother-tongue. He a true nationalist and a champion of national education he argued instruction through mother tongue. He visualised to indianise the Indian education. He also wanted to spread spiritual education via the mother tongue so that it will reach to everyone. Although Swamiji is of the opinion that mother tongue is the right medium for spiritual education, he prescribes that learning of English and Sanskrit also, because while English is necessary for mastering western science and technology, Sanskrit leads one into the depths of our vast store of classics.

Methods of Teaching

Lecture Method: Spiritual ideas are abstract ideas. It becomes difficult on the part of a child to understand spiritual doctrines. So, Swamiji advocated for the introduction of lecture method to explain the spiritual ideas in a simple way to the students.

Activity Method: Swamiji accepted learning through activities as an ideal method of teaching. It can provide direct experience to the children. He advocated that activities like singing, storytelling, drama and dancing should be performed by the students in the spirit of Ramayana and Mahabharata. He also advocated for the introduction of other activities like excursion, camps, etc., to help the students to understand the value of social service. He also advocated questioning and answering and Deductive and Inductive method in his educational system.

Finding(s)

Most of the pupils were unable.

1. To control fleeting mental faculties by the practice of Yoga.
2. To develop the mind by concentration and deep meditation.
3. To gain knowledge through lectures, discussions, self-experience and creative activities.
4. To imitate the qualities and character of the teacher with intelligence and clear understanding.
5. To lead themselves on the right path by means of individual guidance provided by the teacher.

Conclusion

As all knowledge is within an individual and learning is only a function of their minds, the children should only be made active. Meditation and concentration were also considered important by him as through them the mental powers of the child is developed. It was also emphasised by him that the teacher should encourage children and develop in them self-confidence for learning. Thus, along with the teaching the teacher was advised to develop in children those qualities which are necessary for learning. The learner must be able to control the internal and external senses. He should control his lower nature and concentrate on learning. It is high time that we give serious thought to his philosophy of education and remember his call to everybody — 'Arise, awake, and stop not till the goal is reached.' His contribution for service to Mankind, and Spiritual, Mass and Women education is immemorable. He propagated Vedanta all over the world and it is open to all irrespective of country, race, colour, religion, rich or poor and politics. He believes in simple living and with high thinking. All around there pervades a spiritual and religious atmosphere. Swami Vivekananda's personality reflected conception of the education process as an effective harmony of relationship. Swami Vivekananda dedicated himself to the welfare of the essential unity of all faith and religions, and the need for spiritual pursuits for achieving higher goals of human life. He presented the true Indian to the whole world.

References

- Avinashilingam, T.S. (1957), Education complied from speeches and writings of Swami Vivekananda Sri Ramakrishna Math, Mylapore, Chennai.
- Behera, S.K. (2010), Educational ideas of Rabindranath Tagore: Preception of the Essential Nature of a Teacher the Taught and the Discipline, Journal of Edcuational Research and Extension, Sri Ramakrishna Mission Vidyala College of Education, Coimbatore, Vol. 47(3).
- Complete works of Swami Vivekananda, Advaita Ashram, Kolkata, 1962, (Hereafter cw) 4.358; 3.302.; 7.232; 5.366; 5.224; 4.24; 1.28 and 1.24.
- Dash, B.N. (1994) Foundation of Educational Thought and Practice, New Delhi, India, Kalyani Publishers.
- Gupta, S. (2009), Education in Emerging India, New Delhi, Shipra Publications.

Index

D